How to Create an Intimate C

THE
Dream
HOME

Kendall Hunt
publishing company

Elias Moitinho, PhD • Denise Moitinho, PhD
Liberty University

www.kendallhunt.com
Send all inquiries to:
4050 Westmark Drive
Dubuque, IA 52004-1840

Getting love and marriage right has been a challenge for couples since Adam and Eve. Yet, God's heart is for us to taste of what it truly means to love and be loved. In *The Dream Home,* Elias and Denise anchor their message in God's heart and plan for close, meaningful relationships and ultimately lead us to a strong Christ-centered marriage. Soak it up. . . together.

—Dr. Tim Clinton, President of the American Association of Christian Counselors (AACC)

The word "home" has a warm, wonderful ring to it. . . as does the word "marriage." However, growing up at home your parents could have been positive or negative—helpful or harmful.

While you cannot change the past, you can change your choices about the future. By applying the principles in this book, *The Dream Home* will not just help you manage your marriage . . . but also help you have the *marriage of your dreams.* What a deal!

—June Hunt, Founder of Hope for the Heart and author of
How to Forgive When You Don't Feel Like It

All of us know marriage can be a difficult road for most people. The constant pressure from outside the home, as well as the internal pressures, can lead to a challenging marital relationship. That's why I am excited about Elias and Denise Moitinho's new book, *The Dream Home.* Their common-sense approach to dealing with the challenges of marriage from a Biblical perspective is refreshing and life-giving. I am praying God uses this book to speak into the lives of many to help build stronger, God-honoring marriages in our churches today.

—Jonathan Falwell, Senior Pastor, Thomas Road Baptist Church

Want to strengthen your marriage? Grow closer to your spouse? Become a better husband or wife? *The Dream Home* shows you how. Filled with eye-opening insights and practical how-to's, *The Dream Home* is a must-read for anyone who wants to improve his or her marriage.

—Sam Hodges, Vice President of Publishing, Church Initiative

One of the most comprehensive and practical books you will ever read on building strong, biblically-based marriages and families. In their book *The Dream Home,* Elias and Denise Moitinho draw upon Scripture, research, case studies, and personal stories and experiences to explore systematically the multiple dimensions of a Christian marriage, from the external appearance to the internal dimensions of communication, self-care, conflict, finances, intimacy, spiritual growth, parenting, and hospitality. Filled with practical advice, assessment tools, checklists, humor, and wise counsel, this book is a must-read for couples, whether they are preparing for marriage, newly-weds, or are in the later stages of marriage. Highly recommended.

—Ian Jones, PhD, Professor of Counseling, New Orleans Baptist Theological
Seminary, and author of *The Counsel of Heaven and Earth*

With warmth and graciousness, the Moitinhos guide readers through the process of constructing and maintaining a strong marriage, one that reflects Christ and points others toward Him. The Moitinhos combine extensive professional knowledge with rich personal experience which results in a practical, down-to-earth guide suitable for every couple or for those who work with couples in ministry settings. I am pleased to see this valuable contribution to the marriage enrichment field.

—Scott Floyd, PhD, Senior Fellow and Director of Counseling Programs, B.H. Carroll Theological
Institute, and author of *Crisis Counseling: A Guide for Pastors and Professionals*

Endorsements on this page and the back cover are reprinted with the permission of their respective authors.

Acknowledgements

Writing this book was a process that involved not only us, the writers, but also a God-sent team and support system. We are thankful to God for giving us the vision, inspiration, motivation, and energy to write and complete this project. We pray that God will use this book to inspire many couples to create an intimate Christian marriage and indeed have a *Dream Home*.

We were amazed at how God led us to our publisher, Kendall Hunt Publishing Company. We have much to thank Curtis Ross, Senior Acquisitions Editor at Kendall Hunt, who showed excitement when we shared our book proposal with him and he gave us the opportunity to make this book a reality. We are thankful to Noelle Henneman who patiently guided us through the writing process by happily answering our questions and helping us every step of the way. We thank Dr. Kristy Ford, who assisted us with careful revisions and editing. We are also grateful for Brett Hartley's skills in recording the videos and to Joby Anthony for creatively editing them.

We want to thank the faculty at the School of Behavioral Sciences of Liberty University for cheering us through our book-writing journey. We are particularly thankful to our colleagues Dr. John Durden, Dr. John Thomas, Dr. Steve Johnson, Dr. Dwight Rice, and Dr. Suzanne Mikkelson for graciously giving of their precious time and reading some of our drafts and providing valuable and insightful feedback. We want to thank Kristin Hauswirth, a doctoral student, for assisting us with research and editing. She carefully read each chapter and provided thoughtful feedback. We also want to thank everyone who believed in this project and gladly endorsed the book.

We are thankful to our precious and amazing children, Victor and Eliana, for their love and for allowing us to take over the basement to write each chapter. They often checked on us to see how far along we were in our writing. We also want to thank our extended family in Brazil, our friends, and our students for their prayers, encouragement, and excitement about the book. We indeed felt their prayers as we started and completed this book.

Contents

Introduction

Creating Your Dream Home

The American dream is alive, but it seems to be in trouble. The average wedding in the U.S. costs $33,391.[1] The price tag of a wedding certainly

 ". . . and they lived happily ever after" can be your story.

varies around the country, but it shows that people tend to invest a lot of money on their precious wedding day. Millions of people are pursuing the American dream, and for most, the American dream also includes having a dream home. Yes, a beautiful home in a nice neighborhood with an impressive curb appeal, open floor concept, spacious bedrooms for the kids, a comfortable and relaxing master bedroom, and a nice backyard with a fantastic pool. Unfortunately, the problem is that many people are living in struggling and conflicted marriages, and several even get divorced. In fact, according to the American Psychological Association, "about 40 to 50 percent of married couples in the United States divorce [and] the divorce rate for subsequent marriages is even higher."[2] They may have a beautiful home, but it is no longer a dream home.

You may have picked up *The Dream Home* book because you want your marriage to be a dream marriage. Like most people, you want to experience the joy, fulfillment, and excitement of an intimate, lasting marriage. You want to experience true intimacy, to love and to be loved. You want to enjoy a sex life that is vibrant and exciting like an endless honeymoon bliss. You want the theme, *"and they lived happily ever after"* to be part of your story in the marriage of your dreams. This is great! We were thinking of you when we wrote *The Dream Home* book. So, keep on reading.

Maybe you are struggling in your marriage and want more out of your relationship with your spouse. Deep inside, you still have a desire to have a dream home. It is also possible that you may be in a conflicted or hopeless marriage. You and your spouse may have had good and bad times. However, you may feel that, lately, you only experience the bad ones.

You may also have picked up *The Dream Home* book because you are engaged and are planning to get married soon. Excitedly, you are on your way to creating your dream home. You want to experience happiness in your new life and believe that this book can help you create a dream marriage. No matter your reason for picking up this book, we believe that it can give you hope and encouragement to create your dream home.

In this book, we use the metaphor of a home to describe the various areas of marriage in a creative way. We start our journey to create a dream home by going house hunting, finding the best location, and examining the curb appeal. Then, we enter the house and check out each room carefully. By using metaphors and analogies, we make essential concepts about Christian marriage easier for you to understand. We include flow charts and graphs to help you grasp some new concepts and visualize how they relate to each other. More importantly, these concepts will help you create your dream home.

What Is This Book About?

This book is about giving you not only hope and encouragement but also providing knowledge and skills to help you create your dream home. We know that this may sound like a bold claim. And yes, it is. But, hear us out first. I (Elias), a licensed marriage and family therapist, licensed professional counselor, and counseling professor with many years of experience in the counseling field, and many years of church ministry, bring my expertise to this book. I (Denise) bring my expertise and experience as a Christian educator, having taught in the seminary setting and human services field for many years, along with church ministry experience. Above all, we are Christians and have been married for over 29 years; we are creating an intimate Christian marriage, though not perfect, and we have two beautiful adult children. Most importantly, we want to let you know that you can create your dream home and have an intimate Christian marriage. We believe it can be done with God's help and wisdom.

You May Ask How?

We know that the landscape of marriage and family in the U.S. has changed due to a high rate of divorce. You may have experienced divorce or seen it happening in your family. You may even have personal experience with the pain, suffering, and the instability that divorce brings to families and the emotional turmoil it creates for individuals and their children.

In a world filled with an ebb and flow of changes, multiple answers are available. This book will provide a stable way for you to pursue your dream marriage from a Christian perspective. There are three main elements that will be helpful in advancing your personal dream of a happy marriage. *The Dream Home* book provides solid biblical principles, insights from research, and wisdom gained from life, professional and ministry work with couples, church ministry, and teaching in seminary and graduate school.

This book also includes many research findings on what works or does not work in marriage and relationships. We will share with you findings that are consistent with Scriptures to help you create your dream marriage. By no means are we saying that the Word of God is not sufficient or that it is not superior to human research or human wisdom. However, we also acknowledge that God has given all humans a brain and intelligence. Many have made their life goals to research what works on relationships and marriage with the end goal to help couples and families.

 When you implement the principles, strategies, and relationship skills presented in this book, you will have a better chance to succeed in creating an intimate Christian marriage.

Your Dream Home	Metaphor	How each part of the Dream Home contributes to your intimacy
House Hunting	House hunting: Creating a vision for your marriage	A shared vision ignites excitement in the present and creates hope for your future as a couple.
Location	Location: Bringing stability to the home	The ideal location in Christian marriage is when both husband and wife are close to God and growing in intimacy with Him. Then, meaningful intimacy happens.
Curb Appeal	Curb appeal: Creating your reputation and testimony as a couple	Your intimate marriage becomes a beautiful testimony to those around you of Christ's redemptive grace and love.

(Continued)

(*Continued*)

Your Dream Home	Metaphor	How each part of the Dream Home contributes to your intimacy
Living Room	Living room: Communicating effectively is essential	Communicating openly and meaningfully grows your intimacy more deeply.
Kitchen and Dining	Kitchen and dining: Taking care of your body, mind, soul, and relationships	When you take care of yourself holistically, you give your spouse your best self or the best version of yourself.
Home Office	Home office: Managing finances according to biblical principles	Creating a budget and developing healthy money management habits bring you and your spouse together.
Laundry Room	Laundry room: Cleaning up conflict effectively	Resolving conflict effectively restores your emotional bond and revives the relationship.
Master Bedroom	Master bedroom: Enjoying multidimensional intimacy	Expressing multidimensional intimacy: Mental (connection of Minds), Emotional (connection of Hearts), Relational (connection of Bodies), Spiritual (connection of Souls).
Closet	Closet: Growing spiritually together as a couple	As each of you grows closer to God, you become closer to each other.
Kids' Room	Kids' room: Parenting with purpose	Together as a couple, you fulfill your God-given responsibility to teach and model your faith in God to your children.
Guest Room	Guest room: Practicing Christian hospitality	Together you and your spouse express God's love and compassion toward others.

We are confident that when you implement the principles, strategies, and relationship skills presented in this book, you will have a better chance to succeed in creating an intimate Christian marriage. Even though we cannot guarantee results, we are excited to share with you what we have learned over the years from the Bible, research, professional experience, and life lessons.

Best wishes,

Drs. Elias and Denise Moitinho

Endnotes

1. "The Average Wedding Cost in America Is Over $30,000-But Here's Where Couples Spend Way More Than That," accessed October 3, 2019, https://www.businessinsider.com/averagewedding-cost-in-america-most-expensive-2018-3.
2. "Marriage & Divorce," American Psychological Association, 2019, accessed September 27, 2019, https://www.apa.org/topics/divorce/.

PART I

THE SEARCH: Finding Your Dream Home

CHAPTER 1

House Hunters: Creating a Shared Vision for Your Marriage

"Then the Lord answered me and said,
Write a vision, and make it plain."
Habakkuk 2:2 (CEB)

The popular HGTV show *House Hunters* has a captivating plot that involves a couple searching for a house that, sometimes, will be their dream home. During the first few minutes of the show, the couple shares their vision for their future home. Typically, they have different views based on their needs, wants, preferences, and expectations. They often have different opinions regarding the location, type, size, model, floor plan, or price of the house. After they tour a few houses accompanied by a knowledgeable realtor, the couple has some time alone to discuss their options, analyze their wish lists, and consider the pros and cons of each property. Finally, they negotiate their preferences and usually make some compromises because, in the end, they have to agree and select only one house. As expected, the episode ends with the couple agreeing on a vision and enjoying their new home with family and friends.

In this chapter, we use the house-hunting experience as a metaphor for the process that you and your spouse engage in when creating a vision and mission for your marriage. We discuss how your values provide the guiding principles for your marriage vision and mission. Next, we guide you through the process of writing vision and mission statements that align with your Christian worldview. Finally, we help you set SMART goals and develop a strategic plan of action to implement a compelling vision and mission for your marriage.

A Shared Vision and Mission

Generally, people enter marriage with some kind of vision for their marriage. A vision, or an imagined future life together, creates expectations for the relationship. As you read this chapter, clarify and share your new and old expectations with your spouse, so that together you may create an inspiring vision and exciting mission for your marriage. If you already have written vision and mission statements for your marriage, we congratulate you on that. We encourage you to use this chapter to review, evaluate, revise, and even solidify your marriage vision and mission statements. We believe that having a compelling vision and mission for your marriage will strengthen the relationship, impacting your life and the lives of those around you positively. The shared vision process model helps visualize the path we will follow in this chapter.

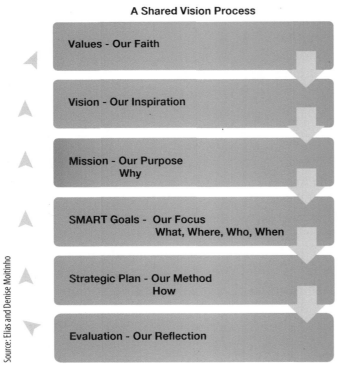

A Shared Vision Process

Values - Our Faith

Vision - Our Inspiration

Mission - Our Purpose
Why

SMART Goals - Our Focus
What, Where, Who, When

Strategic Plan - Our Method
How

Evaluation - Our Reflection

Source: Elias and Denise Moitinho

A vision is a description of a desired or preferred future. In the corporate or business world, organizations envision the future, imagine possibilities, find a common purpose, and create a picture of what they want to be and accomplish.[1] They develop a well-crafted vision based on their values. They also clarify their mission, set goals, and implement strategies to reach their goals and fulfill their vision.[2]

Similarly, Christian married couples need to have a clear vision and mission for their marriages. You may have heard that "Where there is no vision, the people perish" (Prov. 29:18 KJV). Interestingly, some translations use the word *revelation* instead of vision (NIV, NKJV) to represent God's will for His people.[3] Thus, without a godly vision, a Christian marriage can miss the opportunity to become the marriage God has envisioned for the couple.

For the Christian, a vision starts with God's revelation of His will and purposes for His people. Therefore, Christian couples need to begin the process of developing a vision and mission for their marriages with prayer. We

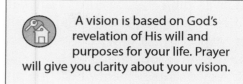

> A vision is based on God's revelation of His will and purposes for your life. Prayer will give you clarity about your vision.

encourage you to pray with your spouse and ask God to reveal His will and purpose for your lives as individuals and as a couple. Prayer will give you clarity about your vision.

Why do you need a vision for your marriage? First, a vision gives you a picture of the type of marriage you want to have in the future based on your understanding of God's will and purpose for you and your spouse. Second, a vision clarifies your expectations and ensures that you direct your lives toward the same destination with a common purpose. Third, a vision becomes a compass to your marriage and prevents it from drifting in the sea of twisted ideologies that will compete for your heart, mind, and soul.

The challenge in creating a shared vision is that spouses must infuse aspects of their own personal visions into one solid vision. In other words, couples need to blend their desired individual and marriage goals. Thus, a shared vision for marriage does not disregard a spouse's vision or imposes a one-sided vision.

Checking Your Marriage Expectations

People come into marriage with a set of expectations. These expectations are often unrealistic, underdeveloped, and even unspoken. Chances are that you and your spouse went into your marriage with different expectations. Consequently, as you go through your married life, you may experience conflicts and disappointments because of unmet expectations. The discrepancies between what you expected and what is actually happening in your marriage can be frustrating. Perhaps, it is a good time to reevaluate your expectations.

My Expectations:

Relationship with Spouse

- Spouse's roles
- Communication and conflict resolution
- Quality time
- Expressing love
- Sexual intimacy
- Recreation and vacation
- Technology and social media use

(Continued)

Developing a vision statement requires that you review and discuss your expectations for your marriage, no matter how long you have been married. As we already mentioned, you and your spouse may also be operating with unspoken expectations and assumptions. So, look at the list and consider your own expectations, adding more items to the list as needed. Ideally, you and your spouse could complete this activity together, as this might inspire the start of the conversation on creating a vision for your marriage.

Shared Core Values

A vision flows out of shared core values. James Kouses and Barry Posner, authors of the well-acclaimed book *The Leadership Challenge*, note that for-profit and non-profit organizations intentionally define the core values that guide their organizations.[4] The same is true when it comes to the development of vision and mission statements for your marriage. While you and your spouse may have different values and beliefs, it is essential to come together and find some common ground. Thus, we encourage you and your spouse to reflect on your values and beliefs, especially those related to marriage and family life since they influence your vision for your marriage.

Another point to consider is that Christian values are based on a biblical worldview. A worldview is a lens that helps you interpret and make sense of reality. We discuss the concept of worldview in Chapter 2, where we emphasize

(Continued)

- Faith, church commitment and participation
- Personal and professional goals

Relationship with Family and Friends

- Spending time with family-of-origin and in-laws
- Spending time with friends of the opposite sex
- Talking with ex-spouses if divorced

Parenting

- Disciplining children
- Taking children to activities

Household Responsibilities

- Grocery shopping
- Preparing meals
- Household chores
- Managing finances
- Yardwork
- Home improvement

Celebrating the Holidays

- Where
- With whom
- For how long

Cultural Engagement (especially for interracial/interethnic couples)

- Language use
- What traditions to keep and which ones to discard from each culture

how your worldview helps create a dream marriage. Based on this definition of worldview, we conclude that your values influence how you view your spouse and your marriage. Your core values include your beliefs about God, people, salvation, the Bible, marriage, family, parenting, church, and evangelism. As both of you consider your values, you become aware of ideas that shape and challenge your vision and mission. Let us explore some of these ideas.

I, Me, Mine vs. We, Us, Ours

Marriage is about creating intimacy by transitioning from "I" to "we." It is about focusing on the "we" as a guiding force in the relationship. By using language that denotes teamwork and commitment, you create oneness that leads to becoming "one flesh" (Gen. 2:24). This, of course, happens while still respecting each other's individuality. Therefore, your identity and your spouse's identity need to be preserved while you develop a couple identity. Above all, embracing the concept of *Agape* love (1 Cor. 13:5), which is self-sacrificial and others-focused, will help you become less self-centered and place your spouse first.

Agape Love

1 Corinthians 13:5	Meaning and Application
Love is not self-seeking (NIV)	It's not about me
Does not seek its own (NASB, NKJV)	It's not about what I want
Does not insist on its own way (ESV)	It's not my way
It does not demand its own way (NLT)	I do not put pressure on you
Is not selfish (HCSB)	It's not "do it for me," it's "I do it for you"
Love cares more for others than for self (MSG)	It's about you

Needs vs. Wants

A conversation about needs versus wants may involve many areas of a couple's life. Ideally, a couple has to clarify their needs and wants and come to an agreement. Otherwise, they may experience conflict or pursue their wants instead. For example, having reliable transportation is a need; having a sports car or a brand new car may be a want. Having a house in a safe neighborhood is a need; having a house with a swimming pool and a large backyard may be a want. Therefore, you and your spouse need to make crucial decisions regarding your needs and wants in the various areas of your marriage to find a healthy balance.

Obedience vs. Sacrifice

What do we mean by obedience versus sacrifice? You may remember the Bible verse, "To obey is better than sacrifice" (1 Sam. 15:22 NIV). In this verse, God was speaking to Saul after he had disobeyed Him by not waiting for Samuel to arrive and perform the sacrifice. The sacrifice was the ceremony performed by the priest as a religious practice, or an act of worship. God emphasized that He wants people to obey Him, rather than simply go through religious activities meaninglessly. Obedience is relational; God wants a relationship with us. Therefore, the vision needs to reflect your desire to obey God as a couple in all areas of your life. So, your obedience flows out of your relationship with God.

Holiness vs. Happiness

A few years ago, Gary Thomas wrote the book *Sacred Marriage*, asserting that marriage can be an instrument that God uses to draw spouses "closer to God and to grow in Christian character."[5] We agree that marriage is the context in which you can be thoroughly known by another, namely your spouse, and it provides an opportunity for your flaws and sins to be exposed and dealt with by the Holy Spirit. Thus, expanding your awareness of the spiritual dimension of your marriage and engaging in spiritual practices will help you grow closer to God and each other in holiness and happiness.

The ABC's of Vision

A vision has several intertwined foundational elements. These elements can help guide your thoughts as you develop your vision for your marriage. We call them the ABC's of a vision for the Christian marriage and discuss them below.

 A vision ignites excitement in the present and creates hope for the future.

Amplify

A God-given vision for your marriage will amplify your influence on your marriage and other people's lives. For instance, when you look at the great leaders of the Old Testament, you see that they received a calling and a vision to do something not for themselves, but rather for God's people. You also note that many times they were unable to comprehend the magnitude of the vision, yet by faith they accepted it. Thus, a God-given vision is not self-centered, egotistical, or materialistic. It is others-focused as it starts with God and His purpose for your life, and as it spreads to touch those around you. Hence, ask yourself what impact you want to make in your spouse's life and on other people's lives.

Become

A vision is about becoming the person and the couple God wants you to be. As a Christian, you want to become a genuine Christ-follower who strives to be more like Christ daily. Therefore, ask yourself the following questions: What kind of person do you want to become? What kind of husband or wife do you want to become? What kind of father or mother do you want to become? Thus, having a vision is transformational; it shapes us as we make the commitment to embrace it.

Communicate

Every vision communicates a message to the world. As a couple, what kind of message do you want your lives to communicate? Your vision can communicate a Christ-centered message to those around you like letters to the world (2 Cor. 3:2). It can communicate the sacrificial commitment you have for one another and how you invest your lives to become one flesh. Moreover, you have the power to design the message your marriage conveys to those around you.

Do

The vision becomes the catalyst that propels you to take action to create the marriage of your dreams. However, these actions need to be strategic and match the multidimensional aspects of the vision. A well-developed strategic plan of action helps materialize the vision while simultaneously strengthening it. For instance, if your vision calls for a change in your career, as a couple, you need to take the necessary steps to make it happen.

Engage

Engage wholeheartedly with the people who are part of your vision. In marriage, couples engage each other to create the most intimate human relationship. This involves intentionally spending both quantity and quality time together. Engaging is about communication. Your daily interactions need to be positive and constructive, reflecting your specific vision for your dream marriage. In fact, John Gottman, a famous marriage researcher, and his team found that *harsh start-up*, "which is the habit of beginning your interactions with criticism or contempt,"[6] can create barriers between you and your spouse. Conversely, they recommend a *softened start-up* which means that you will start a conversation positively, even if it is a complaint.[7] Therefore, building and strengthening intimacy needs to be part of your focus through all kinds of engagements.

Feel

A vision ignites excitement in the present and creates hope for the future. When you are living the vision for your marriage, you can experience positive feelings and a great sense of well-being. When you give and receive true love in your marriage, you feel joy, excitement, peace, and happiness. You also have a sense that you are living your vision to its fullest. Additionally, a vision provides an emotional and mental shelter for you when you face adversities in your marriage or in life.

——————— Vision in Seven Areas of Life ———————

In the counseling field, counselors use a multidimensional model called the bio-psychosocial-spiritual approach, a holistic methodology that looks at life from a multifaceted perspective. The **biological** facet focuses on the body, physical health, neurobiology, and illnesses. The **psychological** area addresses mental health, including the thoughts, emotions, and behaviors. The **social** dimension centers on romantic/intimate relationships, friendships, family, peers, and social influences. Finally, the **spiritual** area focuses on religious beliefs, spirituality, and practices. As expected, for Christian counselors, the spiritual area emphasizes a relationship to Christ.

The National Wellness Institute promotes six dimensions of wellness, which include the emotional, occupational, physical, social, intellectual, and spiritual areas.[8] Other models of wellness focus on even more areas. Many counselors and life coaches use the Wellness model, which focuses on helping people make choices to promote a healthy and fulfilling lifestyle. Both models, the biopsycho-social-spiritual approach and the wellness approach, emphasize the importance of developing a healthy lifestyle from a holistic perspective.

Since vision is a multidimensional concept, we will borrow from these models and focus on the following seven areas of life: physical, psychological, relational, financial, professional, recreational, and spiritual. These areas are interdependent and influence each other. For example, not feeling well physically might affect your mood and, consequently, the interaction with your spouse. Having marital problems and unresolved conflict may affect your attitude, and you may feel depressed. These problems might affect other relationships as well as productivity at work. On the other hand, if you are doing well physically, psychologically, and spiritually, chances are that you are going to be more productive and relate to others more positively. Thus, your vision for your marriage needs to be all-encompassing so that it includes these seven areas of life. Additionally, these seven areas might change in the different seasons of the marriage life cycle.

Vision in Seven Areas of Life?

Physical
- Your health and fitness

Psychological
- Your thinking and feeling

Relational
- Your spouse and others

Financial
- Your money and budget

Professional
- Your vocation and career

Recreational
- Your leisure and fun

Spiritual
- Your faith and spirituality

Vision through the Marriage Life Cycle

As you think about the vision for your marriage and the future, you may be aware that you will be going through different seasons in your marriage. Sociologists and counselors call these seasons the marriage life cycle.[9] We have created our adapted version of the model for intact families.

Newly Married	Child Rearing Years			Launching	Middle Aged	Aging
Visioning	Parenting			Sending	Revisioning	Retiring
	Preschool	Child	Teen			
Creating a Vision	Bonding	Guiding	Coaching	Sending Child to College	Reassessing Life and Marriage	Accepting Aging
Forming a Couple Identity	Caring for Children	Parenting	Instructing	Providing Support	Grandparenting	Failing Health
Commitment	Discipline	Discipline	Supervision	Encouragement	Repurpose	Reminisce
Housing and Finances	Busyness and Fatigue	Child's Activities	Freedom and Protection	Financial Challenges	Empty Nest and Sandwich Generation	Loss of Friends and Relatives
Relating to In-Laws	Relating to Teachers, Doctors, and Other People in Child's Life			Investing in Child	Fulfilling Vision and Mission	Loss of Spouse
Becoming "one flesh"	Raising Child to Love God and Love People			Empowering Child	Gaining Meaning	Finishing Well

As you contemplate your future as a couple, we recommend that you begin to prepare for the changing realities that you will face in the different stages of the marriage and family life cycle. For example, if you do not have children yet but plan to have them, you can start now to prepare for parenting. Chapter 10 covers some essential concepts that are helpful for those who have children as well as for those couples who plan to have children someday. Since you have to make many major financial decisions throughout the life cycle, we encourage you to look at Chapter 6 where we discuss the importance of financial planning and preparing for these different phases of marriage.

Mission Statement Equals Purpose

When you embark on a house-hunting journey, you are on a mission to find your dream home. In the field of administration and leadership, the words *mission* or *purpose* are used interchangeably to justify the existence of an organization.[10] When applying the concept of mission to marriage, a mission statement invites couples to move out of their comfort zone, so they can identify and implement a plan of action to fulfill their mission. The mission also provides a sense of direction, especially when couples have a clear vision for their marriage. Clint and Penny Bragg, in their book *Your Marriage, God's Mission*, point out that "just as no two marriages are alike, God's mission for each marriage is also unique."[11] Thus, the mission provides the unique *why* for your actions in your marriage.

Having a compelling mission statement can be beneficial to your marriage for a variety of reasons. First, it helps you and your spouse stay the course, pursuing your marriage goals despite challenges. It also prevents you from wasting energy and resources on things that will lead you and your spouse away from your purpose. For instance, if your dream is to send your children to college, it will be unwise to try to spend the money on a big boat. According to John Bryson, in his book *Strategic Planning for Public and Nonprofit Organizations*, a mission "fosters a habit of focusing the discussion on what is truly important."[12] We agree with Bryson and believe that couples can experience similar benefits by having a mission statement.

Second, defining your mission will also help you and your spouse clarify the strategic plan or course of action. The plan might involve details on how you will organize your lives as a married couple, the types of jobs and hobbies you will pursue, and how you will allocate your resources to support your actions. It helps you anticipate and prepare for some challenges you may face.

Third, having clarity about your mission helps you deal with internal and external conflicts effectively. It makes you less prone to allow the unnecessary escalation of conflict to impact your marriage negatively. Bryson believes that having a mission statement "eliminates a great deal of unnecessary conflict ... and it can channel discussion and activity productively."[13]

Finally, having a mission statement helps you focus on values that are dear to your family. It also creates private and public value, as you and your spouse interact with and serve people in your community. This helps you consider how to live out your vision and mission in your community. By the way, we explore the metaphor of curb appeal as your Christian testimony in your neighborhood in Chapter 3.

Stepping Out of Your Comfort Zone

As you and your spouse think about a clear vision and a captivating mission for your marriage, you will probably begin to realize that this process might be challenging for you. It might require that you step out of your comfort zone. The comfort zone is a model discussed in the fields of counseling and education,[14] and it is widely used in the self-development arena.[15] The comfort zone is a place that includes what is familiar to you; a place that is known and predictable. Usually, in your comfort zone there are no challenges, risks, or changes. Therefore, you feel safe, secure, and comfortable. Even if you are not satisfied with where you are in life, it is easier to stay in the comfort zone than to try something new.

According to the comfort zone model, dreams or goals are outside of the comfort zone. Some people even say that outside the comfort zone is where "magic happens." Michael Hyatt, author of *Your Best Year Ever*, states, "If you are going to accomplish significant things in your life, you are going to be spending a lot of time outside your Comfort Zone."[16] Therefore, it is possible that your dream marriage is outside of your comfort zone. Consequently, getting out of the comfort zone involves taking risks and facing new challenges. However, the payoff can be achieving significant things such as deeper intimacy with your spouse.

If dreams are outside of the comfort zone, you may ask, "Why do people stay in the comfort zone?" We believe that people stay in their comfort zone because of fear, lack of self-efficacy, and the cost of stepping out. First, stepping out of the comfort zone creates varying levels of anxiety and apprehension.

Some people may also experience fear of failure, fear of what others might think, and fear of the unknown. Second, some people lack self-efficacy, as they do not believe they have the skills and abilities required to perform the tasks at hand.[17] Finally, there is a price to pay when stepping out of the comfort zone. For example, we have some friends who stepped out of their comfort zone. They moved abroad to serve as missionaries, and, in the process, made significant sacrifices and overcame challenges as a couple. These types of changes can be very challenging and yet rewarding.

Three tips to help you step out of your comfort zone

- **Develop a growth mindset**. A growth mindset believes that you can learn new things and develop new abilities. Unfortunately, many individuals have a fixed-mindset and tell themselves self-limiting messages that discourage growth and learning, such as "you cannot teach an old dog a new trick." A growth mindset considers more possibilities and believes that you can indeed learn new tricks.
- **Replace your negative thoughts with God's truth.** You need to be aware of your negative thoughts that represent a fixed-mindset. God's truth gives hope and can inspire you to think positively.
- **Take the leap of faith**. Faith is "the confident assurance that something we want is going to happen" (Heb. 11:1 TLB). You need to use your faith in God and prayer to help you each step of the way. Faith will fuel hope that God can do above and beyond our expectations (Eph. 3:20).

Setting SMART Goals

Once you clarify your vision and determine your mission, you can move into the specifics of setting goals for your marriage. Obviously, we cannot presume upon the future, but planning is essential for a successful life because "careful planning puts you ahead in the long run" (Prov. 21:5 MSG). However, you need to avoid the pitfall of setting vague goals or abandoning your goals prematurely.

Vague goals do not provide specific direction. For example, you may say that your goal is to lose weight. However, this goal is not specific because you are not stating how many pounds you want to lose. Let us say that you and your spouse want to save some money. This is an important goal; however, you need to determine how much money you want to save. For instance, if you want to improve your marriage, you must consider which specific areas of your marriage you want to improve. As you can see, vague goals are not specific; consequently, they are difficult to measure.

Another challenge with goal-setting is that couples tend to abandon their goals as the year progresses. This may be due to a lack of motivation or purpose. The SMART goal technique can be an extremely helpful tool for couples. The acronym SMART stands for Specific, Measurable, Attainable, Relevant, and Time-bound. Counselors often use this technique or tool to help clients set SMART goals[18] because it gives direction, purpose, focus, and motivation for couples to stay the course. Let us examine each one of them briefly.

SMART Goals

S SPECIFIC - What? Who? Where?

M MEASURABLE - How can you measure it?

A ATTAINABLE - Do you have the resources?

R RELEVANT - Is it part of your life's purpose?

T TIME-BOUND - When?

Specific

Specific goals give clarity. So, you and your spouse need to be able to answer the *what, who,* and *where* of the goal. First, you need to determine *what* behaviors or actions you want to start, change, increase, decrease, or even stop. Second, you need to consider *who* is involved in your goal. Since marriage goals are relational, your spouse is directly or indirectly involved in your goal. Keep in mind that you cannot set a goal for another person even when your goal involves him or her. Finally, consider the *where* or the context of your goal. Will this goal take place at home, work, or school? For example, if your goal is to get a promotion or a raise, then the setting of this goal is your workplace.

Measurable

Measurable goals let you know whether you are making progress. You and your spouse need to be able to measure your goal. But, how can you measure it? For example, if you want to pay off your mortgage, you will need to determine how much of the mortgage you want to have paid at the end of the year. If you want to save money, you will need to decide how much. Without thinking of specific amounts, you will never know how close or far you are from achieving your goal. Consequently, you will not put in the required effort to accomplish it.

Attainable

The goal needs to be within your reach; otherwise, it will be unrealistic. You need to think in terms of having the resources you need to reach the goal and being able to access those resources. For example, if your goal is to celebrate your next anniversary with a trip to Europe, but you do not have the finances or a strategic plan to accomplish it, your goal is unachievable. However, we are not saying that you cannot set ambitious goals that require faith.

Relevant

The goal needs to be connected with your overall sense of purpose in life and align with your shared values. How will this goal contribute toward the vision and mission for your marriage? For example, going back to school to get a Master's degree to further your career may be relevant to your overall personal and professional growth, finances, and marriage.

Time-Bound

Goals need to have a beginning and an end. As a couple, you will need to determine a realistic time frame to reach your goal. This helps you answer the *by when* question. For instance, a SMART financial goal may be stated, "We want to save $ 10,000.00 by the end of the year." However, you will need to ensure that the time frame is realistic.

As you continue to read this book, you will gain knowledge, insights, and relational skills that you can include in your strategic plan to achieve your dream marriage. In the following chart, we provide some examples of SMART goals in each of the seven areas. Use them to inspire you to set your own SMART goals as a couple.

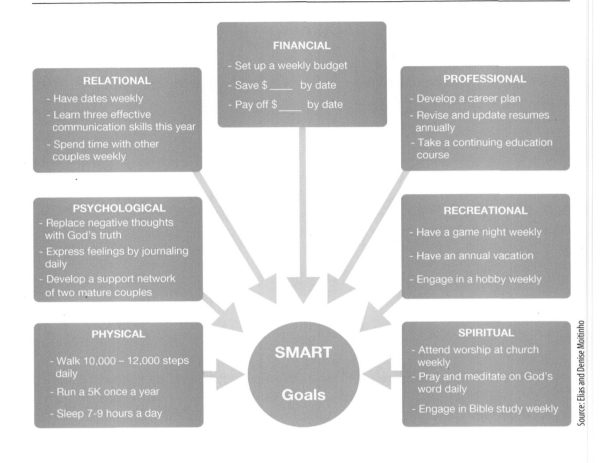

FINANCIAL
- Set up a weekly budget
- Save $ _____ by date
- Pay off $ _____ by date

RELATIONAL
- Have dates weekly
- Learn three effective communication skills this year
- Spend time with other couples weekly

PROFESSIONAL
- Develop a career plan
- Revise and update resumes annually
- Take a continuing education course

PSYCHOLOGICAL
- Replace negative thoughts with God's truth
- Express feelings by journaling daily
- Develop a support network of two mature couples

RECREATIONAL
- Have a game night weekly
- Have an annual vacation
- Engage in a hobby weekly

PHYSICAL
- Walk 10,000 – 12,000 steps daily
- Run a 5K once a year
- Sleep 7-9 hours a day

SMART Goals

SPIRITUAL
- Attend worship at church weekly
- Pray and meditate on God's word daily
- Engage in Bible study weekly

Source: Elias and Denise Moitinho

Developing a Strategic Plan

Once you have your SMART goals in place, you need to develop a strategic plan. You may have heard that a goal without a plan is only a wish. Based on our work experience, we created this helpful acronym, the S.AF.E. plan, to help you reach your SMART goals. The S.A.F.E. plan includes Short-term objectives, Action steps, Faith-building practices, and Evaluation of progress.

Short-term objectives are smaller goals that lead toward each SMART goal. For example, your SMART goal is the destination. The short-term objectives are the stops along the way. If your SMART goal is to buy a house, some short-term objectives would include elements such as saving for a down payment, qualifying for a mortgage, and deciding on a location. These objectives lead toward the SMART goal of buying a house. Some short-term objectives may require multiple action steps.

Action steps are the specific actions or behaviors that you engage in as a couple to accomplish a short-term objective. For example, some action steps when buying a house would involve setting up a plan for saving money, meeting with a realtor and a mortgage lender, and researching the desired neighborhoods. Action steps also need to have specific due dates.

Faith-building practices such as prayer and worship help you deal with challenges that come along the way as you work on your S.A.F.E. plan toward your SMART goal. Awareness of potential challenges helps you and your spouse pray and prepare. We believe that God can do above and beyond our expectations (Eph. 3:20) and He can help us when we face life challenges.

Evaluation of progress allows you and your spouse to know how fast or slow you are moving toward the SMART goal. It also helps you determine if you are moving in the right direction and how much progress you are making or if you are experiencing a setback. Evaluation lets you determine whether you need to adjust your plan of action or even your goals. It may also lead to a revision of your vision.

We acknowledge that life is unpredictable and things or events beyond your control may happen. Events such as accidents, job loss, health challenges, and natural disasters can derail your goals and strategic plan. Therefore, being flexible and adaptable will be essential in this process. Being unable to reach your goals due to unforeseeable life events does not mean that you have failed in your marriage. We encourage you to regroup, rethink, revise your vision and goals, and keep on trusting God for a brighter future. Additionally, we also want to emphasize that setting SMART goals for your marriage does not mean you cannot have individual goals. We do encourage you to have individual as well as marriage goals.

Writing Your Vision Statement

When we decided to move to Virginia, we were blessed to find a house near the foothills of the amazing Blue Ridge Mountains. As a result, every summer and fall, we often visit the Peaks of Otter and enjoy a scenic drive on the Blue Ridge Parkway. While driving on the parkway, we reach elevations over 3,000 feet and stop at the various overlooks to contemplate breathtaking views of the mountains and the valleys below. Standing there on the mountain, we see far away in the distance, but when we look through our binoculars, we are able to see more details and discover towns that we never knew existed.

A vision is similar to this scenario. Right now, we want to invite you to climb up figuratively to a higher elevation as a couple. We want to invite you to imagine that you are looking far away into the distant future. Perhaps you need to get your own binoculars to look with more focus into a particular area of your life and imagine details of your marriage life that you want to see transformed in the future. By doing so, you will be able to formulate a comprehensive and transformational vision statement for your marriage. We do not assume that you do not have a vision or goals for your marriage. So, as you go through the process of looking upward, inward, outward, and forward, consider the vision and goals you already have and the progress you are making.

As you contemplate your vision, consider these elements:

- Look **UPWARD** – Acknowledge your dependence on God.
- Look **INWARD** – Identify your strengths, gifts, and talents.
- Look **OUTWARD** – Recognize your influence and support network.
- Look **FORWARD** – Envision a bright future.

Step 1. Start with Prayer

We recommend that you and your spouse make time to pray for your marriage and ask God to show you His purpose for your lives and things He wants to do in and through your marriage. In Jeremiah 33:3 (NIV) God says, "Call to me and I will answer you and tell you great and unsearchable things you do not know." Therefore, we believe that as God's children, when we ask Him, He will reveal to us His plan and purpose for our lives. We realize that some people are married to spouses who are not believers. If this is your case, we still encourage you to pray.

Step 2. Share Your Expectations

Review the list of expectations you read at the beginning of this chapter. Be as specific as possible as you discuss the various areas of your marriage with your spouse. Moreover, be sure to listen to your spouse as well.

Step 3. Ask the Miracle Question and Dream Big

The *miracle question* created by Steve DeShazer, creator of Solution-Focused Brief Therapy (SFBT), can be a catalyst to help you develop your vision. The miracle question is the following:

"Suppose you were to go home tonight, and while you were asleep, a miracle happened, and the problem that brought you here was solved. How will you and those around you know the miracle happened?"

"What will be different?"
"What would you do differently?"
"What would your spouse, your friends notice you were doing differently?"[19]

Here is our adaptation of the miracle question to help you in the process of developing your vision.

Suppose a miracle happened and you were 10 years into the future and your dream marriage is a reality, what would it look like?
What would you and your spouse be doing?
What types of conversations would you be having?
What types of activities would you be engaging together?
What feelings would you be experiencing?

By asking the miracle question and taking the time to answer the follow-up questions, you will gain clarity. You can begin to envision your dream marriage in ultra-high definition in the seven areas of life as well as in the different stages of the marriage and family life cycle.

Step 4. Consider the Seven Areas of Life and the Stages of the Marriage Life Cycle

Considering the seven essential areas of life will assist you to develop a realistic vision. When envisioning your marriage moving through the stages of the marriage life cycle, you can identify actions you need to take to ensure a brighter future ahead.

Step 5. Reflect on Essential Questions

- What is God's purpose for your marriage?
- What are your values as a couple?
- What kind of marriage do you want to have?
- What kind of couple do you want to be?
- What do you want to accomplish in your lives as a married couple?
- What kind of couple do you want to be 5 years from now?
- What do you want to be doing 5–10 years from now?
- What kind of life do you envision for yourselves in the different stages of the marriage life cycle?
- What legacy do you want to leave?

By asking and answering these essential questions, you and your spouse can create a vision statement that addresses various aspects of your lives. Rick Warren in his popular book, *The Purpose Driven Life,* uses the acrostic SHAPE to highlight the importance of understanding spiritual gifts, passions, abilities, personalities, and experiences to discover your purpose in life.[20] Thus, the process of developing a vision statement will help you to see the full picture of your life as a couple.

Step 6. Write a Vision Statement

Here is a couple of concise vision statement examples to inspire you:

- "To become a marriage that brings honor and glory to God in all seven areas of life: physical, psychological, relational, financial, professional, recreational, and spiritual."
- "To maintain a growing, successful, and intimate marriage that inspires couples to do the same."

We encourage you to come up with your own and ensure that your statement aligns with your Christian values.

Writing Your Mission Statement

A mission statement flows from your understanding of your vision for your marriage. It is usually no longer than a page and, once established, can be captured in a slogan[21] so that you and your spouse can easily remember it. This is important, especially during times when conflict arises so that you do not lose focus on the things that matter the most.

Perhaps, it is a good idea to post your mission slogan somewhere in your house where both of you can see it, the same way organizations keep their mission statement in front of their employees. For instance, many Christians use the following verse "But as for me and my house, we will serve the Lord" (Jos. 24:15 NKJV) as their marriage or family mission statement and display it proudly in their homes. The marriage mission statement "To have a Christ-centered marriage in which our love for God is displayed in how we treat each other and those around us with unconditional and redemptive love" is another example based on the Great Commandment (Matt. 22:35–40) and the Great Commission (Matt. 28:19–20).

As you live out your vision and mission statement by implementing your strategic plan to reach your goals, it is essential to evaluate your progress. We encourage you and your spouse to have what we call *Couple Time* to meet regularly to discuss your progress in each SMART goal in the seven areas of your life. House-hunting for a dream home and envisioning and creating a dream marriage can be and overwhelming yet exciting and rewarding task. Our prayer is that this book will be a helpful guide to you in this process.

Next, we invite you to consider the location of your dream home.

Check out the chapter video at: www.grtep.com

Endnotes

1. James M. Kouzes and Barry Z. Posner, *The Leadership Challenge: How to Make Extraordinary Things Happen in Organizations*, 6th ed. (New York, NY: John Wiley & Sons, 2017).

2. John M. Bryson, *Strategic Planning for Public and Nonprofit Organizations: A Guide to Strengthening and Sustaining Organizational Achievement*, 5th ed. (New York, NY: John Wiley & Sons, 2011).

3. Paul Koptak, *Proverbs: The NIV Application Commentary from Biblical Text to Contemporary Life* (Grand Rapids, MI: Zondervan Academic, 2014).

4. Kouzes and Posner, *The Leadership Challenge*.

5. Gary Thomas, *Sacred Marriage: What If God Designed Marriage to Make Us Holy More Than to Make Us Happy?* (Grand Rapids, MI: Zondervan, 2015), 11.

6. John M. Gottman, Julie Schwartz Gottman, and Joan DeClaire, *Ten Lessons to Transform Your Marriage: America's Love Lab Experts Share Their Strategies for Strengthening Your Relationship* (New York, NY: Three Rivers Press, 2006), 178.

7. Gottman, Gottman, and DeClaire, *Ten Lessons to Transform Your Marriage*.

8. National Wellness Institute, "The Six Dimensions of Wellness," accessed January 14, 2019, https://www.nationalwellness.org/page/Six_Dimensions.

9. Irene Goldenberg, Mark Stanton, and Herbert Goldenberg, *Family Therapy: An Overview*, 5th ed. (Boston, MA: Cengage Learning, 2017); Jack O. Balswick and Judith K. Balswick, *The Family: A Christian Perspective on the Contemporary Home*, 4th ed. (Grand Rapids, MI: Baker Academic, 2014).

10. Bryson, *Strategic Planning for Public and Nonprofit Organizations*.

11. Clint Bragg and Penny Bragg, *Your Marriage, God's Mission: Discovering Your Spiritual Purpose Together* (Grand Rapids, MI: Kregel Publication, 2017), 24.

12. Bryson, *Strategic Planning for Public and Nonprofit Organizations*, 104.

13. Bryson, *Strategic Planning for Public and Nonprofit Organizations*, 38.

14. Mike Brown, "Comfort Zone: Model or Metaphor," *Australian Journal of Outdoor Education* 12, no. 1 (2008): 3–12.

15. John C. Maxwell, *No Limits: Blow the Cap off Your Capacity* (New York, NY: Center Street, 2017).

16. Michael Hyatt, *Your Best Year Ever: A 5-Step Plan for Achieving Your Most Important Goals* (Grand Rapids, MI: Baker Books, 2018), 145.

17. Albert Bandura, *Social Foundations of Thought and Action: A Social Cognitive Theory* (Englewood Cliffs, NJ: Prentice Hall, 1986).

18. Ronald Hawkins, Anita Knight, Gary Sibcy, and Steven Warren, *Research-Based Counseling Skills: The Art and Science of Therapeutic Empathy* (Dubuque, IA: Kendall Hunt, 2019).

19. Gary J. Oliver, "Solution-Focused Counseling," in *The Popular Encyclopedia of Christian Counseling: An Indispensable Tool for Helping People with Their Problems* (Eugene, OR: Harvest House Publishers, 2011), 492; Christine E. Murray and Thomas L. Murray Jr., "Solution-Focused Premarital Counseling; Helping Couples Build a Vision for Their Marriage," *Journal of Marriage and Family Therapy* 30, no. 3 (July 2004): 349–358.

20. Rick Warren, *The Purpose Driven Life: What on Earth Am I Here for?* (Grand Rapids, MI: Zondervan, 2009).

21. Bryson, *Strategic Planning for Public and Nonprofit Organizations*, 120.

CHAPTER 2

Location Is Everything: Providing Stability

"Where does God say you need to be?"
Ian F. Jones

When we decided to move from Texas to Virginia, we knew our house-hunting experience was going to be challenging. Although we started our online house-hunting months before we actually visited the beautiful city of Lynchburg, we had no idea what areas were safe, friendly, and convenient for our family. Additionally, since we were coming from the flatlands of North Texas, we were unaware of the rolling hills and

curvy roads and how these geographic features would affect our daily commute. Nevertheless, we knew that we wanted to live in the best possible location within 5–10 miles from our children's school and our place of employment. Needless to say, location was a driving force in our house-hunting experience.

The phrase *location, location, location* has become a standard in real estate, and it has been around since the 1920s.[1] Many people believe that the location is as important as the house itself. But why is it so important? First, location is a significant factor in determining the value of a home. Second, it represents the ideal place where you and your spouse desire to live. Third, it means access to things that are important to you and meet your needs and preferences. These needs and preferences may include a safe neighborhood, excellent schools, and hospitals. It may also involve access to popular places, shops, restaurants, public transit, and highways.[2] Thus, it is not surprising that when house hunting, most couples place the location of the house at the top of their wish list. Buying a dream home is a long-term commitment and a costly investment that can bring stability to the family for years to come.

In this chapter, we use the concept of location as a metaphor to spiritual location in life. We also explore how this spiritual location can give you a sense of stability to your marriage. Such stability arises from the understanding of a sound biblical view of marriage and family, which helps you create your dream home, an intimate Christian marriage, consistent with God's design.

Spiritual Location

Ian Jones in his book, *The Counsel of Heaven on Earth,* discusses three essential dimensions of location that he believes need to be considered in Christian counseling. Jones uses Genesis 3, the account of the Fall of Adam and Eve in the Garden, to develop the following dimensions of location: location in relationship to self, location in relationship to others, and location in relationship to God.[3]

Regarding location in relationship to self, Jones explains that by hiding from God, Adam had become egocentric and displayed self-interest. He points out that when Adam sinned against God, he became separated from God, and his sin led him to develop a distorted view of self. Next, the Fall also affected Adam and Eve's location in relationship to each other. By covering their bodies, Adam and Eve lost the openness they had with each other; distrust and blame invaded their relationship. In addition, sin disrupted Adam and Eve's location in relationship to God, and it caused them to engage in deception and idolatry. Consequently, sin separated them from God. Thus, we conclude that people need to know where they are located in relationship to self, others, and God to experience a healthy and balanced life.

We agree with Jones and we want to expand on the concept of location and its implications for marriage. For instance, regarding location in relationship to self, we need to be aware of our fallen human nature and our natural tendency to be self-centered in the marital relationship. Perhaps it is time to consider how we may be displaying self-centeredness in our daily interactions with our spouse. Are we mainly looking at our own interests rather than the interests of our spouse (Phil. 2:4)?

Regarding your location in relationship to others, it is a good idea to examine how you are doing in your interactions with your spouse and family. You may want to consider how much mistrust, conflict, and blame may be a regular part of your relationships. You may also want to reflect on your interactions with others and determine if they have been positive and uplifting or negative and destructive.

Finally, we encourage you to examine your location in relationship to God. How would you describe your relationship with God? How much are you growing spiritually? How are you and your spouse growing in your relationship with God together? This self-reflection can be beneficial to you and your marriage. Next, let us expand on this idea of location in relationship to God.

Location in relationship to God implies having a close connection to God and an understanding of the biblical teaching on marriage. This is significant since research shows that religion has a mostly positive influence on marriage. For instance, a study examined the relationship between religion and four variables including marital relationship quality in 11 countries, which also included the United States.[4] In the study, researchers used data from the World Values Survey (WVS) and the Global Family and Gender Survey (GFGS) and found that "Men and women who share an active religious life, for instance, enjoy higher levels of relationship quality and sexual satisfaction compared to their peers in secular or less/mixed religious relationships."[5] Since our focus is on the Christian faith, we emphasize a biblical worldview in this chapter.

Location Equals Stability

The wedding industry has influenced our society in such a way that many couples believe that they need a big and expensive wedding to have a happy marriage. However, is this really true? Andrew Francis-Tan and Hugo Mialon in their article, *A Diamond Is Forever and Other Fairy Tales: The Relationship between Wedding Expenses and Marriage Duration,* attempted to answer this question. They evaluated data from a survey of over 3,000 married couples in the U.S. to determine if there was a correlation between how much money people spend on their wedding and the duration of their marriages.[6] They concluded that there is "little evidence to support the validity of the wedding industry's general message that connects expensive weddings with positive marital outcomes."[7] In other words, having an expensive wedding will not necessarily create a happy marriage.

Randy Olson in his article on marriage stability highlights research-based factors that make a solid marriage in the U.S.[8] Dating at least three years before getting married, attending church together, and having a wedding followed by a planned honeymoon are some of the factors that help provide stability for the marital relationship. Interestingly, an expensive wedding is not on the list, though Olson mentions a wedding with more than 200 people, which does not necessarily mean an expensive wedding.

As you read this information, do not assume that your marriage is doomed to fail if you dated for only a few months, had a small wedding, or did not have a traditional honeymoon. The reality is that you cannot change the past. However, you can inevitably focus on the things that are part of your present and future, such as your location in relationship to yourself, your spouse, and God. Finding the right location in those areas will help you create the stability your marriage needs to continue to grow and thrive. We will continue drawing from this location metaphor to discuss key foundational principles related to marriage stability.

Understanding Worldview

Everyone has a worldview, and a worldview influences one's location. A worldview is a filter or a lens through which you view, understand, and make sense of reality and the world around you. John Thomas and Lisa Sosin in their book, *Therapeutic Expedition: Equipping the Christian Counselor for the Journey,* define worldview as "an internal map that consciously or unconsciously provides direction to life ... [and] contains the assumptions, beliefs, and principles on which we build our lives."[9] More recently, James Sire, in his book *The Universe Next Door: A Basic Worldview Catalog*, proposes a revised definition of worldview. He states,

> A worldview is a commitment, a fundamental orientation of the heart, that can be expressed as a story or in a set of presuppositions (assumptions that may be true, partially true or entirely false) that we hold (consciously or subconsciously, consistently or inconsistently) about the basic constitution of reality, and that provides the foundation of which we live and move and have our being.[10]

Although you may not be fully aware of your worldview or the specific sources of your beliefs and assumptions, your worldview still guides your decision-making and behaviors. To put it succinctly, your worldview is your core beliefs. In fact, your worldview is an amalgamation of various worldviews, and it may or may not be entirely consistent with a biblical worldview. We believe that when Christians look at the Bible for guidance, their worldview becomes anchored in God's perfect revelation and truth. Then, they can live out the life-changing biblical principles.

Thomas and Sosin explain that a worldview has four components: cosmology, teleology, epistemology, and axiology.[11]

Worldview Component	Focus	Key Questions
Cosmology	Totality of reality: Physical and non-physical reality	• Where did I come from? • Is there a God?
Teleology	• Purpose • Meaning	• Why am I here? • Where am I going?
Epistemology	• Knowledge • Truth	• What can I know for sure? • How can I know it?
Axiology	• Morality • Values	• Why do I do what I do? • How do I live

Source: John C. Thomas and Lisa Sosin, *Therapeutic Expedition: Equipping the Christian Counselor for the Journey* (Nashville, TN: B&H Academic, 2011), p. 14.

We believe that these four elements are also present in a worldview on marriage. Based on the chart provided, *axiology* refers to morality and values as it addresses how you live and why you act the way you do. This includes how you view marriage and family and how you live as husband and wife. You may also believe that God is real (*cosmology*) and He created you and your spouse for a purpose (*teleology*). You may believe that the Bible is God's revelation of Himself and it provides divine guidance and truth for you to live your marriage life (*epistemology*). As a Christian, you can use your faith and reason to ensure that your worldview aligns with a biblical worldview.

A Cognitive Perspective

We want to use a cognitive approach to expand further on the concept of worldview. From a *cognitive* perspective, a worldview is made up of core beliefs or schemas, also known as *schemata*, which develop from life experiences, including both positive and negative experiences.[12] A worldview may also include intentional learning from formal educational environments as well as from daily interactions with others and the media. Your worldview includes what you have learned from your individual experiences, family, culture, religion, and society. Consequently, the core beliefs you have about marriage and family give rise to your thoughts, including automatic thoughts, assumptions, attitudes, and biases that influence your behaviors in marriage. The following picture illustrates and helps us understand this process.

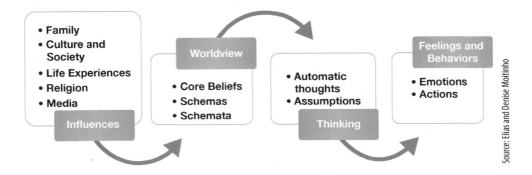

Source: Elias and Denise Moitinho

A Theological Perspective

From a *theological* perspective, Scriptures command us to renew our minds (Rom. 12:2) and set our minds "on things above" (Col. 3:1–2 NIV). Proverbs 23:7 states, "For as he thinks within himself, so he is" (NASB). Many Christians believe that according to this verse, our minds are at the core of who we are and that we are engaged on a battle of the mind, called spiritual warfare (Eph. 6:10–18). Therefore, because Satan can also influence our minds, we need to be alert (1 Pet. 5:8). We also need to acknowledge that our core beliefs may or may not be in agreement with Scriptures, and that our minds are bombarded daily with messages contrary to the Bible. Hence, we must practice the renewing of our minds because, ultimately, our beliefs and thoughts will influence how we live our lives and how we interact with our spouses daily.

A Call to a Transformed Worldview

God calls us to live a transformed life with a renewed mind. The Bible says, "do not conform to the pattern of this world, but be transformed by the renewing of your mind. Then you will be able to test and approve what God's will is—His good, pleasing and perfect will" (Rom. 12:2 NIV). The word *transformed* in this verse is the Greek verb *metamorphoo,* which means "to change into another form, [or] to transform."[13] Interestingly, we get our English word *metamorphosis,* which means transformation, from this verb. Moreover, Paul is challenging believers to be transformed from the inside out into a new creation and to develop a worldview that is consistent with God's truth. In 2 Cor. 5:17 he writes, "Therefore, if anyone *is* in Christ, *he is* a new creation; old things have passed away; behold, all things have become new" (NKJV). Clearly, Paul views a transformed life as the result of salvation and an abiding relationship with Christ through the work of the Holy Spirit (2 Cor. 3:18) as the believer studies the Bible.

Throughout Paul's letters, we also see an emphasis on the importance of having a biblically based worldview. According to scholars, Paul's letters to the Romans, Ephesians, and Colossians follow a similar pattern in which they contain extensive teaching of foundational doctrine (orthodoxy) that is

 As Christians, we are to have a worldview that is not shaped by the world (Rom. 12:2) so that we may put into practice (orthopraxy) what we know and believe about God (orthodoxy).

followed by practical application (orthopraxy). In summary, Paul teaches that we are sinners (Rom. 3:23; Eph. 2:1–2), who accepted God's redemptive plan through faith in Christ (Rom. 5:8; 6:23; 10:9–10; Eph. 2:8–9) and gained a new identity as Christians (Eph. 2:4–7; Cor. 5:17). He emphasizes that the only way we can experience the power of Christ in our lives (Gal. 2:20) is through the indwelling and filling of the Holy Spirit (Gal. 5:16–26; Eph. 5:18). Moreover, the goal of the Christian life must be spiritual maturity and, ultimately, to conform to the likeness of Christ (Col. 1:28; Eph. 4:13). Thus, as Christians, we are to have a worldview that is not shaped by the world (Rom. 12:2) so that we may put into practice (orthopraxy) what we know and believe about God (orthodoxy).

A Biblical Worldview on Christian Marriage

Now, let us expand our understanding of Christian marriage by focusing on some foundational principles from three key Bible passages. While we do not position ourselves as the ultimate authority on biblical hermeneutics and on a theology of marriage, we believe that our many years of seminary education have helped us develop a sound, conservative biblical understanding of marriage. We hope that the following discussion will enhance your biblical worldview on Christian marriage.

Location: In the Garden – God's Design for Marriage (Genesis 2:24–25)

The well-known passage of Genesis 2:24–25 needs to be considered in the context of the biblical narrative of God's creation. The passage states, "Therefore a man shall leave his father and mother and be joined to his wife, and they shall become one flesh. And they were both naked, the man and his wife, and were not ashamed" (NKJV). In the first two chapters of Genesis, we read about the creation of all humankind and God's perfect plan for marriage and family. The creation of all humanity starts with the equality between Adam and Eve who were created in the *Image of God* (Gen. 1:26–28). Consequently, Adam and Eve had equal worth, and Eve was not lesser than Adam or inferior to him.

Looking at the account of how God created Eve, we see the principle of men and women having the same worth in God's eyes. Genesis 2:18 says, "It is not good for man to be alone. I will make a helper suitable for him" (NIV). This verse demonstrates Adam's need for companionship and shows that the woman is an equal companion to the man by the use of the term helper. Interestingly, the Hebrew term *ezer* (helper) was also applied to God himself multiple times in the Old Testament.[14] Thus, the helper is not a subordinate. As Kenneth Matthews, a Bible scholar, carefully explains, "in the case of the biblical model, the 'helper' is an indispensable 'partner' to achieve the divine commission"[15] to be "fruitful and multiply, and fill the earth, and subdue it" (Gen. 1:28 NASB). Consequently, we can see that the man and the woman have "equal worth but differing roles."[16] This concept is called complementarity. Therefore, we believe that the assertion held by some that the Bible teaches that the man is superior to the woman is a misunderstanding and misinterpretation of Scriptures.

From a biblical perspective, marriage is a monogamous, permanent, intimate, and exclusive covenant-based relationship between a man and a woman. Genesis 2:24 states, "a man shall leave his father and mother and be joined to his wife" (NKJV). Leaving is a public act implying that as the man leaves his family, the woman becomes the new focus and priority in his life. Traditionally, Christians believe that this act takes place in the presence of God and other witnesses. Joining or cleaving represents a private union. Interestingly enough, Paul quotes Genesis 2:24 in Ephesians 5:31. The Greek word he uses has been translated as "be joined" (NASB), "be united" (NIV), or "hold fast" (ESV), which means gluing or cementing two things together.[17] Thus, we believe that the Bible emphasizes the concept of a permanent commitment.

When you got married, you made a declaration that you were leaving your family and joining your spouse. This commitment made your spouse the priority in your life. You may have recited the following vows, "from this day forward, for better, for worse, for richer, for poorer, in sickness and health, 'til death do us part." Therefore, you made a promise and gave your word before many witnesses. You made a lifelong commitment to be faithful to your spouse and to be present in times of joy as well as during challenging times. Your wedding ring is the symbol of your commitment.

From an evangelical perspective, marriage is a covenant relationship between the husband and the wife before God. The Hebrew terms leave (*azab*) and cleave or cling (*dabaq*) are used in the context of a covenant.[18] Therefore, they imply marital faithfulness and commitment for life. Tony Evans, a popular pastor and Bible teacher, asserts,

> the marriage covenant can never operate to its fullest potential without the ongoing involvement of God. Biblical, spiritual, and theological covenants assume God's integration into every aspect of the relationship in order for that covenant to maximize its purposes. But when God is dismissed from the marital covenant, it becomes an invitation to the devil to create havoc in the home.[19]

As we turn our focus to the phrase "and they become one flesh" (v. 24), we see a representation of the sexual union to solidify the intimacy between Adam and Eve since both were created as sexual beings. Therefore, sex and sexuality are intrinsically part of God's creation, and God declared that the creation of Adam and Eve "was

 Multidimensional Intimacy

Emotional – A connection of the hearts
Intellectual – A connection of the minds
Spiritual – A connection of the souls
Physical – A connection of the bodies

very good" (Gen. 1:31 NIV). Additionally, Genesis 2:25 states, "Adam and his wife were both naked, and they felt no shame" (NIV). In fact, in the Hebrew culture this nakedness "was shameful because it was often associated with guilt . . . [Thus,] it would have been remarkable to the Hebrews that the couple could be naked without embarrassment."[20] This nakedness requires a deeper level of intimacy. Intimacy means to know and to be known. It carries the connotation of being connected and it requires self-disclosure, vulnerability, trust, closeness, and no fear of rejection. Furthermore, intimacy is a multidimensional experience.

Perhaps, at your wedding, a minister read and even explained the meaning of becoming one flesh. The concept of becoming one flesh refers to the most intimate connection between a man and a woman, which goes beyond the physical relationship. In fact, emotional intimacy precedes physical intimacy. As a couple, you create intimacy in your marriage by how you show love to your spouse, how you connect emotionally, intellectually, physically, and spiritually. When you engage in this multidimensional intimacy, physical intimacy will reach deeper levels. We will discuss these levels of intimacy in-depth in Chapter 8.

Location: Outside the Garden – Still God's Design (Ephesians 5:21–31)

Another pivotal passage of Scriptures that deals with marriage is Ephesians 5:21–31. You may have heard that much debate and controversy exist over the concept of a wife's submission to the husband as expressed in this passage, particularly in verses 22 and 23. However, we need to understand the meaning of the word submission. First, it is essential to highlight that Paul writes to Christians and describes the Christian life in the context of being "filled with the Spirit" (Eph. 5:18 NASB). Furthermore, Paul uses the Greek word *hupotasso* in verse 21, which carries the understanding of "a voluntary attitude of giving in, cooperating, assuming responsibility, and carrying a burden."[21] Thus, the word implies that the wife chooses to submit voluntarily. She is neither forced nor coerced into submission. Second, it is essential to consider that verse 21 calls for mutual submission, as Paul writes, "Submit to one another out of reverence for Christ" (NIV). Harold Hoehner, a Christian theologian, expands on the meaning of submission, and he adds that "one is willing to submit to those who have authority whether it be the home, church, or in the society."[22] Finally, it is worth noting that this passage does not imply that the wife is inferior, since her submission is described, "as you do to the Lord" (v. 22). Moreover, it does not mean that the husband has the same authority that the Lord has; rather, it means that her submission comes out of her obedience to Jesus Christ.

In Ephesians, Paul gives an example of the submission of the church to Christ and presents it as a model for the wife's submission in marriage. He states, "just as the church is subject to Christ, so *let* the wives *be* to their own husbands in everything" (Eph. 5:24 NKJV). However, submission "in everything" does not mean to engage in behaviors or activities that violate God's principles in Scriptures. As we know, the church benefits from Christ's sacrificial love, guidance, protection, and blessings. Ideally, the wife should receive the same type of love and blessings from her husband exemplified in Christ's love for the church. Additionally, submission does not mean that a husband is never to consult with his wife or that the wife's ideas and opinions are no longer valid. As previously stated, both have equal worth in God's sight.

The concept that the husband is the head of the house is another biblical concept that can be easily misunderstood. Bible scholars have debated whether in Scriptures (Eph. 4:15; 5:23) the word *head* means source, leadership, or authority over. Hoehner shed some light on this debate by stating

For the man to be the head of the house does not imply that he may abuse, intimidate, or control his wife. Doing so would be contrary to and a violation of the command God gave the husband to love his wife as Christ loved the church.

that Ephesians 5:23 "speaks of two manifestations of power: first, God has subjected everything in creation under Christ's feet; and second, God gave Christ to the church as head over everything which thus implies that he is head over the church."[23] Similarly, Andreas Köstenberger and David Jones assert, "this headship implies both the wife's submission to her husband's authority and the husband's loving, sacrificial devotion to his wife."[24] For the man to be the head of the house does not imply that he may abuse, intimidate, or control his wife. Doing so would be totally contrary to and a violation of the command God gave the husband to love his wife as Christ loved the church (v. 25). Furthermore, when both husband and wife choose to follow God's plan rather than the distorted cultural views of marriage, they relate to each other as equals and experience the joys and fulfillment of marriage in a significant way.

The picture of a Christian marriage includes a loving husband who follows God's command to love his wife "as Christ loved the church" (Eph. 5:25 NIV). This is the *Agape* love that is exemplified by the sacrificial love of Christ for His church. Agape love is the highest form of love and it focuses on another person's well-being and not on oneself. Paul emphasizes that Agape "love is patient [and] kind. It does not envy, it does not boast, it is not proud. It does not dishonor others, it is not self-seeking, it is not easily angered, it keeps no record of wrongs" (1 Cor. 13:4–5 NIV).

The biblical concept of covenant marriage established in the Garden of Eden is still relevant outside the Garden. In fact, Christians have attempted to influence society in the U.S. to accept this concept. A few years ago, Rachele Cade examined the Christian movement called Covenant Marriage. This movement sought to strengthen the institution of marriage and advance traditional Christian values regarding marriage by developing legislation to make stricter requirements such as premarital counseling for a marriage license and delay in the divorce process. Some states, including Louisiana, Arizona, and Arkansas developed legislation that allowed couples to choose to have this Covenant Marriage license. Cade noted that the distinctive features of the covenant marriage are showing a lifelong commitment, viewing marriage as a covenant and not a contract, having God as part of the marriage, and understanding gender roles based on evangelical principles.[25] She concluded that the Covenant Marriage movement has been criticized by some groups including feminists and those who advocate for non-traditional marriage.

Location: On the Rock or on the Sand (Matthew 7:24–27)

At the end of the famous Sermon on the Mount, Jesus indicates that there are two types of people and two types of foundations in life. He states that people can be wise or foolish, based on the kind of foundation they use to build their lives. According to Jesus, a wise person is someone who hears His teaching and puts it into practice (v. 24). Such a person is portrayed as a wise builder who built his or her house upon a rock, which withstood the storms, winds, and floods. Interestingly, this reminds us of a news story about a house that survived Hurricane Michael, which wrecked the Florida coast in 2018. According to the Weather Channel, "The house stayed upright because it was built last year to codes that were even more strict than laws required . . . It took reinforced concrete walls, 40-foot pilings driven deep into the ground and other factors to keep the house safe in the storm."[26] Similarly, you want to create a dream home or, in other words, a dream marriage that withstands the storms of life.

Now concerning the foolish builder, Jesus teaches that someone who does not apply His teaching to his or her life is a fool. He points out that this person is like a builder who chose to build on sand. When the storms, winds,

 For sure, you do not want to create a dream home on a shaky foundation that will not provide the stability that your marriage needs to last through the storms of life.

and floods came, the house was destroyed (v. 27). Jesus shows that we have two options in life. First, we may choose to listen to His teaching and obey, thus, living wise lives. Second, we can also choose to ignore His message and live our lives according to worldly philosophies or erroneous worldviews and, consequently, build our lives on a weak foundation. For sure, you do not want to create a dream home on a shaky foundation that will not provide the stability that your marriage needs to last through the storms of life.

As Christians, we are not immune to life stressors such as health challenges, relational conflict, and financial struggles. Life storms can come up suddenly in many ways, shapes, and forms, and they can surprise us when we are not ready. However, Jesus teaches that we have a choice regarding location, to build our dream marriage either on the rock or on the sand. Therefore, we believe that when you implement the principles we share in this book, you are better prepared to face life's fiercest storms. So, our prayer is that you will continue to focus on your decision to be a faithful Christ-follower who seeks to put into practice Jesus' teaching in your life and marriage daily.

The Ideal Location in Christian Marriage

Source: Elias and Denise Moitinho

A popular triangular picture depicting a couple's relationship with each other and with God is a perfect representation of this concept of location in relationship to self, others, and God. In this triangular picture, you can see God's ideal design for a Christian marriage, which is a covenant relationship between the couple and God. When the husband and the wife decide to pursue a growing relationship with God, they both move closer to Him. Consequently, as they worship, study the Bible, pray, and serve God, they move toward God together and get closer to each other naturally as a result. On the other hand, when a spouse moves toward God, but the other spouse does not, a natural distance forms between them. This gap may be clearly seen in the way they find meaning and purpose in life and how they organize their spiritual priorities. As expected, the ideal location in Christian marriage is when both husband and wife are close to God and growing in intimacy with Him. Then, meaningful marital intimacy happens as well.

A Psychological Perspective on Love

Since we are multidimensional beings with emotions, intellect, soul, and a physical body, it is essential to understand love more comprehensively. Several years ago, American psychologist Robert Sternberg developed his popular *Triangular Theory of Love.*[27] According to Sternberg, the highest type of love is called *Consummate Love*, which is a combination of three components: intimacy, passion, and commitment. Intimacy represents closeness and connection. Passion represents the physical attraction in the relationship evidenced by sexual fulfillment. Commitment exemplifies the long-term decision to maintain the love and the relationship. Based on this theory, seven types of love result from different

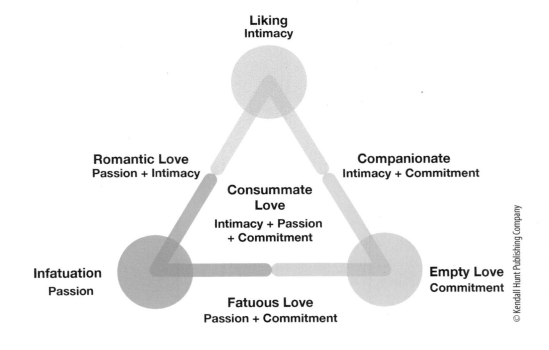

© Kendall Hunt Publishing Company

possible combinations: consummate love, empty love, companionate love, liking, infatuation, romantic love, and fatuous love.

According to Sternberg, *Consummate Love* is the ideal combination of the three types of love. It is a love in which a couple experiences intimacy, passion, and commitment to the highest levels. Certainly, you want to feel close and connected to your spouse. You want to know that your spouse finds you attractive and wants to be intimate with you sexually. You want to know that your spouse honors the marriage vows and will be with you "till death." This is the type of love that you probably desire to experience in your dream marriage.

Empty Love happens when a couple shows commitment and neither spouse plans to leave the relationship. However, intimacy and passion are no longer part of their relationship. For Christian couples, the decision to stay in the marriage may be mainly due to their belief in the permanence of marriage and that divorce is not God's ideal. They may also stay together for the sake of the children, extended family, and social status. These couples desperately need help to deal with the issues that have driven them apart. Unfortunately, many couples, including Christians, experience *Empty Love*.

Other couples may find themselves experiencing *Companionate Love*. In this type of love couples develop a good friendship and are committed to their marriage. Unfortunately, passion or sexual intimacy is lacking. This may be due to a variety of reasons. However, no matter what those reasons might be, again, we believe that these couples need to seek professional help to address this vital area of their marriage.

The other types of love, as expected, will not lead to a successful, intimate marriage because they lack the elements required for multidimensional intimacy. *Liking* and *Infatuation* have only one component each. Therefore, they will not sustain a marriage. Similarly, *Romantic Love* has the elements of a Hollywood movie with intimacy and passionate sexual relationship. However, it lacks commitment, which leads to a marriage that has a fire, but it does not last. Next, *Fatuous Love* has passion and commitment, but because it lacks intimacy, it may become a marriage based only on physical attraction and sexual pleasure. In this type of love, one may wonder what happens to the marriage when physical beauty fades. If you find yourself not experiencing *Consummate Love*, we recommend that you get help from your pastor or a Christian marriage counselor. There is still hope for you and your spouse to develop *Consummate Love* and enjoy an intimate Christian marriage.

—————————— **A Biblical Perspective on Love** ——————————

Amid multiple challenging and competing worldviews in the world today, we need a clear understanding of love from a biblical perspective. We would be remiss not to articulate a biblical view of love. You may have heard that the Bible uses different words for love. Although the Greek word **Eros** is popular in Christian circles, it was not used in the Greek New Testament. The main focus of our brief discussion will be on the three Greek terms used in the New Testament to describe love: fileo, storge, and agape. First, *Fileo* is a common word in classical Greek that means to show love, demonstrate affection, and offer hospitality.[28] Next, the word *Storge* appears to be used in classical Greek to represent the love of a father for a son.[29] Finally, the third word is *Agape* which represents sacrificial love that is steadfast and undeserved.[30] Agape also represents God's love and love that is part of the fruit of the Spirit.

Paul describes Agape love beautifully.

Love is patient, love is kind. It does not envy, it does not boast, it is not proud. It does not dishonor others, it is not self-seeking, it is not easily angered, it keeps no record of wrongs. Love does not delight in evil but rejoices with the truth. It always protects, always trusts, always hopes, always perseveres (1 Cor. 13:4–7 NIV).

The New Testament highlights the supremacy of love. Love is the first virtue listed by Paul as part of the fruit of the Spirit (Gal. 5:22). Paul charges husbands to love (Agape) their wives with the same type of sacrificial love that Christ loved the church (Eph. 5:25). He urges older women to "admonish the young women to love their husbands" (Titus 2:4 NKJV). Similarly, John the Apostle encourages his readers to show love in action, and not only with words (1 John 3:18). Both Paul and John reinforce the idea that in marriage, spouses need to display selfless and sacrificial love toward each other in words and in actions daily.

——————— **Aligning Your Mindset with a Biblical Worldview** ———————

As we have discussed, understanding a biblical perspective on marriage, intimacy, and love helps build a solid foundation for marriage. When the location of our dream home is close to God, in other words, based on God's principles in the Garden, our marriage can experience more stability as we live our lives outside the Garden. As previously stated, life events can shape our worldview positively and negatively. Unfortunately, many people have experienced abuse, trauma, pain, and suffering in their lives. These life experiences may have led some of them to a place of bitterness, resentment, or even depression, which can impact marriage negatively. From a mental health perspective,

> Adverse Childhood Experiences (ACEs) is the term used to describe all types of abuse, neglect, and other potentially traumatic experiences that occur to people under the age of 18 . . .[These] have been linked to risky health behaviors, chronic health conditions, low life potential, and early death . . . [However], The presence of ACEs does not mean that a child will experience poor outcomes.[31]

You or your spouse may have grown up with pain and suffering in your own lives before getting married. Perhaps, by God's grace, you lived most of your life devoid of much suffering, and now you may even consider that you have a comfortable life. However, people who grew up in divorced or abusive homes may develop a negative or distorted view of marriage. A study found:

> In general, those young adults that had experienced stressful family situations as they were growing up tended to report gaining messages about the negative side of intimate relationships. Specifically, the results indicated that people with divorced parents were more likely to see the messages of Relationships Are Not Permanent, Approach Relationships with Caution, and Relationships Are Beset by Lack of Trust and Fidelity, as typical of what they gained from their families of origin. Furthermore, people who rated their parents' marriages as less happy were more likely to rate the messages of Relationships Are Not Permanent, Relationships Are Beset by Lack of Trust and Fidelity, and Divorce Is Hard on Families as more typical and influential. These negative messages also were seen as influencing their attitudes toward and experiences in romantic relationships.[32]

As previously discussed, our life experiences, including the good, the bad, and the ugly, shape our worldview including core beliefs, ideas, and concepts about God, life, marriage, and family. Now, we want to invite you to explore your beliefs, ideas, and attitudes about marriage and determine how closely they align with a biblical worldview. We recognize that Christians also differ in their interpretation and understanding of Scriptures, and that we have shared a traditional, conservative Christian perspective on marriage in this book. We believe that when our worldview aligns with God's Word, we live a life that pleases God. In turn, we enjoy the blessings that come from living according to His design for marriage and family.

It is also important to acknowledge that from a neurobiological perspective, our brains are ever-changing. Caroline Leaf, a Christian cognitive neuroscientist, in her book, *Switch on Your Brain: The Key to Peak Happiness, Thinking, and Health,* describes neuroplasticity and her approach on how we can change our minds, more specifically, our thoughts. She defines neuroplasticity as the brain's ability to be "malleable and adaptable, changing moment by moment of every day."[33] She thoughtfully and skillfully developed an approach that connected brain plasticity with Paul's teaching on mind renewal (Rom. 12:2). Her approach involves the process of becoming aware of our thoughts and identifying them (Gather), engaging in disciplined thinking (Focused Reflection), writing down thoughts (Write), redesigning thoughts (Revisit), and practicing the new healthy thoughts to solidify the new thinking (Active Reach).[34]

Similarly, we conceptualize mind renewal as a process of changing and aligning our thoughts and thinking patterns with a biblical worldview. However, we provide a simple, less complex approach here. In fact, our mind transformation process is a combination of biblical application and practical actions similar to what counselors call cognitive restructuring.

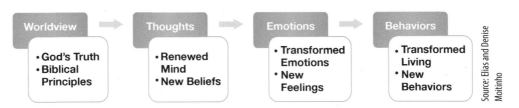

Worldview		Thoughts		Emotions		Behaviors
• God's Truth • Biblical Principles		• Renewed Mind • New Beliefs		• Transformed Emotions • New Feelings		• Transformed Living • New Behaviors

Source: Elias and Denise Moitinho

We believe that you can renew your minds by implementing the following steps:

1. ***Saturate your mind with the Word of God.*** You can accomplish this step through regular Bible reading, daily devotional, weekly Bible study, and listening to inspiring sermons on a regular basis. The purpose of this step is to

develop a biblical worldview and become familiar with what God says about the various areas of life including marriage.

2. *Identify your core beliefs (worldview) and automatic thoughts that are contrary to the Word of God.* This process requires reflection, introspection, and monitoring your inner dialog or self-talk. You may even write your beliefs and automatic thoughts down. Writing them down helps you articulate your beliefs about the various areas of life and marriage.

3. *Challenge your core beliefs (worldview) and automatic thoughts with the truth of God's Word and replace them with God's truth.* This process involves a close examination of your thoughts and assumptions to determine how they align with Scriptures. Probe them by asking yourself how realistic or unrealistic these thoughts are. More importantly, challenge the thoughts to see if they align with biblical teaching, which you are learning by saturating your mind with God's Word. We recommend that you get help from your spouse or a trusted mature Christian friend who can help you examine and determine the validity of these beliefs or thoughts and how to align them with a biblical foundation. Whenever you identify discrepancies between your beliefs or thoughts and God's Word, change them so that they align with God's truth.

4. *Internalize biblical principles.* Make God's truth personal in your life, just like uninstalling software programs from your computer (secular worldview) and installing new software (biblical worldview). By internalizing principles, your output, including your words, attitude, and behaviors can be a representation of God's truth and the Holy Spirit living inside of you.

5. *Practice new behaviors based on the teaching of Scriptures.* Engage in behaviors that reflect God's principles and are the results of the new

Check out the chapter video at: www.grtep.com

beliefs and thoughts that are now consistent with a biblical worldview.

As we come to the end of our discussion on how spiritual location can give a sense of stability to your marriage, we want to emphasize that this stability is the result of having a sound biblical view of marriage and family. It is our hope that as you renew your mind, you continue to create your dream home, an intimate Christian marriage, consistent with God's design.

Now, let's look at the curb appeal.

Endnotes

1. Brendon DeSimone, "Why Location Matters in Real Estate," *Fox Business*, October 22, 2013, accessed May 28, 2019, https://www.foxbusiness.com/features/why-location-matters-in-real-estate.

2. DeSimone, "Why Location Matters."

3. Ian Jones, *The Counsel of Heaven on Earth: Foundations for Biblical Christian Counseling* (Nashville, TN: Broadman & Holman Publishers, 2006), 33–34.

4. "World Family Map 2019: Mapping Family Change and Child Well-Being Outcomes," Institute for Family Studies, 2019, accessed May 28, 2019, https://ifstudies.org/ifs-admin/resources/reports/worldfamilymap-2019-051819final.pdf.

5. "World Family Map 2019."

6. Andrew Francis-Tan and Hugo M. Mialon, "'A Diamond is Forever' and Other Fairy Tales: The Relationship between Wedding Expenses and Marriage Duration," *Social Science Research Network*, September 15, 2014, accessed August 28, 2019, https://papers.ssrn.com/sol3/papers.cfm?abstract_id=2501480.

7. Francis-Tan and Mialon, "'A Diamond is Forever' and Other Fairy Tales."

8. Randy Olson, "What Makes for a Stable Marriage?" *Huffpost*, accessed May 28, 2019, https://www.huffpost.com/entry/what-makes-for-a-stable-m_n_5969946.

9. John C. Thomas and Lisa Sosin, *Therapeutic Expedition: Equipping the Christian Counselor for the Journey* (Nashville, TN: B&H Academic, 2011), 11.

10. James W. Sire, *The Universe Next Door: A Basic Worldview Catalog*, 5th ed. (Downer's Grove, IL: IVP Academic, 2011), 8.

11. Thomas and Sosin, *Therapeutic Expedition*, 14.

12. Judith S. Beck, *Cognitive Behavior Therapy: Basics and Beyond*, 2nd ed. (New York, NY: The Guildford Press, 2011), 228.

13. The KJV New Testament Greek Lexicon, s.v. "metamorphoo," accessed June 1, 2019, https://www.biblestudytools.com/lexicons/greek/kjv/metamorphoo.html.

14. Andreas J. Köstenberger and David W. Jones, *God, Marriage, and Family: Rebuilding the Biblical Foundation*, 2nd ed. (Wheaton, IL: Crossway Books, 2010), 25.

15. Kenneth A. Mathews, *The New American Commentary: Genesis 1-11:26*, vol. 1A Nashville, TN: B&H Publishing Group, 1996), 214.

16. Köstenberger and Jones, *God, Marriage, and Family,* 38.

17. William Barrick, Nathan Busenitz, and James Mook, eds., *Biblical Doctrine: A Systematic Summary of Bible Truth* (Wheaton, IL: Crossway, 2016).

18. Mathews, *The New American Commentary*, 222.

19. Tony Evans, *The Kingdom Agenda: Living Life God's Way* (Danville, VA: LifeWay Press, 2013), 227.

20. Mathews, *The New American Commentary*, 225.

21. The KJV New Testament Greek Lexicon, s.v. "Hupotasso," accessed June 7, 2019 https://www.biblestudytools.com/lexicons/greek/nas/hupotasso.html.

22. Harold Hoehner, *Ephesians: An Exegetical Commentary* (Grand Rapids, MI: Baker Academic, 2002), 717.

23. Hoehner, *Ephesians*, 289–90.

24. Köstenberger and Jones, *God, Marriage, and Family,* 67.

25. Rochelle Cade, "Covenant Marriage," *The Family Journal* 18, no. 13 (2010): 230, accessed June 10, https://doi-org.ezproxy.liberty.edu/10.1177/1066480710372072.

26. Sean Breslin, "Here's How That One Mexico Beach House Survived Hurricane Michael," *The Weather Channel*, October 17, 2018, accessed June 5, 2019, https://weather.com/news/news/2018-10-16-mexico-beach-home-survives-hurricane-michael.

27. Robert J. Sternberg and Rachel Hall Sternberg, *The Triangle of Love: Intimacy, Passion, Commitment* (New York, NY: Basic Books, 1988); Robert J. Sternberg, "A Triangular Theory of Love," *Psychological Review* 93, no. 2 (1986): 119–35.

28. William D. Mounce, *Mounce's Complete Expository Dictionary of Old and New Testament Word*s (Grand Rapids, MI: Zondervan, 2006).

29. Ceslaus Spicq, *Agape in the New Testament Vol. 1: Agape in the Synoptic Gospels* (Eugene, OR: Wipf & Stock Publishers, 2006).

30. Mounce, *Mounce's Complete Expository Dictionary.*

31. "About Adverse Childhood Experiences," Centers for Disease Control and Prevention, accessed June 6, 2019, https://www.cdc.gov/violenceprevention/childabuseandneglect/acestudy/aboutace.html.

32. Daniel J. Weigel, "Parental Divorce and the Types of Commitment Related Messages People Gain from Their Families of Origin," *Journal of Divorce & Remarriage* 47 (2008): 28, accessed June 1, 2019, https://doi.org/10.1300/J087v47n01_02.

33. Caroline Leaf, *Switch on Your Brain: The Key to Peak Happiness, Thinking and Health* (Grand Rapids, MI: Baker Books, 2013), 22.

34. Leaf, *Switch on Your Brain.*

PART II

THE WALKTHROUGH: Checking Out Every Room

CHAPTER 3

Curb Appeal Counts: Creating an Influential Marriage

"A good reputation and respect are
worth much more than silver and gold."
Proverbs 22:1 CEV

© Artazum/Shutterstock.com

An eye-catching curb appeal helps make a great first impression and, certainly, adds value to a home. A manicured yard, colorful flowers, unique boulders, and a calming water feature can add a lot of charm to a yard and make a statement about the property. Even if you live in an apartment, probably the building where you live has some type of curb appeal.

The curb appeal creates the reputation of a home. This may help explain why homeowners tend to spend a reasonable amount of time and money caring for their front yard in an effort to make their home inviting and pleasant. Unfortunately, when a yard has overgrown bushes and plants, dead flowers, or even patches of weeds on the lawn, it becomes unattractive to neighbors or to others who might pass by. Moreover, a house with a neglected curb appeal affects the neighborhood negatively, and it may even play a role in the market value of the home.

In this chapter, we use the curb appeal as a metaphor for the married couple's reputation in the community. From a Christian perspective, a reputation is your testimony as a believer. As you build your dream home, your curb appeal, metaphorically speaking, may draw people toward or away from your dream home. Thus, we discuss the value of building a positive reputation in the community and ways to use this reputation to glorify God and influence people with the gospel of Jesus Christ.

Couple Identity and Reputation

According to the Merriam-Webster dictionary, reputation is an "overall quality or character as seen or judged by people in general."[1] It is "how we see ourselves seen"[2] and part of our social identity. Reputation carries a sense of how others perceive, judge, and evaluate us.[3] In fact, our behaviors and actions build our reputation. The same way it takes time to create a curb appeal, it takes time to build a reputation. However, it takes very little time to lose it if we are not wise in our actions. As Warren Buffet puts it, "It takes 20 years to build a reputation and five minutes to ruin it."[4]

A beautiful and complex aspect of marriage is the development of a couple identity. In marriage, the man and the woman come together and bring their own individual identities, and through meaningful daily interactions, they create a couple identity. Together, in a sense, they form their curb appeal, their reputation. For instance, they may be known in their neighborhood as the Johnsons, the Moitinhos, the Kims, and so forth. The couple may also be viewed by family, friends, and neighbors as happy, kind, mature, organized, friendly, or frugal, to name a few.

We believe that couples form a couple identity in the same way people form an individual identity. For instance, a psychological theory explains that a person's perception of self (real self) may be different from what the person would like to be (ideal self). According to this theory, if the self-perception differs from the ideal self, then the person would have low self-esteem, as the real self would be incongruent with the ideal self.[5] For example, if in your own life you viewed yourself as timid, quiet, and weak in your faith (real self), but you wanted to be confident, assertive, and mature in your faith (ideal self), then there would be a discrepancy between how you viewed yourself and what you would like to be.

We will apply the psychological concept of real versus ideal self to marriage. Think of who you are as a couple (couple identity) in the areas listed in the chart. Consider each area on a scale from 1 to 10. For example, feeling neglected would be 1, whereas feeling loved and accepted would be a 10. Then, check where you believe you and your spouse are as a couple (real couple identity) and compare it to what you and your spouse would like to be as a Christian married couple (ideal couple identity). Note any discrepancies. Often, when there is a discrepancy between what is (the real) and what couples desire (the ideal), they may experience an abundance of negative emotions. They may feel discouraged, disappointed, frustrated, sad, and even angry with themselves or with each other.

Areas of Couple Identity	Real Couple		vs		Ideal Couple (the Dream)		
Love:	Feel Neglected				Feel Loved and Accepted		
	1 2 3	4	5	6	7 8 9		10
Vision:	Competing Visions				Shared Vision		
	1 2 3	4	5	6	7 8 9		10
Goals:	Separate Goals				Mutual Goals		
	1 2 3	4	5	6	7 8 9		10
Relationship:	Independence: I, Me				Interdependence: We, Us		
	1 2 3	4	5	6	7 8 9		10
Commitment:	Uncertain				Faithful		
	1 2 3	4	5	6	7 8 9		10
Communication:	Poor Communication				Open Communication		
	1 2 3	4	5	6	7 8 9		10
Intimacy:	Emotionally Distant				Multidimensional Intimacy		
	1 2 3	4	5	6	7 8 9		10
Needs:	Unaware, Ignoring				Meeting Needs		
	1 2 3	4	5	6	7 8 9		10
Teamwork:	Independent				Collaborative		
	1 2 3	4	5	6	7 8 9		10
Finances:	In Debt				Debt Free		
	1 2 3	4	5	6	7 8 9		10
Parenting:	Reactive & Detached				Intentional & Relational		
	1 2 3	4	5	6	7 8 9		10
Faith:	Stagnant Spiritually				Growing Spiritually		
	1 2 3	4	5	6	7 8 9		10
Community:	Disconnected				Connected		
	1 2 3	4	5	6	7 8 9		10

Source: Elias and Denise Moitinho.

As you complete this activity, you will have a glimpse into how you perceive your marriage in these various areas. It would be a good idea to ask your spouse to complete this activity with you, and then, you can talk about it together. It can be a productive exercise for your marriage. Perhaps neighbors and friends may have witnessed poor interactions between you and your spouse. This would undoubtedly affect their perception of you as a couple and, consequently, affect your reputation negatively in your family and community. This exercise will help increase your self-awareness.

No couple is perfect; we all need to work on our curb appeal. We would like to encourage you to continue reading this book to learn some key strategies that you can implement in the various areas of your marriage. For instance, you may want to go over Chapter 1 and review your vision, mission, goals, and plans for your marriage. This will ensure that you indeed have a plan for your dream marriage that directly enhances your reputation as a Christian couple. Therefore, you can take appropriate actions to improve your marriage curb appeal so that it, ultimately, glorifies God and points people to Him.

Even Bible Characters Had a Reputation

You may think of several people in the Bible whose reputation followed them to this day. For example, Abraham is known for his obedience and faith (Heb. 11:8). King David is considered "a man after God's own heart" (Acts 13:22 NIV). Barnabas is viewed as "a good man, full of the Holy Spirit and faith" (Acts 11:24 NIV). The apostle Paul, before his conversion, was seen as the persecutor of the church (Acts 8:3; 9:1–2), to the point that even shortly after his conversion, Christians were still afraid of him (Acts 9:26). However, because of his change of attitude and conduct, he is viewed as one of the greatest defenders of the Christian faith. Additionally, we could not leave Priscilla and Aquila out of this list. They were a hospitable and mature Christian couple whose ministry touched those around them. These are only a few examples, but they allow us to see the importance of our reputation.

Since we are focusing on the couple's reputation, let us expand a little more on Priscilla and Aquila. This couple's reputation exemplifies integrity of character and service to the Lord. In fact, the apostle Paul met Priscilla and Aquila in Corinth and stayed with them for a while since they were also tentmakers (Acts 18:2–3). Eventually, Priscilla and Aquila joined Paul's ministry (Rom. 16:3) and served the Lord faithfully. For instance, when they were in

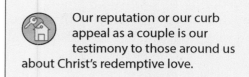

Our reputation or our curb appeal as a couple is our testimony to those around us about Christ's redemptive love.

Ephesus, they met and discipled Apollos (Acts 18:24–26). Because of their commitment to Jesus Christ and His church, they even opened their house to become a church (1 Cor. 16:19). They were also willing to take risks for the sake of the gospel (Rom. 16:3–4). Indeed, their life as a couple is of such relevance to the history of the early Church that Jim Schnorrenberg, in his book *Couples in the Bible: The Good, the Bad, and the Downright Evil*, highlights Priscilla and Aquila's example as a Christian married couple. Schnorrenberg believes they were a ministry team whose example needs to be followed by couples today.[6] They were undoubtedly an influential couple whose home had a beautiful curb appeal.

Reputation Equals Testimony

Our reputation or our curb appeal as a couple is our testimony to those around us about Christ's redemptive love. Paul was clear when he proclaimed to Christians to live "in a manner worthy of the gospel of Christ" (Phil. 1:27 NIV). The Living Bible puts it this way, "remember always to live as Christians should" (TLB). The standard is the gospel of Christ. Therefore, all Christians must strive to live their lives based on the gospel. In Romans 12:2 Paul encourages Christians to be different. He states, "Don't copy the behavior and customs of this world, but be a new and different person with a fresh newness in all you do and think" (TLB). We know that to be salt and light in the world (Matt. 5:13–16), we must engage our culture and community with the realization that the gospel is counterculture. Consequently, the challenge for Christians is to live according to the gospel and avoid being shaped by the lifestyle of the secular culture.

Several years ago, Richard Niebuhr wrote the classic book *Christ and Culture*, in which he proposed a paradigm for viewing the possible relationships between

Christianity and culture.[7] Using Niebuhr's paradigms, we will briefly mention the various ways in which Christian couples seem to engage the secular culture. You may find yourself engaging in culture according to one of these paradigms.

Christ against culture – In this approach, Christian couples reject the culture they live in.

Christ of culture – In this position, Christian couples show a stronger loyalty to the culture, rather than to Christ.

Christ above culture – In this model, Christian couples synthesize Christ and the culture by getting the best of both worlds together.

Christ and culture in paradox – In this approach, Christian couples emphasize that humanity is fallen and sinful, while God is holy and full of grace. They place humanity in between Christ and the culture.

Christ the transformer of culture – In this model, Christian couples focus on attempting to influence and transform the culture.

Most Christians agree that believers should not compromise their testimony. Instead, Christians are to make a difference in the world by influencing culture. For instance, David Platt, in his book, *Counter Culture: Following Christ in an Anti-Christian Age*, emphasizes that Christians need to be consciously counter-culture, and that "This is the only possible posture for individuals, families, and churches who have any hope of following Christ in contemporary America."[8] Platt challenges believers not to compromise their faith despite cultural pressure and opposition, but rather they should live focused on eternal values.[9]

Character, Ethics, and Integrity

When we think of a reputation, certain intertwined concepts come to mind, including character, ethics, and integrity. These concepts are intrinsically part of what a reputation is all about.

Character

According to the Merriam-Webster dictionary, *character* means "the complex of mental and ethical traits marking and often individualizing a person,

 As Christian couples, we are called to have high moral standards that flow out of our relationship with Christ.

group, or nation . . . moral excellence and firmness."[10] Klaus Issler, author of *Living into the Life of Jesus: The Formation of Christian Character*, points out that Christ-centered spiritual formation and spiritual growth leads to building Christian character.[11] He emphasizes the importance of focusing on the heart rather than on outward behavior. So, a Christian's character centers on a heart that is fully devoted to Christ.

As Christian couples, we are called to have high moral standards that flow out of our relationship with Christ. Living a life that pleases God is only possible when we are filled by the Holy Spirit. Being filled with the Spirit will result in displaying the fruit of the Spirit (Gal. 5:22–23) in our daily interactions with our spouses and others. Hazel Offner, in her book *A Deeper Look at the Fruit of the Spirit: Growing in the Likeness of Christ,* asserts,

> Nothing attracts unbelievers and believers alike to God as much as seeing a life lived out in love, joy, peace, gentleness and so forth even though that person may be suffering. A life exhibiting these beautiful qualities can be a powerful tool of evangelism as well as for promoting harmony and unity in the body of Christ.[12]

We agree that when we display the fruit of the Spirit, we have a positive impact on people's lives. Thus, we encourage you to focus on guarding your heart and being filled with the Spirit.

Ethics

The way we live makes or breaks our reputation. Ethics is about principles that guide behavior. Therefore, we would like to borrow some concepts from our field of work, counseling and human services, to emphasize the importance of living an *ethical life*. Being ethical contributes positively to the development of a solid reputation. As you may know, similar to other professionals, counselors must abide by codes of ethics that describe a counselor's ethical guidelines, expectations, and responsibilities to clients and other professional relationships. Codes of ethics also emphasize some specific ethical principles that guide decision-making in the counseling relationship.[13] Below, we are going to list some of these ethical principles and briefly discuss how we believe they can be applied to your interactions with your neighbors as you strive to build a positive reputation as a married couple.

Autonomy – A person's self-determination and freedom to make decisions.

Applying this definition of autonomy to your relationship with your neighbors means that you will need to respect their freedom to be themselves and make their own decisions about their lives. As a Christian, you want your neighbors to develop a relationship with Christ and move away from any destructive behaviors or sinful lifestyle. Understandably, you may feel sad when neighbors display unhealthy lifestyles and unwise choices that might be detrimental to their marriages and families. However, you cannot force nor coerce them to become Christians or even change their attitudes and habits. You can certainly pray for your neighbors and find creative ways to show Christ's love to them, but you cannot change their hearts. Only the Holy Spirit can. However, if you know your neighbors pose a threat to themselves or others, you will need to take appropriate action such as calling the proper authorities.

Nonmaleficence – Avoid causing harm to others.

As a responsible member of your community, you desire to help your neighbors and not harm them. However, you need to be aware of your limitations even as you seek to help those in your community. For example, you may want to give advice to a friend or a neighbor. However, the advice-giving can potentially create problems because you may not understand the whole picture of your neighbor's situation. Besides, what would happen if your neighbor followed your advice and the results were negative? Who would be responsible for the outcome? Perhaps connecting your neighbor to resources might be better than trying to solve their problems on your own.

Beneficence– Doing what is in the best interest of others.

The Bible is clear that we are to show love to our neighbors by performing good deeds. The Parable of the Good Samaritan (Luke 10:25–37) is an excellent example of tangible help that one can give to someone in need. Being a Good Samaritan in your neighborhood can help your neighbors see God's goodness as well. It can be something as simple as welcoming those who just moved into the neighborhood or helping elderly neighbors with yard work. Of course, you would not be helping others with the intent of earning points with God, but as a genuine concern for your neighbor and as an overflow of your desire to serve people in Jesus' name.

Justice – Act with fairness toward others.

Being fair means that you will look for what is right to take place in your community, and you will not take advantage of your neighbors. It also means that you will strive to treat all your neighbors equally and that you will be sensitive to their diverse backgrounds. Additionally, avoiding bias, establishing boundaries, and maintaining fair interaction are ways to express a sense of justice and treat everyone with respect and kindness.

Veracity – Being truthful and honest in your interactions with others.

The Bible teaches that we are to speak the truth in love (Eph. 4:15) and "put off falsehood and speak truthfully to your neighbor" (Eph. 4:15 NIV). Therefore, it is essential to avoid gossiping about neighbors and engaging in online interactions that lead to the spreading of negative information about neighbors and the neighborhood.

Fidelity – Being loyal and keeping one's promises to others.

Living by the golden rule, "do to others what you would have them do to you" (Matt. 7:12 NIV), is an excellent way to express love. You will need to be attentive to your neighbors' needs and make an effort to be helpful to them. You may be helpful by meeting small needs such as picking up your neighbors' mail or keeping an eye on their property when they are traveling. You may also help them in tangible ways when they go through a major crisis, such as the loss of a loved one.

Integrity

The Merriam-Webster dictionary defines integrity as "firm adherence to a code of especially moral or artistic values: incorruptibility."[14] Henry Cloud in his book, *Integrity: The Courage to Meet the Demands of Reality*, defines being a person of integrity as "being a whole person, an integrated person, with all our different parts working well and delivering the functions that they were designed to deliver. It is about *wholeness* and *effectiveness* as people."[15]

From a biblical perspective, integrity means living in a way that pleases God. In Psalm 15, King David describes

A Person of Integrity - Psalm 15

[1] Lord, who may dwell in your sacred tent? Who may live on your holy mountain?

[2] The one whose walk is blameless, who does what is righteous, who speaks the truth from their heart;

[3] whose tongue utters no slander, who does no wrong to a neighbor, and casts no slur on others;

[4] who despises a vile person but honors those who fear the Lord; who keeps an oath even when it hurts, and does not change their mind;

[5] who lends money to the poor without interest; who does not accept a bribe against the innocent.

Whoever does these things will never be shaken.

a life of integrity. He emphasizes integrity in relational terms by pointing out the remarkable positive and God-honoring behaviors toward others. These actions represent obedience to the covenant relationship with God.

Integrity also includes authenticity, which is living consistently with one's faith. It is a life without masks. God wants us to be real Christ-followers who live authentic Christian lives, in other words, to be people who do not wear masks or simply pretend to be kind to others.

The opposite of integrity is hypocrisy. This is when we say the right things but live a life that is contradictory to our faith or statements. Jesus condemned the Pharisees and called them hypocrites (Matt. 23:13–39). The Pharisees had a fake spiritual life; they only put on a show to be seen and praised by others. As a result, Jesus stated that in reality, they were dead on the inside. We certainly do not want to earn this label. We think that you likely do not want it either.

Who Is My Neighbor?

We want to take some time to explore some important concepts that we believe will help you understand your community better and your Christian responsibility to honor God in your community.

Understanding My Neighborhood

Generally, people define a neighborhood as a geographical area with homes and buildings that may be in rural, urban, suburban, or exurban areas. Depending on where your neighborhood is located, the interactions among neighbors will vary from daily to occasional ones. Urban, metropolitan areas tend to encourage more daily interaction among people since they are more densely populated. On the other hand, rural areas tend to limit daily interactions since homes are more geographically apart in the community.

Knowing your neighbors provides a sense of security and interdependence. It reminds you that you are part of a community, a system in which you and your spouse play a role. However, the question is: How many of us know all our neighbors? The Pew Research Center surveyed 2,258 adults and found that less than 50% of them knew the majority of their neighbors.[16] The number got even smaller, to about 19%, when they considered how many of the surveyed people knew their neighbors' names.[17] This may be the result of people's desire for anonymity and privacy[18] and also due to the fact that our society is predominantly individualistic. Consequently, people avoid having their public life in full view of those who live next to them, isolating themselves from the rest of the community.

You may have witnessed people's desire for anonymity, privacy, and individualism when you walk through the streets of your neighborhood. You may notice people on their cellphones, in their own world. Some may even avoid making eye contact or having small talks. For instance, when we lived in Fort Worth, Texas, all houses in our subdivision had garages. We would see people come home, park in their garage, and close the garage door. Then, we would not see them again until morning when they would leave for work. Although the homeowners association (HOA) made efforts to create a sense of community in the neighborhood by organizing neighborhood events such as movie nights and pool parties, most neighbors preferred to maintain their anonymity and privacy. We acknowledge that not all neighborhoods or parts of the country may be this way. In fact, in our current neighborhood in rural Virginia, we see more interactions among neighbors. They seem to have more friends over to their homes for social gatherings and Bible study groups.

Technology has affected how we interact with our neighbors and even how we gather information about our community. Although many neighbors do spend time talking to each other while standing on their lawns or driveway, many take advantage of technology, such as Facebook, to stay connected to their neighborhood groups.[19] Other social media and internet tools allow neighbors to know what is happening in the community and take a peek at their neighbors' lifestyle. For instance, websites like Zillow and Trulia even provide pictures and virtual tours of neighbors' houses from the time the house was on the market. They also show information about property value and taxes. Additionally, concerned neighbors may check government websites that provide valuable information about public schools and registered sex offenders living in the neighborhood.

Geographic Mobility

When we came to the USA in 1992, we noticed that American families were more mobile than Brazilian families. We also noticed that many of our American friends had lived in different states before we met them. Of course, the robust American economy makes it easier for citizens to enjoy this geographic mobility. Perhaps you know a family who is about to move away from or into your neighborhood. In fact, statistics show that around "35.5 million Americans move each year."[20]

People move for various reasons. Some want to downsize while others want to upgrade. Still, others move because of a new job, marriage, military service, or a desire to live in a better neighborhood. Additionally, moving sometimes reflects a couple's financial status transitioning to either upper or lower class.[21] Nevertheless, moving is a daunting task that involves the couple's financial, physical, mental, and emotional energy and resources.

Interestingly, some couples who move frequently may find it exciting to experience a new neighborhood, a new house, and a new social system. Sometimes people may move because they may experience conflict with their neighbors. While this may not apply to you or to your neighbors, you need to be aware of it. Sometimes people avoid building meaningful relationships with neighbors because they plan to move soon. They prematurely conclude that getting to know their neighbors will be a waste of time. As you know, not investing in new relationships can make you miss many ministry opportunities or prevent people from blessing you. We need to keep in mind that relationships with others make room for divine interruptions in our marriage.

Intentional Connections

Isolation for the sake of privacy sometimes can be detrimental to your sense of community. Relying solely on superficial social media interaction can be detrimental to your marriage, family, and relationship with neighbors. Perhaps we need to view the doorbell

 Perhaps we need to view the doorbell rings or knocks on our front doors as more important than the clicks or likes on our Facebook pages by those who are miles away from us.

rings or knocks on our front doors as more important than the clicks or likes on our Facebook pages by those who are miles away from us.

We need to be intentional to connect with our neighbors and build meaningful relationships with them. Doing so will help us mature and develop an appreciation for diversity and individual differences. If your neighbors seem isolated, perhaps that is one more reason for you to pray and take the initiative to reach out to them so that they can experience a more fulfilling life in the community. For Christian couples, connecting with neighbors and developing new friendships create the opportunity to influence them spiritually. Thus, being intentional is key.

Probably, location was one of the most important considerations when you were looking for a house or an apartment. Therefore, you may already have some knowledge about the neighborhood you live in. Now, the next step is for you to spend some time seeking to understand your own neighborhood or community. Since neighborhoods vary based on their geographical location, regional culture, and social-economic status, you need to get to know your neighborhood. We encourage you to take steps to get to know how you can play a positive role in your specific neighborhood or community.

Recently, we had the privilege of attending a community roundtable event in our city, Lynchburg, Virginia,[22] led by Rashad Jennings, a former New York Giants NFL running back and winner of Dancing with the Stars, Season 24. We were excited about it because the purpose of the event was to discuss ways to improve the community. The panel included leaders of the community, such as the mayor of Lynchburg and the chief of the police. They discussed some of the challenges they see in the community and steps they are taking to address them. Other leaders of non-profit organizations also described their initiatives to improve the community. Being a part of this event helped us connect with people who care deeply about our city and want to make a difference in the lives of the residents in the various neighborhoods of Lynchburg. Similarly, you can be involved in a church or organization that seeks to give back to your

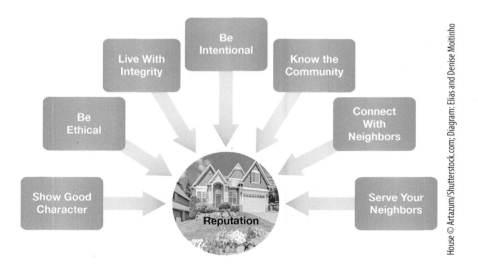

neighborhood. This would be an excellent way for you to show God's love to your neighbors in a tangible way. As we shared in this chapter, reputation has many elements, including showing good character, being ethical, living with integrity, being intentional, knowing the community, connecting with neighbors, and serving them.

Curb Appeal Makeover

Every spring, we find ourselves wondering how we can improve the curb appeal of our home. You and your spouse probably may have evaluated your home's curb appeal at some point. The internet has what seems like an infinite number of blogs that offer hundreds of tips about how to improve a home's curb appeal. Some tips include minor improvements, such as planting a couple of trees, or significant renovations, such as building a new driveway or changing the roof. Sometimes, with the help of an expert, a realtor, or a landscape contractor, you will determine what changes can be made to improve the curb appeal. Similarly, as you read this book, you will become aware of some areas of your marriage and home life that may need improvement or a makeover. As you gain knowledge, implement tips, and learn new relationship skills, you will make the curb appeal of your dream home even more beautiful. Thus, you and your spouse become more influential in your community.

Creating an intimate Christian marriage is far more than seeking happiness and fulfillment. Indeed, happiness and fulfillment are a by-product of a covenant relationship with God. Christian marriage is also about reflecting God's love and bringing glory to God while making a difference in the community. The foundation for these actions is evident in Jesus' words, "Let your light so shine before men, that they may see your good works and glorify your Father in heaven" (Matt. 5:16 NKJV) and "love your neighbor as yourself" (Matt. 22:29 NIV). Thus, we invite you to consider implementing some of the actions below:

1. Focus on strengthening your marriage and developing a positive relationship with your spouse. When you and your spouse display love, joy, harmony, and fulfillment, it will be evident to your family, friends, and neighbors that you are creating a dream marriage.
2. Build a meaningful relationship with your neighbors. Get to know them by listening to their story with genuine interest. Be available to them in times of need.

3. Show Christ-like compassion and concern for your neighbors and their families. You can do this by checking on them specifically in times of crisis and offering tangible help.
4. Open your home to your neighbors. This is an excellent way to get to know them and for them to know you.

We have heard many testimonies of people who accepted Christ because they saw in a Christian something that, spiritually speaking, they lacked. They saw something different in the way that person talked and interacted with others. They may have seen inner peace, joy, excitement for life, or a strong and growing marriage. The point was that a Christian's lifestyle was appealing and led the person to consider learning more about Christ. In the same way, as you work on your marriage's curb appeal, your ultimate goal is that your marriage will reflect God's love and grace. Thus, your curb appeal will point your neighbors to Christ.

Looking at the Moitinho's Curb Appeal

As we consider our own curb appeal from the time we got married to today, we can say that there were some instances when our curb appeal needed a makeover. We remember a specific time when we still lived in Brazil that we were extremely busy. We worked from Monday to Saturday and participated actively in our church on Sundays. However, we had very little time to spend with members of our extended family. As we looked back at that time and reflected upon it, we realized that we should have made more time to spend with our families, so that they could really see our marriage and testimony.

Spending time with members of the extended family is part of our Latino cultural heritage. However, during the first two years of our marriage, spending time with members of the extended family was not one of our priorities, though we loved them dearly. The truth is that we were extremely busy organizing our marriage life, focusing on our jobs, and investing in our educational goals. However, slowly, we realized that we needed to be more intentional in the way we engaged our extended family, especially because we were planning to move to Texas to continue our studies. We remember going to visit one nephew on his birthday. He was happy to see us even though we had hardly participated in his development from the time he was a baby to the time he was five. When we handed him his gift, we had no idea he had so many toys just like the one we gave him. That would not have been the case, had we spent more time with him.

Little by little, we learned that we needed to become more available to those around us. We also learned that our neighbors observed us and knew that we were Christians. One particular example happened early on in our marriage. I (Denise) clearly remember a time when we lived in our one-bedroom apartment on the fifth floor of a building in Rio de Janeiro. I heard some yelling and intense door banging. It did not take long for me to realize that the couple down the hall was having a very intense argument. I opened the door carefully and poked my head out. To my surprise, my neighbor, whom I knew superficially, was standing in the hallway holding her baby. She looked at me, so I waved at her and whispered an invitation for her to come into my apartment. As she came in and sat down on my couch, she started crying. I had zero counseling skills and training at that time, but I knew she needed a shoulder, a prayer, and some encouragement. I was glad to be available to God and to my neighbor. A few months later, Elias and I moved to Texas.

Fast forward several years, and we have an example of when we lived in Fort Worth, Texas. The subdivision where we lived was diverse, and we Check out the chapter video at: www.grtep.com encountered people from various cultural and religious backgrounds. However, it was similar to what we described in this chapter, neighbors drove in, parked in the garage, and closed the garage door. There was little interaction among neighbors. However, we became friends with a family who lived just a few houses up the street from our house. We enjoyed many walks together with them and had fun in the neighborhood pool to escape the Texas heat. We spent time with these neighbors regularly and participated in sad and joyful moments in their lives. Although our neighbors were not churchgoers, they knew that we were Christians and even came to church with us a couple of times.

One instance, our neighbor was scheduled to have back surgery. He and his wife were both immigrants just like us without the support of any extended family. We were able to visit him and his wife before his surgery and pray with them. On one occasion, we invited them to have dinner with us at our house. We thoughtfully invited another Christian couple whose husband was from the same country as our friends and could speak their native language. When our Christian friend prayed in their native tongue, my neighbors were surprised and touched. They told us that they felt something special at that moment. We believe they felt God's presence. Although we have moved away, we still talk to them and encourage them to focus on God. We believe that these neighbors not only saw our home curb appeal as they drove by our house, but they were also able to witness our marriage curb appeal regularly. These experiences have encouraged us to continue to work on our dream home curb appeal.

Now, let's enter the house and check out the rooms. We will start in the living room.

Endnotes

1. Merriam-Webster, s.v. "Reputation," accessed July 15, 2019, https://www.merriam-webster.com/dictionary/reputation.
2. Gloria Origgi, *Reputation: What It Is and Why It Matters* (Princeton, NJ: Princeton University Press, 2018), 4.
3. Garry Honey, *A Short Guide to Reputation Risk* (New York, NY: Routledge, 2016), 8.
4. James Berman, "The Three Essential Warren Buffett Quotes to Live By," April 20, 2014, accessed July 15, 2019, https://www.forbes.com/sites/jamesberman/2014/04/20/the-three-essential-warren-buffett-quotes-to-live-by/#7ae5cd7b6543.
5. Robert B. Ewen, *Personality: A Topical Approach: Theories, Research, Major Controversies and Emerging Findings* (United Kingdom: Psychology Press, 2013), 200.
6. Jim Schnorrenberg, *Couples in the Bible: The Good, the Bad, and the Downright Evil* (Bloomington, IN: WestBow Press, 2014).
7. H. Richard Niebuhr, *Christ and Culture* (New York, NY: Harper Collins Publishers, 2001); D. A. Carson, *Christ and Culture Revisited* (Grand Rapids, MI: William B. Eerdmans, 2012).
8. David Platt, *Counter Culture: Following Christ in an Anti-Christian Age* (Carol Stream, IL: Tyndale House Publishers, 2017), xi.
9. Platt, *Counter Culture*, 23.
10. Merriam-Webster, s.v. "Character," accessed July 16, 2019, https://www.merriam-webster.com/dictionary/character
11. Klaus Issler, *Living into the Life of Jesus: The Formation of Christian Character* (Downers Grove, IL: IVP Books, 2012), 24.
12. Hazel Offner, Dale Larsen, and Sandy Larsen, *A Deeper Look at the Fruit of the Spirit: Growing in the Likeness of Christ* (Downers Grove, IL: IVP Books, 2012), 8.
13. Gerald Corey, Marianne Schneider Corey, and Cindy Corey, *Issues and Ethics in the Helping Professions*, 10th ed. (Boston, MA: Cengage Learning, 2018).
14. Merriam-Webster, s.v. "Integrity," accessed July 21, 2019, https://www.merriam-webster.com/dictionary/integrity.
15. Henry Cloud, *Integrity: The Courage to Meet the Demands of Reality* (New York, NY: Harper Collins, 2006), 31.

16. Russell Heimlich, "Do You Know Your Neighbors?" *Pew Research Center-Fact Tank: News in the Numbers*, June 18, 2010, accessed June 18, 2019, https://www.pewresearch.org/fact-tank/2010/06/18/do-you-know-your-neighbors/.

17. Heimlich, "Do You Know Your Neighbors?"

18. Marc J. Dunkelman, "Next-Door strangers: The Crisis of Urban Anonymity," *The Hedgehog Review* 19, no. 2 (June 22, 2017): 53, accessed July 28, 2019, http://www.virginia.edu/iasc/publications_hedgehog_review.php.

19. Aaron Smith, "Neighbors Online," *Pew Research Center*, June 9, 2010, accessed July 12, 2019, https://www.pewinternet.org/2010/06/09/methodology-82/.

20. Colin Holmes, "The State of the American Mover: Stats and Facts," April 23, 2018, accessed August 23, 2019, https://www.move.org/moving-stats-facts/.

21. Antwan Jones, "The Health Consequences of Moving from Place to Place," *Scholars Strategy Network*, October 20, 2014, accessed August 29, 2019, https://scholars.org/brief/health-consequences-moving-place-place.

22. Tim Saunders, "Retired NFL Star Rashad Jennings Returns to Lynchburg to Give Back," *WDBJ*, July 11, 2019, accessed July 21, 2019, https://www.wdbj7.com/content/news/Retired-NFL-star-Rashad-Jennings-returns-to-Lynchburg-to-give-back-512597231.html.

CHAPTER 4

The Living Room: Communicating Effectively

"One cannot not communicate."
Paul Watzlawick

I f you watch TV shows such as *House Hunters* or *Property Brothers*, you would likely notice that many couples dream of having a house with an open concept. However, if you look online, you will find a variety of opinions about the pros and cons of open concept or open floor plans: some people like it and others do not. Despite design preferences, you would probably agree that the living room is a place where a couple spends a lot of time communicating, interacting, and enjoying each other's company. Metaphorically, the living room represents open communication. It is a place where a couple can sit together at the end of a busy day to unwind and catch up with each other.

In this chapter, we emphasize that effective communication is key for you to connect with your spouse and grow your marriage. We highlight some essential elements of effective communication, including skills, techniques, and behaviors that can enhance communication. We also discuss behaviors that are detrimental to effective communication, such as criticism and defensiveness. Additionally, we address some foundational biblical principles that can guide your communication and help you connect and grow in intimacy with your spouse. Thus, the goal of this chapter is to help you become a better listener and communicator.

Effective Communication

Effective communication is the key that will unlock your spouse's heart and bring you together. There are several models of communication that fall under the *linear, interactive,* and *transactional* categories.[1] The *Linear model* views communication as flowing in one direction from the sender to the receiver. In this model, the receiver is considered a passive recipient of the message. The *Interactive model* goes beyond the linear model because it recognizes that, in communication, the receiver also responds and provides feedback to the speaker. The *Transactional model* views communication as a dynamic process in which both parties participate actively in communication within a particular context. Both parties have their field of experience that includes all their life experiences, beliefs, values, attitudes, and assumptions.

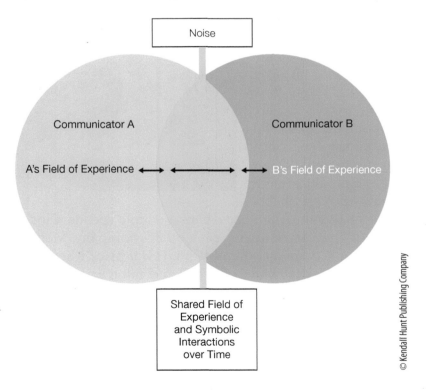

Time is an essential variable in the Transactional model because it allows for relationships to grow and communication to move to a deeper level. We will consider communication from a transactional perspective since your marriage relationship changes and grows through time. In addition to the element of time, external and internal noise or distractions have the potential to interfere with communication. Technology and social media are examples of external noise, while fatigue is an internal physiological noise and anger is an internal psychological noise.

As you reflect on your interactions with your spouse, you may become aware of several implicit and explicit elements influencing your communication both positively and negatively. For instance, there are times when you, the *sender*, may be unaware of your own presuppositions, assumptions, and biases toward your spouse, a particular topic, or a situation. You may also

 Effective communication happens when you and your spouse make the most of each interaction. You share openly and meaningfully, understand each other's messages completely, and provide feedback to each other respectfully. Consequently, you grow in intimacy more deeply.

be unaware that your emotions affect your tone of voice and body language and that your message may be too long, confusing, vague, or even emotionally charged. Similarly, your spouse, the *receiver*, may have presuppositions, assumptions, and biases. Moreover, as you both send, receive, and interpret messages, you filter these messages through your worldview, emotions, and expectations. Communication is a complex process. Please consider the following example.[2]

How the message was meant — **Husband:** "You spent more money on this laptop than is in the budget."

How the message was sent — **Husband:** "You have to stick to the budget; otherwise, we are going to break the bank. Here we go again!"

How the message was received — **Wife:** "You think I don't know how to manage money and you are blaming me for our big debt."

Source: Elias and Denise Moitinho, *People Skills.*

As you can see in the provided example, the husband had an idea of what he wanted to communicate based on his field of experience. However, the message was impacted by noise, which included his emotions, semantics, communication style, and tone of voice. The wife, in turn, felt blamed based on her field of experience and noise. Perhaps, she was tired after a stressful day, or she was feeling the pressure of a previous unresolved marital conflict. Additionally, this interaction could have quickly escalated into an argument if the wife had become defensive and responded in self-protection. The fact is that communication occurs in the context of a relationship and it has the potential for misunderstanding. To maximize communication, the noise needs to be recognized and managed.

Speak the Truth in Love

You may be thinking, "Yes! I want to encourage my spouse; however, there are times we need to talk about serious issues such as money, personal goals, and parenting. How can I encourage my spouse while still sharing my own thoughts when we have different opinions?" The answer is simple. "Speak the truth in love" (Eph. 4:15 NLT) because how you communicate is as important as what you communicate. So, speak kindly, gently, and lovingly to your spouse.

Below is an example of positive communication.

Husband: Honey, when you have a chance, I'd like to sit down and review our budget.

Wife: I have time now. Let's talk.

Husband: I've noticed that you bought a new laptop that was not included in our budget.

Wife: Oh yes, that's true. I can tell you what happened. I decided to buy this laptop because it is faster than the one I have and it was on sale, honey. This new laptop will perform better than the old one. It will make my home business more efficient, and it will help us increase our family income.

Husband: That makes sense. This helps me understand your thinking process, darling. I would like to discuss large purchases or changes in our spending ahead of time to avoid potential misunderstandings.

Wife: That's a good point! I love you, honey!

Two Cycles of Communication

In the living room of life, we recommend that you sit on the *loveseat* when communicating with your spouse, especially when experiencing strong emotions. The *loveseat* represents your desire to provide a loving, kind, and gentle response to your spouse. This, in turn, will probably create a positive cycle because a gentle response has the power to calm down the conversation and produce peace and harmony (Prov. 15:1). The *loveseat*, consequently, leads to positive emotions and interactions. Unfortunately, many couples do not make use of the *loveseat* and respond harshly to each other out of anger and frustration. As expected, this critical and demeaning response only escalates the conflict. Thus, it generates more negative emotions and causes couples to be caught in the negative cycle of communication.

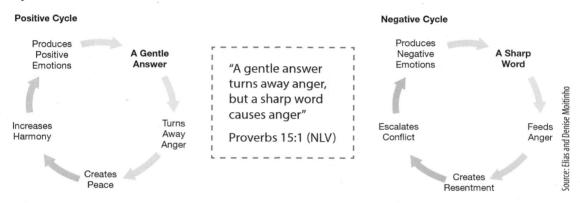

Obviously, most people want to create a positive cycle of communication in their marriage. However, many people are stuck in the negative cycle, especially when they have poor communication skills, lack good examples of positive communication from their family-of-origin, and display a self-centered attitude. Unfortunately, this negative cycle can be exacerbated by the uncontrollable or unhealthy use of technology and social media.

Technology and Social Media Use in Marriage

Technology and social media have become pervasive in our lives. Most of us use computers, smartphones, and engage in social networks such as Facebook, Instagram, and Twitter, to name a few. According to the Pew Research Center, "seven-in-ten Americans use social media to connect with one another, engage with news content, share information and entertain themselves,"[3] by playing online games, watching movies, and YouTube videos. Although technology and social media have certainly improved the way we communicate and get connected, they have also become, to some extent, detrimental to effective communication in marriage.

Negative Impact of Technology and Social Media on Marriage

© Twin Design/Shutterstock.com

Recent research shows that technology and social media can have a negative impact on the quality of the marital relationship.[4] In fact, interactive social media and online gaming may cause individuals to neglect their marriages.[5] A study on couples' use of media found that two patterns of interactions, namely *demand–withdraw* and *criticism–defensiveness*, have adverse effects on couples' relationship satisfaction. The *demand–withdraw* pattern happens when one spouse demands a change in how his or her spouse uses social media, and the other spouse resists by withdrawing. Withdrawing is displayed by leaving the room or being silent. On the other hand, the *criticism–defensiveness* pattern occurs when one spouse criticizes the other spouse's use of technology and media, and the criticized spouse acts defensively.[6]

Interestingly, Facebook use may be the culprit of many marital conflicts, especially for new relationships. A study found that "individuals who are currently in a relationship of 3 years or less are more likely to experience negative relationship outcomes as a result of Facebook-related conflict."[7] Similarly, another study concluded that "Facebook use is correlated with reduced marital satisfaction and divorce rates."[8] The authors of the study explain that

> First, excessive use of social media has been associated with compulsive use, which may create psychological, social, school, and/or work difficulties in a person's life. These phenomena, in turn, may trigger marriage unhappiness and, ultimately, divorce. Second, Facebook, in particular, creates an environment with potential situations that may evoke feelings of jealousy between partners, harming the quality of their relationship. And third, we noted that services like Facebook have unique affordances that may help partners to reduce searching costs for extra-matrimonial affairs and consequently may contribute to cheating.[9]

Social media can be potentially very harmful and even destructive to a marriage.[10] The danger of social media, particularly Facebook, is that communication between married people and individuals of the opposite sex starts informally but may eventually escalate into intimate verbal interaction with the potential to lead to an affair.[11] A study found that individuals who were less satisfied in their marriages or cohabiting relationships were more likely to engage in infidelity-related behaviors through social media.[12]

Benefits of Technology and Social Media for Couples

Couples can intentionally use technology and social media to maximize their communication and learn how to improve their relationship in specific areas such as romance, finances, and faith. In the romantic area, couples can send each other messages throughout the day to show love and appreciation to each other.[13] They may also choose to add images that evoke pleasant memories and positive feelings. For instance, you may send a picture of you and your spouse in your honeymoon spot or on vacation to remind each other of the good times you had together, and your commitment to each other. In the financial area, couples can take advantage of multiple apps available to help them manage their finances. In addition, they can access useful information about money management from experts, listen to financial podcasts together, and talk about them. Finally, in the faith area, couples can benefit from multiple ministry websites and apps that provide sermons, devotionals, and in-depth spiritual resources to help them grow in their faith.

Social Media Boundaries for Marriage

In this technology-driven world, it is smart to set boundaries to protect your relationship from the potentially devastating effects of technology and social media use. Perhaps you need to take some time to discuss this topic with your spouse and agree on some boundaries that can protect and enhance your relationship. Take a look at some of our suggestions below:

- Be wise when you post on social media. Ask yourself, "How will this post motivate and encourage people?" or "How will this post reflect on my marriage?" You may even ask yourself, "What if this post is read in court?" or "What if my boss reads this post?"

- Be wise and careful when you send a text message. Revise and edit it before posting it.
- Engage in social media as a couple.
- Make sure you and your spouse are together in several pictures you post.
- Avoid using technology or social media during meal times.
- Avoid posting private information such as marital conflicts or disagreements on social media.
- Do not be secretive about your social media accounts. Both spouses need to have access to each other's social media accounts.

We encourage you to invite your spouse to evaluate each other's technology and media use by completing this brief survey. Please keep in mind that in the following questions, the term *using media* refers to "using computers, online games, video watching, smartphone, text messaging, etc."[14] Use the following questions to reflect and discuss with each other your thoughts and opinions about how you are using technology and media.

On a scale from 1 to 7, with 1 indicating that you strongly disagree and 7 indicating that you strongly agree, please rate the following items:

1. I feel ignored by my partner when he/she is spending time using media. _____
2. My partner is less interested in me or my conversations when he/she is using media. _____
3. I feel that my partner spends time using media when he/she should be spending time with me and/or the family. _____
4. I feel that my partner wastes too much time using certain types of media. _____
5. My partner's use of media frustrates me. _____
6. I miss having a face-to-face relationship with my partner. _____
7. My partner fails to listen to me when he/she is using media. _____

Source: Todd A. Spencer et al., "Assessing The Mediating Effect of Relationship Dynamics Between Perceptions of Problematic Media Use And Relationship Satisfaction," *Contemporary Family Therapy* 39, no. 2 (2017): 85.

Now that we have addressed technology and social media use in marriage; we will look at how the five levels of communication can enrich your marriage.

Five Levels of Communication

Communication occurs at multiple levels,[15] and awareness of those levels can maximize your communication in your marriage.[16] We created the acronym G.I.F.T.S. to provide an easy way to remember these levels. We hope that the G.I.F.T.S. will inspire you to explore your interactions with your spouse at each level.

G – Greeting

Greeting is the most superficial level of communication. All cultures have different types of greetings whether it is shaking hands, bowing, saying "hello," hugging, kissing on the cheeks, or giving a "high-five." Greeting is important because it communicates that you are glad to see your spouse and that you acknowledge his or her presence. However, there is minimal sharing because it is, by nature, a superficial exchange. For example, when someone asks, "How are you doing?" a brief reply usually follows in the form of "I'm fine."

Communication G.I.F.T.S.

Greetings
Information
Feelings
Thoughts
Self

Maximize the use of greetings in your marriage – Be sure to greet your spouse with a genuine smile. When you greet your spouse, greet him or her in a way that communicates, "I'm so glad to see you, and I love you." This may include hugs, kisses, and yes, guys, even flowers. Remember that you are greeting the person with whom you wanted to spend your life. Thus, greeting each other with kindness communicates that you consider yourself blessed to have your spouse in your life.

I – Information

The second level of communication is information. This involves giving and sharing facts about something or someone. At this level, couples may talk about their work or what they accomplished during the day. They may discuss financial goals, vacation plans, their children's behavior, and education, or even what they want to have for dinner. Although conversations at this level help couples accomplish tasks and administer the household, they do not involve the sharing of emotions.

Provide clear and accurate information – In marriage, it is vital to be truthful with your spouse and ensure that you have accurate information when discussing important issues. For example, if the conversation is about finances, it would be helpful to have the budget numbers in front of you. This will help both of you to talk about specific information and be focused. At this level, make an effort to be detailed and precise by choosing your words carefully.

F – Feelings

Sharing feelings is considered a deeper level of communication. When you share your feelings with your spouse, you decrease your stress levels and improve your mental health. A study suggests that emotional skills contribute to marital health, intimacy, and happiness.[17] Additionally, you are more vulnerable, which helps increase the trust and intimacy between you and your spouse. We acknowledge that for some people sharing feelings may be challenging. This is particularly true for those who were raised in homes where sharing feelings was seldom encouraged, or for those who experienced some sort of emotional trauma, betrayal, or broken trust.

Communicate your feelings effectively by identifying and naming them accurately – Your response to "How are you?" can go beyond "I'm fine" to a deeper self-disclosure. For this reason, we encourage you to become familiar with the Feeling Wheel, which is a tool that helps you and your spouse identify and name your feelings.

The use of "I" statements is another technique to help you communicate your feelings to your spouse effectively. For example, when answering the question "How are you doing?" avoid giving a superficial reply. Instead, you can be more specific with statements such as "I feel lonely" or "I feel unappreciated." Notice the feeling words. This is much better than stating, "I feel that you do not care about me" or "I feel that you are not thankful enough for what I do." The former expresses feelings, whereas the latter expresses opinions or evaluation of the spouse, which can lead to unnecessary arguments. Remember that the goal is to increase dialogue and intimacy through communication.

T – Thoughts

Sharing your thoughts allows people to know you at a deeper level; however, at this level, there is more potential for conflict because people often have different thoughts, beliefs, ideas, and opinions. You may have noticed this in your own marriage. Conflicts often arise because of a difference of opinion on something, whether it is about spending money, raising children, or where and how you should celebrate the holidays.

Speak the truth in love (Eph. 4:15 NIV) – This principle helps minimize conflict when sharing your thoughts, beliefs, ideas, and opinions. This means that you need to use the *loveseat* more regularly and speak lovingly, gently, and kindly to your spouse. You also need to monitor how you react to your spouse when there is a disagreement. Be sure to validate your spouse's right to express his or her opinions. Besides, recognizing the differences in opinions and finding common points of agreement is a great way to build understanding. Perhaps you need to say something like, "Thanks for sharing your thoughts with me. I was unaware of your perceptions about this topic. I'm glad that though we disagree on this point, we agree on the other one."

S – Self

This level involves transparency, vulnerability, and deeper self-disclosure. It means sharing without the fear of rejection, which leads to true intimacy. A definition of intimacy that we learned a long time ago is that intimacy is *to know and to be known*. So, if you want to grow in deeper intimacy with your spouse, you need to share at this level. Perhaps you are wondering how you could share at this deeper level.

Open your heart, take risks, and be vulnerable – You may start by using the "I" statement technique that we discussed earlier in this chapter to share your thoughts and feelings. This is an excellent way to start sharing what is on your mind and heart. At this level, you can share not only your needs, purpose, and goals, but also your fears and insecurities. You become vulnerable and allow your spouse to know you more intimately. This is easier to do when you have developed a trusting relationship. Therefore, we encourage you to give the G.I.F.T.S. of communication to your spouse and watch your relationship grow as you laugh and cry together in the living room of your dream home.

Destructive Patterns of Communication

Destructive patterns of communication can develop in any marriage, but they do not need to be a frequent part of a couple's daily interactions. World-renowned marriage researcher John Gottman has studied the communication of thousands of couples and discovered what he called the *Four Horsemen of the Apocalypse*.[18] According to Gottman, these destructive patterns of communication are predictors of divorce. These patterns include *criticism, defensiveness, contempt*, and *stonewalling*.

Criticism – Criticism happens when a spouse verbally attacks the other spouse's personality or character. Criticism usually starts as a complaint or blame and with "you always" or "you never."

Defensiveness – Defensiveness occurs when a spouse is attacked or feels attacked by the criticism, complaint, or blame by the other spouse. Then, the spouse counterattacks to protect himself or herself. Thus, he or she may act like a victim, blame the other spouse, or complain.

Contempt – Contempt is a negative pattern of communication and includes hostility with the use of insults or abusive language. This verbal abuse may consist of "sarcasm, mocking, name-calling, or belligerence."[19]

Stonewalling – Stonewalling happens when, eventually, one of the spouses withdraws from the conversation and from the relationship. The attitude of being there but not interacting with the spouse is an attempt to hide any verbal and non-verbal reaction to what is perceived as a personal attack.

Fortunately, Gottman and his team of researchers offer some antidotes to these four patterns.

THE FOUR HORSEMEN
AND HOW TO STOP THEM WITH THEIR ANTIDOTES

CRITICISM

Verbally attacking
personality or character.

GENTLE START UP

Talk about your feelings using "I"
statements and express a positive need.

CONTEMPT

Attacking sense of self with
an intent to insult or abuse.

BUILD CULTURE
OF APPRECIATION

Remind yourself of your partner's
positive qualities and find gratitude
for positive actions.

DEFENSIVENESS

Victimizing yourself to ward off
a perceived attack and reverse
the blame.

TAKE RESPONSIBILITY

Accept your partner's perspective and
offer an apology for any wrongdoing.

STONEWALLING

Withdrawing to avoid conflict and convey
disapproval, distance, and separation.

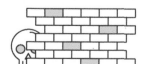

PHYSIOLOGICAL
SELF-SOOTHING

Take a break and spend that time doing
something soothing and distracting.

The Gottman Institute

Interestingly, research conducted at the University of Denver has yielded similar findings and identified four similar destructive patterns to marriages.[20]

Escalation – This is a pattern of arguing in which a spouse responds out of anger and frustration using words that offend and hurt the other spouse. These out-of-control arguments are what couples commonly refer to as big fights.

Invalidation – This negative pattern occurs when a spouse puts down the thoughts, feelings, behaviors, and character of the other spouse. This pattern also includes contempt.

Withdrawal and Avoidance – This pattern occurs when a spouse is unwilling to interact during an argument and, consequently, withdraws by leaving the room or shutting down emotionally. The spouse may also avoid getting into any conversation that is perceived as stressful. This pattern is similar to stonewalling.

Negative Interpretation – Due to the recurring arguments and hostility in the relationship, spouses tend to view the beliefs, motives, and behavior of the other spouse negatively.[21] No matter what positive things the other spouse does, it is always interpreted negatively.

You and your spouse certainly do not want these patterns in your marriage. You want to become encouragers of one another. In the coming pages, we discuss some practical listening skills that can help you deal with these negative and destructive habits of communication.

Do's and Don'ts of Effective Communication

To communicate effectively, you need to practice behaviors that enhance communication and avoid the above-mentioned patterns from developing. The goal is to prevent behaviors that weaken communication in your marriage. Building on Bolton's *People Skills*,[22] we provide a practical list of some Do's and Don'ts of effective communication. We will start with the Don'ts.

Don'ts

Don't interrupt – When you interrupt, you cut your spouse's flow of thought and make it harder for him or her to articulate his or her ideas, opinions, and feelings. This also communicates that you disagree with your spouse or find no value in what he or she is saying.

Don't be thinking about how to respond – When you are thinking about how to respond, you stop listening. Therefore, you stop focusing on your spouse's message and miss essential points your spouse is trying to make.

Don't fake understanding – Sometimes, during a conversation, you may miss something that your spouse is saying. This may be because you got distracted by external factors or by your own thoughts. When you pretend that you understand, you may be lost in the conversation later on. Pretending communicates that you do not care about what your spouse is saying.

Don't take a mental vacation – According to Amit Sood, in his book *The Mayo Clinic Guide to Stress-Free Living*, our brains have a tendency to engage in internally directed thinking when in *Default Mode*.[23] This causes our mind to wander off and daydream. So, when your spouse is talking with you, and you allow your mind to wander, you will certainly miss what your spouse is saying.

Don't be distracted by looking at your phone – As mentioned previously, phones help us to be connected with meaningful people in our lives. However, we have to be careful that in our effort to connect with people who are distant, we do not disconnect from those who are near us. Therefore, when you start looking at your phone, you communicate to your spouse that you are not interested in the conversation. You are saying that other people or things are more important to you. Undoubtedly, this behavior will hurt your spouse's feelings.

Don't divert from the topic – Many topics are uncomfortable to discuss due to a variety of reasons. For example, talking about your extended family or a job situation may evoke strong emotions due to some past experiences. Therefore, even though you may feel uncomfortable with a particular topic, be mindful that your spouse initiated the conversation about it because the topic is important to him or her. So, take the time to learn why the topic is important to your spouse.

Do's

We now move to some essential Do's of effective communication. While we acknowledge that cultural variations may influence what is considered appropriate behavior in communication, we address the most foundational behaviors that need to be implemented for effective communication to happen in your marriage. The Do's will make the living room a more pleasant place in your dream home.

Make appropriate eye contact – When you were dating, you probably made a lot of eye contact and gazed into your spouse's eyes. Eye contact shows interest in the other person and, obviously, interest in what the person is sharing.

Have a posture of involvement – Non-verbal communication is a significant part of any dialogue, making it critically important to be self-aware. Pay attention to your non-verbal behaviors and what they might communicate to your spouse. For example, if you are sitting down, lean forward to convey that you are interested and focused.

Be fully present psychologically – Being present means that you are paying attention to your spouse and avoiding a mental vacation. Focus on your spouse with your mind and heart. Make this moment about your spouse and give him or her your ears and your undivided attention. Then, hopefully, in turn, your spouse will give you his or her heart and mind.

Mirror your spouse's emotional expression – Your spouse will convey a lot of emotions during your interactions. Some conversations might be happy and include a lot of laughter. However, other conversations may be stressful or about sad issues. Therefore, you should convey empathy toward your spouse by making your facial expression match that of your spouse, except when your spouse has an angry facial expression.

Use appropriate head nods – A way to show that you are following the conversation is by using head nods. Whenever you agree with your spouse, let your head nod convey that.

Use minimal encouragers – These are small words or phrases that you can use to show your spouse that you are listening. Additionally, they also encourage the speaker to continue talking by providing evidence that you are listening. For instance, you may use "Uhm," "keep going," "go on," and "I see."

Use Communication to Encourage Your Spouse

Everyone needs words of affirmation and appreciation, including your spouse. You can affirm your spouse for who he or she is. For example, think of your husband's character, work ethic, and commitment to the family. You may tell him that he is a loving, hard worker, committed husband, and provider. You may also appreciate your spouse for what he or she does. For example, you may tell your wife, "honey, thank you for this delicious dinner." To give her bonus points, add, "It's much better than what my mother makes." Doing so can be an encouragement to your spouse. When you encourage your spouse, you are communicating: "You are the best, and I'm proud of you!"

"Let everything you say be good and helpful, so that your words will be an encouragement to those who hear them."
(Eph. 4:29 NLT)

Listen with Your Heart: Active Listening Skills

Listening is an art that includes a set of skills that can be learned and developed through practice. For this reason, we are going to share four active listening skills that counselors use every day to ensure that they understand their clients. These skills are paraphrasing, reflecting feelings, reflecting meaning, and summarizing. Since these are essential skills for effective listening, counselors also teach conflicted couples how to use some of these skills to improve their listening and overall communication.[24] We believe these skills can also improve your communication, minimize conflict, and maximize your ability to resolve conflict when you sit on your *loveseat*. If the skills work for counselors, they can certainly work for you.

Paraphrasing is when you restate concisely in your own words to your spouse what you heard. The purpose of paraphrasing is to ensure understanding of the meaning of your spouse's message. You may start your paraphrase with "What I'm hearing you say is . . ." or "It sounds like you . . ." When you paraphrase accurately, you ensure understanding and your spouse feels understood.

Reflecting feelings conveys empathy to your spouse by showing that you understand how he or she is feeling without saying "I know how you feel."

The purpose is to empathize with your spouse by focusing on your spouse's feelings and emotions. It is essential to keep in mind that your spouse sometimes may or may not use feeling words. However, you will need to identify the feelings your spouse may be experiencing or may have experienced based on the content of the conversation, the tone of voice, and body language. You may have to try to put yourself in your spouse's shoes and ask yourself, "If I were going through this situation, how would I be feeling?" or "If this had happened to me, how would I have felt?" This will help you identify your spouse's feelings and show empathy. You may say something along the lines of, "It sounds like you are feeling overwhelmed" or "I can see that you are frustrated." By doing so, you will validate your spouse's feelings, and in turn, your spouse feels cared for.

Reflecting meaning is a combination of reflecting feelings and paraphrasing. The purpose is to show more profound empathy with understanding. For example, you may say to your spouse, "You are feeling overwhelmed because we have too many bills to pay and our budget is very tight." When you reflect meaning, you let your spouse know that you understand how he or she feels and the reason behind his or her emotions. In turn, your spouse feels nurtured.

Summarizing involves a recap of the conversation, especially when much has been shared. When summarizing, you may restate the main topics or themes of the conversation. You may highlight a pattern or the primary concern that you noticed as your spouse shared. Summarizing is also helpful when closing a conversation. When you summarize, you ensure comprehension and your spouse feels heard and understood.

 ### Be a Good Listener

Being a good listener starts with a willingness to listen and understand your spouse's message. It is essential to realize that in a conversation, you will have your opportunity to talk and share. So, during the conversation, remind yourself that it is vital for you to be attentive and focused on what your spouse is saying.

"You must all be quick to listen, slow to speak."
(James 1:19 NLT)

When you interrupt and respond to your spouse before you take the time to listen, you show a lack of wisdom. By interrupting your spouse, you do not have a chance to hear the whole story or argument. Consequently, you do not hear all the facts before responding.

"If one gives an answer before he hears, it makes him foolish and ashamed."
(Prov.18:13 NLV)

A Practical Listening Technique

Now that you have a better understanding of communication and listening, we recommend that you start practicing what you learned in this chapter. First, establish what we call *Couple Time*, a specific set time once a day or once a week, depending on your schedule, to have meaningful conversations with your

Rules for Both	Rules for the Speaker	Rules for the Listener
The speaker has the floor	Speak for yourself	Paraphrase what you hear
Share the floor	Talk in small chunks	Don't rebut
No problem-solving	Stop and let the listener paraphrase	

spouse. During the *Couple Time*, we encourage you to sit on the *loveseat* and use the *Speaker–Listener Technique*[25] with your spouse. This technique provides the basic rules for both the speaker and the listener. We also recommend that you select topics that are easy for you to talk about and less likely to create conflict. We want you to gain confidence in improving your skills. As you practice this technique, praise each other once you have positive communication.

Check out the chapter video at: www.grtep.com

Now, let's walk into the kitchen and dining area.

Endnotes

1. Julia T. Woods, *Interpersonal Communication: Everyday Encounters* (Boston, MA: Cengage Learning, 2016).
2. Adapted from Robert Bolton, *People Skills: How to Assert Yourself, Listen to Others, and Resolve Conflict* (New York, NY: Simon & Schuster, Inc., 2011).
3. "Demographics of Social Media Users and Adoption in the United States," *Pew Research Center: Internet, Science & Technologies*, February 5, 2018, accessed May 4, 2019, https://www.pewinternet.org/fact-sheet/social-media/.
4. Jeffrey Dew and Sarah Tulane, "The Association between Time Spent Using Entertainment Media and Marital Quality in a Contemporary Dyadic National Sample," *Journal of Family and Economic Issues* 36, no. 4 (2015): 621–32, doi:10.1007/s10834-014-9427-y.

5. Dew and Tulane, "The Association between Time Spent Using Entertainment Media and Marital Quality."

6. Todd A. Spencer et al., "Assessing the Mediating Effect of Relationship Dynamics between Perceptions of Problematic Media Use and Relationship Satisfaction," *Contemporary Family Therapy* 39, no. 2 (2017): 80–86, doi:10.1007/s10591-017-9407-0.

7. Russell B. Clayton, Alexander Nagurney, and Jessica R. Smith, "Cheating, Breakup, and Divorce: Is Facebook Use to Blame?" *Cyberpsychology, Behavior, and Social Networking* 16, no. 10 (2013): 719, doi:10.1089/cyber.2012.0424.

8. Sebastián Valenzuela, Daniel Halpern, and James E. Katz, "Social Network Sites, Marriage Well-Being and Divorce: Survey and State-Level Evidence from the United States," *Computers in Human Behavior* 36 (July 2014): 100, doi:10.1016/j.chb.2014.03.034.

9. Valenzuela, Halpern, and Katz, "Social Network Sites, Marriage Well-Being and Divorce," 99.

10. Zackery A. Carter, "Married and Previously Married Men and Women's Perceptions of Communication on Facebook with the Opposite Sex: How Communicating through Facebook Can Be Damaging to Marriages," *Journal of Divorce and Remarriage* 57, no. 1 (January 2016): 36–55, doi:10.1080/10502556.2015.1113816.

11. Carter, "Married and Previously Married Men and Women's Perceptions of Communication on Facebook with the Opposite Sex."

12. Brandon T. McDaniel, Michelle Drouin, and Jaclyn D. Cravens, "Do You Have Anything to Hide? Infidelity-Related Behaviors on Social Media Sites and Marital Satisfaction," *Computers in Human Behavior* 66 (2017): 88–95, doi:10.1016/j.chb.2016.09.031.

13. Katherine M. Hertlein, "The Integration of Technology into Sex Therapy," *Journal of Family Psychotherapy* 21, no. 2 (2010): 117–31. doi:10.1080/08975350902967333.

14. Todd A. Spencer et al., "Assessing the Mediating Effect of Relationship," 85.

15. Gary D. Chapman, *Covenant Marriage* (Nashville, TN: Broadman & Holman, 2003), 51–60; John Powell, *Why Am I Afraid to Tell You Who I am?* (Grand Rapids, MI: Zondervan, 1999).

16. Chapman, *Covenant Marriage*, 51–60.

17. James V. Cordova, Christina B. Gee, and Lisa Z. Warren, "Emotional Skillfulness in Marriage: Intimacy as a Mediator of The Relationship between Emotional Skillfulness and Marital Satisfaction," *Journal of Social and Clinical Psychology* 24, no. 2 (2005): 218–35, doi:10.1521/jscp.24.2.218.62270.

18. John Mordechai Gottman, Julie Schwartz Gottman, and Joan DeClaire, *Ten Lessons to Transform Your Marriage* (New York, NY: Three Rivers Press, 2006).

19. Gottman, Gottman, and DeClaire, *Ten Lessons to Transform Your Marriage*, 5.

20. Scott M. Stanley et al., *A Lasting Promise: A Christian Guide to Fighting for Your Marriage* (San Francisco, CA: Jossey Bass, 2014); Howard J. Markman, Susan L. Blumberg, and Scott M. Stanley, *Fighting for Your Marriage* (San Francisco, CA: Jossey-Bass, 2013).

21. Stanley et al., *A Lasting Promise.*

22. Robert Bolton, *People Skills: How to Assert Yourself, Listen to Others, and Resolve Conflict.*

23. Amit Sood, *The Mayo Clinic Guide to Stress-Free Living* (Boston, MA: Da Capo Press, 2013).

24. K. Daniel O'Leary, Arthur E. Jongsma, and Richard E. Heyman, *The Couples Psychotherapy Treatment Planner, With DSM-5 Updates*, 2nd ed. (Hoboken, NJ: Wiley, 2015).

25. Stanley et al., *A Lasting Promise*, 77–78.

CHAPTER 5

The Kitchen and Dining Room: Feeding Body, Mind, Soul, and Relationships

"It takes more than bread to stay alive."
Matthew 4:4 (MSG)

© wavebreakmedia/Shutterstock.com

We love visiting model homes! We clearly remember a five-bedroom model home we visited multiple times in the subdivision where we used to live in Fort Worth, Texas. The house was a showstopper. The kitchen was spacious with long granite counter tops, modern stainless-steel top of the line appliances, custom cabinets, and high-end light fixtures. As you might have guessed, these items were all expensive upgrades that we could only afford in our dreams. It was indeed an open concept dream kitchen flowing into a large dining area, just the way most homeowners like it. In fact, the National Association of Home Builders reports that 84 percent of recently built homes have some form of open concept design.[1] As expected, the open layout combined with upgrades and creative use of spaces made our tour of this particular model home kitchen even more exciting.

For many American families, the kitchen and dining room are places where families prepare and serve delicious meals. These rooms are also places where family members start their morning as they greet one another and share their plans for the day. So, metaphorically, the kitchen and dining room represent our need to be nourished physically, mentally, spiritually, and relationally.

The commonly used phrase *body and soul* refers to "every part of you, including your mind and your emotions"[2] which leads to the idea that nourishing the body and soul involves taking care of oneself holistically. Therefore, in this chapter, we discuss multidimensional self-care and the importance of taking care of yourself and your spouse physically, mentally, spiritually, and relationally.

 When you take care of yourself holistically, you give your spouse your best self or the best version of yourself.

We believe that when you take care of yourself holistically, you give your spouse your best self or the best version of yourself.

Cooking Up Stress: Busy Lives

Stress is a reality in our fast-paced 21st-century lives and, if we do not manage it well, it can be detrimental to our physical, mental, spiritual, and relational health, including our marriages. In fact, ongoing, chronic stress can lead to burnout.[3] According to the 2017 Stress in America Survey™ sponsored by the American Psychological Association (APA), Americans continue to report high levels of stress including psychological and physical symptoms such as anxiety, anger, and fatigue. The survey highlights that Millennials, ages 18–38, report the highest levels of stress when compared to other age groups.[4]

Research shows that the first years of marriage are an adjustment period for most couples. This adjustment generally involves an elevated level of stress.[5] This makes sense since newly married couples are sharing the same household and learning a lot about each other's personalities, habits, routines, money management, and overall lifestyle. Thus, the first years of marriage can be both a joyful and a stressful time for couples.

Many factors contribute to the intensity of the flow of stress in the lives of married couples. According to research, many couples are dual career or dual income families, meaning both spouses work outside the home.[6] As a result, they may be exhausted or may not have time to engage in family or leisure activities, such as going to the movies or entertaining friends at home at the end of a long day. In addition, some couples may be in school trying to further their education and the little time they have is divided between work, family, and their homework. In some cases, couples are also overly committed to church activities during the week and on weekends. Younger couples may have small children, making parenting a vital task in the early years of their marriage. Still, other individuals who are in their second marriages may have to manage stressful relationships with ex-spouses and stepchildren. All these factors have the potential to create an additional layer of challenges. Thus, transitions, adjustments, and the busyness of life may affect a couple's relationship negatively and intensify the flow of stress.

Ongoing stress may cause couples to become frazzled and emotionally disconnected, which may lead them to experience a decrease in sexual intimacy. Unfortunately, when a couple is disconnected emotionally and physically, unless they are intentional about restoring their relationship, they may slowly drift apart. For this reason, couples need to be aware of possible high-stress factors that can affect the quality of their marriage negatively. Once couples are aware of those factors, they can be strategic about protecting themselves and their marriage by managing stress effectively.

Perhaps you relate to the reality of living a busy life and being caught up in the rat race. You may even find yourself looking for extra hours in the day to accomplish all that you have in your to-do list. For some, sleep-deprivation becomes problematic, leading to unhealthy coping methods such as energy drinks loaded with caffeine. If you and your spouse are frequently tired and cranky, you may not give each other your very best. You certainly do not want to experience the emotional or physical disconnect that all these factors can bring. Now may be the time to find some balance through self-care. However, if you believe you are doing well in all areas of your marriage, we congratulate you. As you know, there is always room for improvement. Hence, we encourage you to consider the nuggets of wisdom found in this chapter to continue to improve your well-being as an individual and as a couple.

Mind Your Priorities

What are some of your priorities in life? An essential aspect of taking care of yourself is to determine your priorities and, then, to live by them. Most Christians will agree that their number one priority is God. Indeed, this is what Jesus taught when He emphasized that the greatest commandment is to love God (Matt. 22:37–38) and that his disciples should "seek first the kingdom of God" (Matt. 6:33 ESV). We agree that having a vibrant relationship with God feeds our soul with joy. We also believe that caring for your soul is the place to start in your self-care, so that you may give the best of yourself to your spouse and other significant people in your life.

If the number one priority is God, what needs to come next? We believe that the next step is to take care of yourself so you can be in the best position to care for your spouse and other family members. Therefore, making time to take care of yourself holistically involves adopting strategies that target your body, mind, soul, and relationships. Although in this chapter, we discuss these areas separately, we must remember that they are interconnected and multidimensional. When these areas are harmonized, they can enhance your most crucial horizontal relationship, your marriage.

Multidimensional Self-Care

Self-care involves understanding priorities and caring for yourself, so you can give the best of yourself to your spouse and to others. For example, you may remember that every time you board an airplane, a flight attendant makes pre-flight safety announcements, which often include the following:

> *Oxygen and the air pressure are always being monitored. In the event of a decompression, an **oxygen mask** will automatically appear in front of you. To start the flow of oxygen, pull the mask towards you. Place it firmly over your nose and mouth, secure the elastic band behind your head, and breathe normally. Although the bag does not inflate, oxygen is flowing to the mask. If you are travelling with a child or someone who requires assistance, secure your mask on first, and then assist the other person. Keep your mask on until a uniformed crew member advises you to remove it.*[7]

The purpose of self-care is to make you a better giver and lover, and ultimately a more nurtured, refreshed, and rejuvenated spouse. Therefore, in a way, you are securing your mask on first, and then assisting your spouse.

 Secure your mask on first, and then assist your spouse.

Jesus set the example of self-care. He encouraged his disciples to get away and rest "because so many people were coming and going that they did not even have a chance to eat, he said to [his disciples], 'Come with me by yourselves to a quiet place and get some rest'" (Mark 6:31 NIV). You may also remember that Jesus even took a nap on the boat (Mark 4:38). These moments are snapshots in Jesus' life that serve as reminders of our own need to practice self-care.

The Bible teaches that our "bodies are temples of the Holy Spirit" and that we must honor God with our bodies (1 Cor. 6:19–20 NIV). John Dunlop, in his book *Wellness for the Glory of God*, defines wellness as "that blessed state of experiencing all spheres of life functioning in harmony with God's ordained purpose."[8] Consequently, self-care is a matter of good stewardship; it is not intended to turn you into a self-centered or narcissistic person. Rather, it helps you live in harmony with God just like Jesus did.

Multidimensional self-care is an ongoing, deliberate practice of strategies that mitigate stress and promote wellness. In other words, it means taking care of the various areas of your life so you may experience optimal well-being by feeding your body, mind, soul, and relationships. Furthermore, self-care protects and helps you flourish in all areas of your life to reach your God-given potential. Now, we turn our attention to these four areas.

 Multidimensional self-care means caring for yourself as a masterpiece created by our Heavenly Father.

Feeding the Soul

Throughout this book, we emphasize the importance of living life based on a biblical worldview. This worldview involves feeding your soul. As abovementioned, we believe that God should be the number one priority in our lives. For this reason, we want to remind you briefly that feeding your soul is essential to living a life that connects with God and reflects His love to others daily.

You probably remember that God delivered the Israelites from Egypt, and they made their way through the desert towards the Promised Land. As they experienced hunger, they complained to Moses, who then presented their complaints to God. God's solution to the situation was the miraculous manna, His daily provision to feed His people (Exod. 16). However, the Israelites were supposed to gather only enough manna for each day. Then, before the Sabbath, they could gather enough for the Sabbath. The main point of the story is that God provided for their physical needs, but they needed to gather manna every day.

We need to feed our souls every day with spiritual food, not only once a week at church. When we feed our soul daily, we become wiser and more mature spiritually. A well-nourished soul is like a well-nourished body, it is healthy and full of energy. When you feed your soul with the Word of God, you grow in your understanding of who God is and who you are. You also grow in your knowledge of God's purposes for humanity, your life, and your marriage and family. Thus, the constant feeding of your soul leads to spiritual growth and maturity.

Throughout the New Testament, Christians are called to grow and mature spiritually (Eph. 4:13–14; 2 Pet. 3:18). Spiritual maturity is not about following a set of rules, becoming legalistic, or accumulating Bible knowledge; it is not a matter of how much you know. Rather, spiritual maturity is a lifelong process that involves becoming more like Jesus Christ in your character, attitude, and behaviors.

Spiritual maturity does not happen automatically. It is a process that results from engaging deliberately in some spiritual practices. For the sake of brevity, we will discuss three essential spiritual disciplines you need to develop to feed your soul. These practices are worship, prayer, and meditation on the Word of God.

Worship is a spiritual encounter with God in which we acknowledge who God is, what He has done, and the things He has promised He will do for us. There

Spiritual maturity is a lifelong process of becoming more like Jesus in your character, attitude, and behavior.

Character: Display the fruit of the Spirit.

Attitude: Show Christ-like humility and compassion.

Behaviors: Perform actions that honor and please God.

are multiple examples of worship experiences in the Bible. Worship can happen at church, at home, or wherever you are. If you participate actively in a local church, you probably have engaged in worship multiple times. If you are new to the Christian faith, you are perhaps learning how to worship God in spirit and truth (John 4:24).

Prayer is our communication with God. According to the Pew Research Center, "More than half (55%) of Americans say they pray every day."[9] Jesus taught that prayer was essential for spiritual maturity. In fact, Jesus not only taught his disciples how to pray, but he also set the example for them to follow by spending time in prayer.

A pastor once said that prayer is a running conversation with God. We agree with him because we can pray all the time in our hearts and minds expressing to God our thoughts, feelings, and needs. This definition is in agreement with Paul's statement, "pray without ceasing" (1 Thess. 5:17 ESV). Thus, we encourage you to make some time to pray every day and connect with your Heavenly Father. In chapter 9, we discuss more in-depth how prayer can strengthen your life and marriage.

Meditation has become a buzzword in our society. Many Americans practice some type of meditation that reflects an *Eastern* perspective. However, in this chapter, we look at meditation from a Christian-Judeo perspective. The Bible teaches us to meditate on God's Word day and night. The word *meditation* comes from a Hebrew word *hagah*, and it means to "speak in an undertone."[10] Therefore, Christian meditation, also known as devotionals, involves reading the Word of God, seeking to understand the meaning of the Bible passage, reflecting on how the message of the Bible relates to our lives, and then, determining how to apply the message to our daily lives. In chapter 9, we discuss specific tips on how to meditate on God's Word as a tool to strengthen your life and marriage.

Feeding the Body

Multidimensional self-care involves caring for our bodies, which is also a biblical principle. The Bible teaches that the body is a temple of the Holy Spirit (1 Cor. 6:19) and that we are called to honor God with our bodies. Developing a biblically-based and balanced understanding about the physical body will lead us to care for the body without engaging in self-worship.[11] As Christians, we give our bodies adequate nourishment, rest, and sleep in order to carry out God's mission in the world and, in this way, glorify and honor him with our bodies.

In today's culture, we witness the extremes that range from an obsession with thinness or bodybuilding to severe levels of obesity. According to the National Eating Disorders Association, "national surveys estimate that 20 million women and 10 million men in America will have an eating disorder at some point in their lives."[12] Obesity is also a major health concern. According to the Centers for Disease Control and Prevention (CDC), "The prevalence of obesity was 39.8% and affected about 93.3 million of US adults in 2015~2016."[13] Obesity can cause multiple health problems including heart disease, stroke, and type 2 diabetes diseases. However, numerous factors such as biological, psychological, and sociocultural may contribute to eating disorder issues. Additionally, many people believe that the media is responsible for causing eating disorders. However, Simona Giordane, director of the medical ethics at the Medical School in Manchester, UK, claims that simply blaming the media for causing eating disorders is "a misanalysis of the problem."[14] She asserts that a core factor is to understand why people believe and connect their sense of self-worth with being thin.[15]

Although there is a growing awareness of the need for physical activity and healthier eating habits, lack of physical activity is still prevalent in our society. For instance, a study discovered that people in the U.S. walk an average of only 4,774 steps a day[16] and noticed that this is a worldwide problem, a "global pandemic of physical inactivity."[17] According to the Mayo Clinic, physical activity, such as exercise or walking, has numerous benefits including the ability to maintain a healthy weight, better management of current health issues, and prevention of other health problems such as high blood pressure and heart disease.[18] In fact, the U.S. Department of Health and Human Services recommends that adults ages 18–64

> do at least 150 minutes (2 hours and 30 minutes) to 300 minutes (5 hours) a week of moderate-intensity, or 75 minutes (1 hour and 15 minutes) to 150 minutes (2 hours and 30 minutes) a week of vigorous-intensity aerobic physical activity, or an equivalent combination of moderate- and vigorous-intensity aerobic activity.[19]

The purpose here is not to shame you, challenge you to get a gym membership, or add losing weight to your New Year's resolutions. Rather, we want to encourage you to discover how you can become more physically active by engaging in enjoyable activities with your spouse. Thus, benefitting not only your overall physical health, but also your marriage. Here are a few things that medical professionals recommend regularly to help people care for their bodies.

Active Lifestyle

Having an active lifestyle needs to be a team effort for couples. Thomas Bradbury and Benjamin Karney, in their book *Love Me Slender: How Smart Couples Team Up to Lose Weight, Exercise More, and Stay Healthy Together*, assert that "the choices and decisions that two partners make will affect each other and the environment they inhabit, the foods that are in their homes, and the inclination to be active."[20] Moreover, to see meaningful changes and positive results in this area, spouses need to encourage each other and make a personal effort to live an active lifestyle as much as possible.

Going for a walk in our neighborhood has been for us a great way to be physically active, talk about life, and meet new neighbors. During our walking, we share our thoughts about ourselves, our marriage and family, and God. We try to make walking a fun activity. We intentionally take our cell phones with us to take pictures of anything interesting we may find along the way. As a result, we have countless pictures of cute deer, interesting clouds, and amazing sunsets. These beautiful pictures often end up in our electronic picture frame in our living room. Most of the year, our walks in the neighborhood are relatively easy to maintain. However, during the winter, we trade the streets of our neighborhood for our treadmill. Still, we try to make it fun by listening to our favorite songs or watching inspiring shows and YouTube videos while walking on the treadmill.

Healthy Diet

Having a healthy diet includes developing healthy eating habits. Fortunately, there is plenty of help available to all of us. For instance, the www.choosemyplate.gov website is a valuable source of information on nutrition and healthy eating. However, changing our eating habits sometimes does not happen as easily as we want. Most of us are not willing to quit our favorite dessert, mocha, or soft drink. Although information is power, most of us find it challenging to implement it. In our family's case, it has taken us many years to transition from a not-so-healthy breakfast to a healthier one. We discovered that integrating healthy fruit smoothies to our breakfast every morning was not only healthier, but educational and fun. As we created and shared new flavor combinations, we encouraged each other to live a healthier lifestyle.

Adequate Sleep

The National Sleep Foundation recommends 7–9 hours of sleep a night for most adults.[21] But, you may be saying to yourself, "Are you kidding me? Who has time to sleep when there is so much to get done?" We understand this is a major complaint from many people. However, adequate regular quality sleep has numerous benefits including reducing levels of stress and restoring our body's ability to regulate and defend itself against diseases.[22]

So, why is it challenging to get our recommended 7–9 hours of sleep? What are the factors that prevent us from quality sleep? Some challenges to proper sleep may include busy schedules, personality differences (morning person versus night person), small children in the house, a chronically snoring spouse, and even technology and social media. However, that is not all. How you view sleep also influences your sleeping patterns and habits. Greg McKeown, the author of the book *Essentialism*, points out a few interesting beliefs people hold about sleep.

Nonessentialist Thinks	Essentialist Knows
One hour less of sleep equals one more hour of productivity.	One hour more of sleep equals several more hours of much high productivity.
Sleep is for failures.	Sleep is for high performers.
Sleep is a luxury.	Sleep is a priority.
Sleep breeds laziness.	Sleep breeds creativity.
Sleep gets in the way of "doing it all."	Sleep enables the highest levels of mental contribution.[23]

Therefore, when you and your spouse have a positive view of sleep, you will be more inclined to protect it, enjoy it, and probably reap the benefits of full night sleep.

Resting and Relaxation

In our counseling work and ministry, we have seen many couples whose busy and demanding lifestyles have led them slowly into a road of neglected self-care and poor marital relationships. We also noticed that though they were dual earners, had more money and possessions, they seemed to experience low levels of fulfillment in their marriages. One thing was clear to us; they had extremely busy lives, which included a tight schedule that left very little time for resting and meaningful interaction.

Taking time to rest is a biblical concept that is relevant to our fast-paced, stress-filled 21st-century life. In the Bible, more specifically in the Old Testament, we see that one of the goals of the Sabbath, besides a focus on God, was to allow the body to rest and be refreshed (Exodus 23:12). In the New Testament, Jesus himself highlighted the need to rest as He invited his disciples to take some time away from the crowds, so that they could eat and rest (Mark 6:31). Joshua Becker in his book, *The More of Less: Finding the Life You Want under Everything You Own*, suggests that people need to schedule a day during the week for intentional rest.[24] Rest has multidimensional benefits to our lives. It gives us more physical and mental energy, allows us opportunities to develop deeper relationships, enhances our sense of family and community, and makes us contemplative and appreciative of life.

Resting and relaxing at the end of a busy week is an investment not only in our mental health but also in our marital health. For instance, on Friday nights, we often enjoy watching our favorite TV shows or *Shark Tank* reruns while eating our favorite healthy snacks. Watching these shows, especially *Shark Tank*, has inspired our entrepreneurial side. Additionally, doing fun activities on Saturdays such as taking a scenic drive on the Blue Ridge Parkway, going to the local farmers' market, or visiting apple farms have been exciting and fun ways for us to enjoy a weekend and connect as a couple.

Feeding the Mind

According to Scriptures, believers are commanded to renew their minds (Rom. 12:2) and set their minds "on things above" (Col. 3:1–2 NIV). This calls for the development of a worldview that reflects God's truth, an intentional feeding of our minds. Feeding the mind involves protecting, nourishing, and training our thoughts. First, it is about protecting our minds from worldviews that undermine our marriage and family life. Second, it includes nourishing our minds with biblical truth and wisdom. Finally, it involves training our minds to develop a pattern of healthy thinking that influences our emotions and behaviors positively.

Dan Siegel, a clinical professor of psychiatry at the UCLA School of Medicine and prolific author and speaker, has created the healthy mind platter, in which he discusses "daily essential mental activities to optimize brain matter and create well-being."[25] He proposes that similarly to the "choose my plate" approach for a healthy diet, we should have an equivalent daily diet for developing a healthy mind. He recommends that we spend time in the following essential and helpful activities for the brain: focusing on specific tasks, playing and enjoying new activities, connecting with people, engaging in physical activity, reflecting on our thoughts and feelings, relaxing, and sleeping.[26] As you may have observed in his recommendations, we need to be intentional in the process of feeding our minds. Therefore, we need to consider our roles and thoughts and emotions.

Mind Your Roles

Most people want to experience high levels of marital satisfaction and to succeed in their careers without sacrificing their marriage and family. Unfortunately, many people struggle with *role overload* and *role conflict*.[27] Role overload is when a person has too many demands and expectations placed on herself or himself. For example, sometimes a person has many tasks to complete at work and may feel overwhelmed as the job demands much of his or her time and energy. Role conflict, on the other hand, is when the demands of one role conflicts with the requirements of another one. For instance, the role of being a spouse and a student at the same time may conflict.

Many married couples struggle with role conflict because of the multiple new roles they have after they get married. However, once they define their roles earlier in marriage, it becomes easier to determine their priorities. Therefore, as abovementioned, we believe that determining your priorities in life is key to dealing with role *conflict and overload.* By prioritizing your spouse and children above work, you are more likely to make job-related decisions that improve interpersonal interactions and create peace of mind.

Mind Your Thoughts and Emotions

God created us as rational and emotional beings with the capacity to experience a variety of thoughts and feelings throughout our lives. Sometimes, as we interact with our spouses, our thoughts generate feelings that lead to an emotional reaction that can feed and escalate conflict. In those moments, our automatic thoughts and reactions may reflect our lack of self-awareness, reactive mind, and lack of self-control.

When couples get married, they may have many unrealistic expectations including that their spouse will meet all their needs. This type of unrealistic thinking is very detrimental and potentially dangerous to marriage. Unfortunately, disappointments will happen in marriage. Gary and Barbara Rosberg in their book, *Divorce-Proof Your Marriage,* describe the process a couple may go through as they move from wanting a "dream marriage" to becoming emotionally disconnected and eventually divorcing.[28] They contend that disappointments are unavoidable and happen when a spouse does not meet the other's needs.

Disappointments can set a chain of negative events in motion. In fact, unresolved disappointments lead to discouragement, which contributes to a lack of emotional investment in the marital relationship. Discouragement also leads to an emotional distance where the couple "no longer find each other exciting or even interesting."[29] This emotional distance creates a disconnect that leads to discord. As expected, discord includes many unnecessary arguments, fights, and lack of emotional and physical intimacy. Eventually, this leads to an emotional divorce, where the couple has no longer an emotional connection. Sadly, many couples are unable to revert their situation, and they eventually divorce.

As abovementioned, a couple does not fall out of love overnight. Therefore, being aware of your thoughts and emotional reactions and your relational patterns of interaction is key to a successful marriage. You will do well to pay attention to the thoughts you have when your

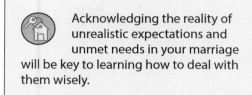

Acknowledging the reality of unrealistic expectations and unmet needs in your marriage will be key to learning how to deal with them wisely.

spouse disappoints you by not meeting your immediate expectations or needs. Again, your thoughts about the event influence your feelings and reactions.

Multiple psychological theories explain emotions and how they happen. Most of these theories emphasize that emotions involve very complex and comprehensive processes that include physiological responses of the body to events, our psychological subjective interpretation of the events and physiological sensations, and the actual behavioral expression of emotions.[30] Since a process of cognitive appraisal or evaluation takes place, emotions become a very subjective experience.

For the sake of our discussion, it is essential to highlight that *emotion regulation* is a person's ability to become aware of and manage or control his or her emotions and feelings and engage in appropriate behaviors to reach a positive outcome.[31] The Bible describes it in terms of self-control and emotional restraint (Prov. 16:32; Prov. 25:28) and indicates that self-control is also a sign of a spiritually mature person who displays the fruit of the Spirit (Gal. 5:22–23).

Your thoughts and decision to get married certainly influenced your emotions. You probably experienced many positive emotions and feelings earlier in the relationship that led you to make your decision. You may have thought of them as butterflies in your stomach or extreme joy. These good feelings or sense of well-being helped you decide to spend the rest of your life with that special someone who makes you feel so good.

The truth is that some situations and interactions between you and your spouse may lead you to experience some negative emotions, such as anger, frustration, hurt, and sadness, to name a few. The thoughts you have about those events or about your spouse may intensify the negative emotions. Therefore, part of minding your thoughts and emotions is to monitor and control your thinking because thoughts influence emotions.

A cognitive perspective can help you understand the interaction between thoughts and emotions. The *ABC theory* of emotions teaches that *A* is the activating event, *B* is your belief about the event, and *C* is the consequence. *A* does not determine *C*, meaning that the event itself does not create the consequence, which can be an emotion or a behavior. Rather, your beliefs (*B*) about the event (*A*) causes (*C*) your emotional and behavioral reaction.[32]

The ABC Theory Examples

Joe spends Saturday afternoon playing online video games with his friends and forgets about his dinner plans with his wife, Sally (A). Sally thinks Joe does not care about her since he forgot about their dinner plans (B). She feels angry, frustrated, and rejected. She withdraws from him and shuts down (C).

Lucy spends most of the evenings on Facebook (A). Dave thinks she is wasting time on the internet when she could help him with the house remodeling project (B). Dave feels angry and alone. He stops working on the project and goes to his parents' house nearby (C).

The Fork in the Road Approach

We would like to share with you an example of a strategy that you can use to deal with your emotions and your thinking process when dealing with disappointments in marriage. We like to call this strategy the *Fork in the Road* approach because it reflects the reality that in life we usually have options. We will apply this strategy to Joe and Sally's situation presented above. In the diagram, we have integrated a couple of concepts from previous chapters, such as the biblical principle of renewing the mind by challenging distorted thinking and the use of "I" statements.

As you can see, Sally is facing a fork in the road. She can choose to think positively or negatively about her situation. Sally's negative thoughts about her interaction with her husband can lead her to the conclusion that Joe does not care about her even though his behavior was simply one of forgetfulness. However, to arrive at such a conclusion, she has to disregard all the positive contributions Joe makes to the marriage. If she chooses this route, she will open up herself to experiencing more negative emotions. These emotions, in turn, will influence her response and affect their relationship in nonconstructive ways. However, to address the situation in a positive way, Sally needs to fuel her thinking with reality-based thoughts and biblical principles. By doing so, she will confirm her belief that her husband loves her and cares for the family. She will also show an understanding that Joe forgot the time for their dinner because he was having so much fun playing with his friends. Since she is thinking positively, she will accept that forgetting about the time to leave for dinner does not equal his lack of love and care for her. Additionally, using the biblical principle of "Speaking the truth in love" (Eph. 4:15 NIV), she can use "I" statements to address her husband and share her concern about being late for dinner. By approaching her husband respectfully, she will establish a constructive interaction with him and probably lead the conversation to a positive direction and outcome.

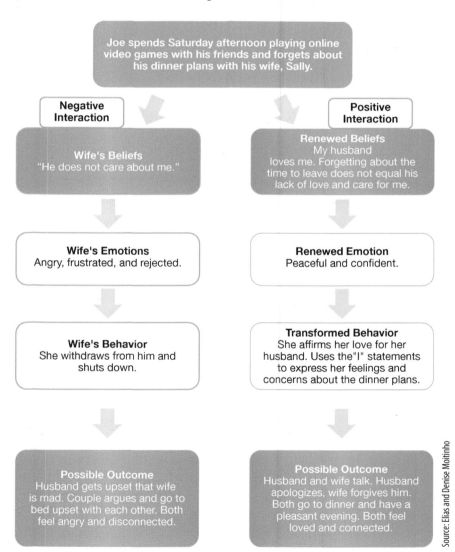

Source: Elias and Denise Moitinho

We encourage you to apply the *Fork in the Road strategy* to the example of Lucy and Dave and consider beliefs, emotions, behaviors, and outcomes to their situation. Hopefully, you will be able to apply this strategy to any of your future personal *fork in the road* situations.

Feeding the Relationships

This book is about investing in your most important relationship: your marriage. As discussed previously, by taking care of yourself, you will be healthy physically, emotionally, and spiritually to give your best to your spouse. Therefore, taking care of your relationships starts with what you are doing right now: reading this book to create a dream marriage. Since the main focus of this book is on your marriage, we will briefly highlight some important aspects of feeding your relationships.

Protect your marriage from infidelity. Some people call it an affair-proof marriage. You may do it by implementing the many principles you are reading in this book. We also recommend that you avoid viewing pornography and set healthy boundaries with the opposite sex.

An important element of relational self-care is learning to say "no." There are many people and activities that compete for your time. However, if you are not careful, saying yes to many people and activities may become detrimental to your marriage. When you say "no" to people and activities that may rob you of your precious time, you are free to say "yes" to your spouse and activities that will enhance your marital intimacy.

If you already have children, be sure to make time for your family. Spending quality time and quantity time with your children will be essential for strengthening your relationships with them. It is important to decide with your spouse what activities are realistic and beneficial to your children to engage in. Unfortunately, many families overcommit to after school activities and sports to the point that parents are stretched thin and have little time and energy left for them as a couple and family.

Cultivate a healthy relationship with your in-laws, extended family, and friends. They can potentially become a strong support network for you and your spouse. Having healthy boundaries with your in-laws and extended family allows for positive interactions while minimizing potential over involvement in each other's lives that may create family conflict. Additionally, having healthy relationships with other couples gives you the opportunity to invest in their lives and at the same time enrich your marriage.

Questions for reflection:

1. What **challenges** do you anticipate when feeding your body, mind, soul, and relationships?

2. What **resources** do you already have that will help you feed your body, mind, soul, and relationships?

3. What **resources** do you need to help you feed your body, mind, soul, and relationships?

4. What **specific issues** do you need to address related to your body, mind, soul, and relationships?

5. What **positive results and emotions** may you experience when you feed your body, mind, soul, and relationships?

Check out the chapter video at: www.grtep.com

We want to encourage you to take a moment and imagine yourself in your kitchen/dining area and let the metaphor and analogies of kitchen/dining used in this chapter to be a reminder to you to take care of your body, mind, soul, and relationships.

Now, let's walk into the home office and talk about finances.

Endnotes

1. Audrey Ference, "Open Floor Plan Homes: You Really Want One? The Pros and Cons," *Realtor.com*, January 22, 2018, accessed August 29, 2019, https://www.realtor.com/advice/buy/open-floor-plan-homes-pros-and-cons/; Paul Emrath, "Economics and Housing Policy," National Association of Home Builders, January 3, 2017, accessed august 30, 2019, https://www.nahbclassic.org/generic.aspx?genericContentID=254919&print=true.
2. "Body and Soul," *Collins Dictionary*, accessed September 20, 2018, https://www.collinsdictionary.com/us/dictionary/english/body-and-soul.
3. Maslach, C., and Leiter, M. P., "Understanding the Burnout Experience: Recent Research and Its Implications for Psychiatry," *World Psychiatry* 15 (2016): 103–11.

4. American Psychological Association, "*Stress in America: The State of Our Union,*" November 1, 2017, accessed September 6, 2019, https://www.apa.org/images/state-nation_tcm7-225609.pdf.

5. "Marriage Study Find Couples Are Happiest Three Years After Wedding," *Huffpost,* September 26, 2013, accessed September 16, 2018, https://www.huffingtonpost.com/2013/09/   26/marriage-study_n_3998429.html?utm_hp_ref=women&ir=-Women&; "Third Year of Marriage Is Happiest Study Shows," *The Telegraph,* September 26, 2013, accessed January 10, 2019, https://www.telegraph.co.uk/news/uknews/10335847/Third-year-of-marriage-is-happiest-study-shows.html; Justin A. Lavner, Benjamin R. Karney, and Thomas N. Bradbury, Relationship Problems Over the Early Years of Marriage: Stability or Change? *Journal of Family Psychology* 28, no. 6 (2014): 979–85, doi:10.1037/a0037752; April A. Buck and Lisa A. Neff, "Stress Spillover in Early Marriage: The Role of Self-Regulatory Depletion," *Journal of Family Psychology* 26, no. 5 (2012): 698–708, accessed September 16, 2018, https://pdfs.semanticscholar.org/21d0/54974296f7fdd4f-219d40effab08b6f4e80b.pdf.

6. "The Rise in Dual Income Families," *Pew Research Center,* June 18, 2015, accessed January, 10, 2019, http://www.pewresearch.org/ft_dual-income-house-holds-1960-2012-2/; Gerami et al., "The Pathology of the Dual-Career Couples: A Qualitative Study," *Global Journal of Health Science* 9, no. 5 (2017): 226–33.

7. Air Odyssey, "In Flight Passenger Announcements," accessed January 2, 2019, https://airodyssey.net/reference/inflight/.

8. John Dunlop, *Wellness for the Glory of God: Living Well After 40 with Joy and Contentment in All of Life* (Crossway, Wheaton, IL, 2014), 21.

9. Michael Lipka, "Five Facts about Prayer," *Pew Research Center,* May 4, 2016, accessed January 2, 2019, http://www.pewresearch.org/fact-tank/2016/05/04/5-facts-about-prayer/.

10. Marvin R. Wilson, *Our Father Abraham: Jewish Roots of the Christian Faith* (Grand Rapids, MI: William B. Eerdmans Publishing, 1989), 154.

11. Ronnie Floyd, *Living Fit: Make Your Life Count by Pursuing a Healthy You* (Nashville, TN: B&H Publishing Group, 2018).

12. "What Are Eating Disorders?" *National Eating Disorders Association,* accessed September 16, 2018, https://www.nationaleatingdisorders.org/what-are-eating-disorders.

13. "Adult Obesity Facts," *Centers for Disease Control and Prevention,* August 13, 2018, accessed September 16, 2018, https://www.cdc.gov/obesity/data/adult.html.

14. Simona Giordano, "Eating Disorders and the Media," *Current Opinion in Psychiatry* 28, no. 6 (November 2015): 478.

15. Giordano, "Eating Disorders and the Media."

16. Althoff et al., "Large-Scale Physical Activity Data Reveal Worldwide Activity Inequality" *Nature* 547, no. 7663 (July 20, 2017): 336–39.

17. Althoff et al., "Large-Scale Physical Activity," 336.

18. "Walking: Trim Your Waistline, Improve Your Health," *Mayo Clinic*, accessed April 14, 2019, https://www.mayoclinic.org/healthy-lifestyle/fitness/in-depth/walking/art-20046261.

19. Department of Health and Human Services, *Physical Guidelines for Americans*, 2nd ed. (2018), accessed April 14, 2019, https://health.gov/paguidelines/second-edition/pdf/Physical_Activity_Guidelines_2nd_edition.pdf.

20. Thomas N. Bradbury and Benjamin R. Karney, *Love Me Slender: How Smart Couples Team Up to Lose Weight, Exercise More and Stay Healthy Together* (New York, NY: Simon & Schuster, 2014), 26.

21. "How Sleep Works, The Science of Sleep: How Much Sleep Do You Really Need?" *National Sleep Foundation*, accessed January 1, 2019, https://www.sleepfoundation.org/how-sleep-works/how-much-sleep-do-we-really-need.

22. "Surprising Reasons to Get More Sleep," *WebMD*, accessed August 8, 2019, https://www.webmd.com/sleep-disorders/benefits-sleep-more#2.

23. Greg McKeown, *Essentialism: The Disciplined Pursuit of Less* (New York, NY: Crown Business, 2014), 96.

24. Joshua Becker, *The More of Less: Finding the Life You Want Under Everything You Own* (New York, NY: Waterbrook, 2018), 196.

25. Daniel J. Siegel, "The Healthy Mind Plater," accessed October 12, 2018, http://drdansiegel.com/resources/healthy_mind_platter/.

26. Siegel, "The Healthy Mind Platter."

27. Wong et al., *Counseling Individuals Through the Lifespan* (Newbury Park, CA: Sage Publications, 2015), 240.

28. Gary Rosberg, *Divorce-Proof Your Marriage* (Chicago, IL: Tyndale House Publishers, 2002).

29. Rosberg, *Divorce-Proof*, 29.

30. Sandra E. Hockenbury, Susan A. Nolan, and Don H. Hockenbury, *Discovering Psychology*, 7th ed. (New York, NY: Worth Publishers, 2016).

31. American Psychological Association, *APA Dictionary of Psychology*, accessed May 4, 2019, https://dictionary.apa.org/emotion-regulation.

32. Daniel David, Steven Jay Lynn, and Albert Ellis, eds., *Rational and Irrational Beliefs: Research, Theory, and Clinical Practice* (New York, NY: Oxford University Press, 2010).

CHAPTER 6

The Home Office: Keeping Your Finances in Check

"Every spending decision is a spiritual decision."
Ron Blue

© GaudiLab/Shutterstock.com

When we embarked on our first house-hunting adventure, it never crossed our minds that we would need to have a room specifically designed, decorated, or organized as a home office. Besides, during that time, the trend was to have home theaters and exercise rooms in newly built homes. We, on the other hand, were thrilled to have a house with bedrooms for each of our two kids. That was our idea of a dream home. However, as we found ourselves placing our junk and regular mail on kitchen counters, side tables, and closets, we realized that we needed a designated place to keep our bills, receipts, and any home-related paperwork. We also realized the importance of having an organized home office space to manage our finances and prevent any unnecessary financial conflicts and headaches in our marriage. Fortunately, nowadays, we do most of our home finances online, but a home office is still a crucial space.

According to a Home Design Trends Survey conducted by the American Institute of Architects (AIA), home offices have grown in popularity. In fact, the survey shows the home office room as the third most important special function room in a house.[1] This is because people believe that the home office provides a quiet space to handle home finances. Additionally, the home office is an essential room for those who work from home. This makes sense since recent government reports show that almost 25 percent of workers work from home, especially those with higher education.[2] As expected, homeowners tend to invest significantly in décor and technology for their home offices[3] to organize their workspace, finances, and, above all, their marriage life.

We use the home office as a metaphor for the couple's finances and we share practical and life-changing financial principles. First, we address the effects of poor financial management on marital satisfaction and how frequent financial conflict can lead to divorce. Next, we review some key biblical principles for wise money management. Then, we share some Christian money-management approaches that can provide you with a system or a plan to manage your home finances well. We agree that "every spending decision is a spiritual decision."[4] Thus, couples need to be intentional in keeping their finances in check.

Financial Management and Marriage

Many couples experience financial conflict. The story of Melissa and Jack in the following example is no exception.

Melissa and Jack have been attending counseling sessions to improve their communication and conflict resolution skills. While Jack was working on becoming less critical and more affirming of Melissa, Melissa was learning how to be more open about her feelings with Jack. One day, Jack was in their home office going over the family finances when Melissa walked in quietly. She seemed hesitant to talk, but indicated that she wanted to share something with Jack. She stated anxiously, "we are in terrible debt." Jack looked at her in disbelief for he thought their finances were under control. Then, with fear in his eyes, he asked the dreaded question, "How much?" After some silence, the answer came. "We are $15,000.00 in debt." Jack was in shock and angry. He could not believe that their situation had spiraled out of control. He had trusted his wife to manage the finances, and now they were in a hole. Melissa shared with him how she had used several credit cards to maintain a lifestyle that, in reality, the family could not afford. Understandably, Jack became angry and said that he could no longer trust her to manage their finances. The situation left them drained mentally, emotionally, and financially. Eventually, they decided to share this situation with their counselor in their next session.

As we step back and look at Melissa and Jack's financial struggles, what insights can we gain from their situation? The major problem we see here is that Melissa overspent, did not seek help, and sadly, hid the debt from Jack. The second issue is that Melissa and Jack did not have a collaborative approach to their finances, and Jack did not provide financial accountability to his wife. Third, on a positive note, they made the wise decision to discuss their financial conflict with their counselor. Fast forward a few months and their situation completely changed. The counselor assisted Melissa and Jack through their emotional and relational healing and guided them through conflict resolution. Consequently, Jack was able to rebuild his trust in Melissa. A key factor in the successful resolution of this conflict was that the counselor also referred Melissa and Jack to a Christian financial advisor, who helped them develop a strategic plan to get out and stay out of debt.

Unfortunately, Melissa and Jack's story is not an isolated case. According to financial experts, the American family's average credit card debt in April 2019 was $8,339.[5] As we saw in Melissa and Jack's story, being in debt creates stress, leads to marital conflict, and decreases marital quality and satisfaction. In fact, research shows that most marital conflict is connected to money.[6] Sadly, arguments about finances are significant predictors of divorce.[7] Financial conflict in marriage occurs frequently and is difficult to resolve.[8] In fact, a researcher found that the higher the frequency of disagreements over money, the higher the likelihood of getting a divorce. He states, "couples who reported disagreeing about finance once a week were over 30 percent more likely to get divorced than couples who reported disagreeing about finances a few times a month."[9]

Consumer debt can also be very detrimental to the health of a marriage. It often creates financial and emotional pressure on couples and increases the frequency of arguments about other areas of marriage.[10] A recent study conducted by Ramsey Solutions found that "the larger a couple's debt, the more likely they were to say money is one of the top issues they fight about."[11] However, for newlyweds, on a positive note, paying off debt early on in the marriage makes a difference in the relationship.[12]

As we discussed in Chapter 2, a biblical worldview provides the best location for us to navigate life and brings stability to a marriage. Your worldview also includes how you view money and material possessions. Being less materialistic influences a couple's overall marital quality positively, whereas when couples are materialistic, they experience more conflict.[13] A biblical view of money and material possessions emphasizes the importance of contentment rather than materialism. Nevertheless, other factors also contribute to financial conflict in marriage. Researchers explain,

> The top predictors of financial conflict for husbands [include] perceptions of a spendy wife, having financial worries, reporting a lower income, having three or more children, and having a wife who thinks he is too spendy. The top predictors of financial conflict for wives [include] having a husband who thinks she is too spendy, feeling a lack of communication with her husband, having financial worries, having a husband with low income, and having perceptions of a spendy husband.[14]

We believe that when couples understand each other and agree on a biblical worldview of money and material possessions, they tend to walk in more agreement and less conflict. Couples who are enjoying their marriage the most "are almost twice as likely to talk about money daily or weekly compared to those who say their marriage is 'okay' or 'in crisis.'"[15]

Money, Money, Money

The Bible has much to say about money and financial management. In fact, the Bible has over 2,350 Bible verses that discuss money, finances, and material possessions.[16] This sheer volume of verses means that managing finances is an essential part of life, and it has spiritual implications as well. Thankfully, God knew that we needed a proper perspective on how to view and handle money responsibly. Therefore, examining a biblical worldview on finances and material possessions can help us become responsible for our money management. We will cover three key principles here.

God Is the Owner of Everything

God is not only the creator of the universe but also the owner of everything. King David proclaimed this truth clearly when he stated, "The earth is the Lord's, and everything in it, the world, and all who live in it" (Psalm 24:1 NIV). In the book of Job, God declares that everything under heaven belongs to him (Job 41:11). Similarly, God speaks through his prophet Haggai, "The silver is mine and the gold is mine" (Hag. 2:8 NIV). During the time of the prophet Haggai, God's people were rebuilding the temple. God wanted to remind them that he was the owner of all treasures and that He would provide for them to rebuild the temple even in difficult economic times.

God's ownership of everything has some significant implications to our lives. First, everything we have or own, technically, belongs to God. This is a very profound truth. This means that our material possessions, whether it is the banking account, the house, or the car, they all belong to God. Second, this redefined ownership changes our view of material possessions. It implies that we cannot and do not own anything because there is already an owner, God. This leads to a third implication or understanding that God has made us managers of His possessions. Next, we will expand on this concept.

> **10** for every animal of the forest is mine, and the cattle on a thousand hills.
>
> **11** I know every bird in the mountains, and the insects in the fields are mine.
>
> **12** If I were hungry I would not tell you, for the world is mine, and all that is in it.
>
> Psalm 50:10-12 (NIV)

God Is the Provider and Giver of All Blessings

Among the many names God has in the Bible, one of the powerful names is *Jehova-Jireh*, which means God will provide. This name appears in the story of Abraham and Isaac. You may remember the account well. In Genesis 22:2 (NIV), God required a sacrifice from Abraham. "Then God said, 'Take your son, your only son, whom you love—Isaac—and go to the region of Moriah. Sacrifice him there as a burnt offering on a mountain I will show you.'" Abraham obeyed God promptly and took Isaac with him. On their way, Isaac questioned his father about the animal that was missing for the sacrifice, to which Abraham answered, "God himself will provide the lamb for the burnt offering, my son" (Gen. 22:8 NIV). Abraham had faith in God as the provider of all blessings, to the point of laying his son on the altar. At that very moment, "the angel of the Lord called out to him from heaven, 'Abraham! Abraham!' 'Here I am,' he replied. 'Do not lay a hand on the boy,' he said. 'Do not do anything to him. Now I know that you fear God, because you have not withheld from me your son, your only son'" (Gen. 22:11-12 NIV). This story reminds us that God provides for our needs in ways that are often surprising to us.

The truth that God is the provider and giver of all blessings is echoed throughout the New Testament as well. For example, the apostle Paul states,

"But my God shall supply all your need according to his riches in glory by Christ Jesus" (Phil. 4:19 NKJV) and "Now he who supplies seed to the sower and bread for food will also supply and increase your store of seed and will enlarge the harvest of your righteousness" (2 Cor. 9:10 NIV). Finally, James emphasizes that every great gift comes from God (James 1:17).

The belief that God is the provider and giver does not absolve us from our responsibilities. It does not mean that we sit idle, pray, and expect God to shower us with money and material blessings. He provides to us through our hard work, education, talents and skills, and even through others. The truth that God is the owner and provider leads us to the realization that we must be responsible managers and generous givers. God is always faithful and will do His part. Now, it is time to focus on our responsibility and the role we play in this process of becoming managers and givers.

We Are Responsible Managers

God has given us the vital role of becoming administrators or stewards of his possessions and the many gifts and blessings He brings into our lives. This responsibility started at the moment of creation when God gave Adam and Eve the job of caring for the Garden of Eden (Gen. 1:28-29). The Parable of the Talents depicts our responsibilities as managers (Matt. 25:14-30). Jesus told this parable to teach us many foundational principles about His kingdom. Purposeful distribution, responsible management, and required accountability are some of these principles. First, the principle of *Purposeful Distribution* means that God is the owner of everything and distributes His talents at His will. This distribution is also based on other principles related to work and diligence discussed in other parts of the Bible (Prov. 12:24; 14:23). Second, the principle of *Responsible Management* indicates that we are His servants and have the responsibility of managing well what He has given us. Finally, the principle of *Required Accountability* emphasizes that we must give God an account of how we manage our material possessions. The expectation is that we will use and invest the resources God has placed in our lives wisely. Thus, we believe that managing money is an issue of the heart. As Jesus stated, "For where your treasure is, there your heart will be also" (Matt. 6:21 NIV).

We realize that we could use many pages to discuss our responsibilities as managers of God's resources. However, for the sake of brevity, we will highlight the following five God-honoring money-management principles: save consistently, spend wisely, avoid debt at all cost, invest prudently, and give generously. Thus, the home office is an essential room in the house.

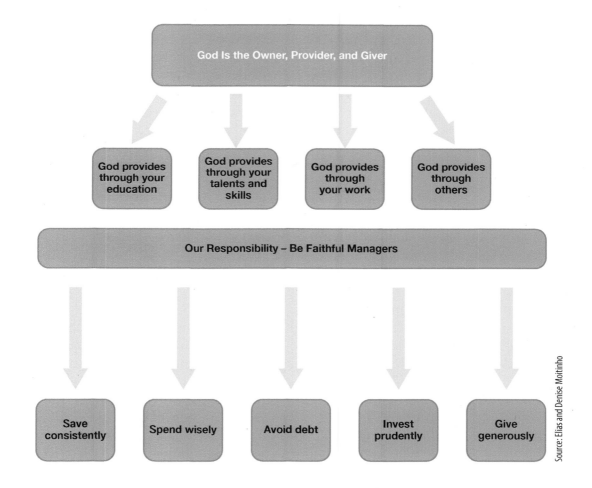

Source: Elias and Denise Moitinho

Save Consistently

Before Dave Ramsey even became popular, we used to listen to the late Larry Burkett, a pioneer Christian financial advisor who had a radio program about finances. Burkett repeatedly emphasized this verse, "be sure you know the condition of your flocks" (Prov. 27:23 NIV). The flocks in the Old Testament represent one's material possessions. Burkett taught us that we need to manage our material possessions and finances wisely. Our material possessions are what we call *assets* such as real estate properties, cars, cash, savings, retirement funds, or investments. We also need to be knowledgeable of our *liabilities*, such as consumer debt, mortgage, and medical bills. Thus, you would be wise to know your *net worth*.

Saving your money is essential and indicates that you do not presume upon the future. The reality is that emergencies will happen; cars and household appliances will break down, and children will get sick. Consequently, you will need to have funds available to cover these unexpected expenses; otherwise, you will incur debt. For this reason, you may want to review the concept of SMART goals in Chapter 1 and, together with your spouse, evaluate your financial situation and discuss some specific financial goals for your marriage.

In Chapter 1, we encouraged you to develop a vision for your marriage. Now, we recommend that you revisit your vision and discuss where you want to be financially, 5, 10, even 20 years down the road. Next, you and your spouse need to set life-changing financial goals. You may already have some big goals such as buying a house, replacing vehicles, or remodeling the home. All of these goals can cost thousands of dollars and, therefore, need to be part of a long-term money-management plan.

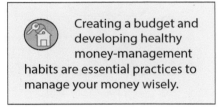

Creating a budget and developing healthy money-management habits are essential practices to manage your money wisely.

Creating a budget and developing healthy money-management habits are essential practices to manage your money carefully. Multiple tools exist to assist you, and we mention a few of them later on in this chapter. The central concept of a budget is to determine needs and wants and to allocate funds to specific expenditures or budget line items. Budgeting helps control spending and minimize impulsive purchases. You and your spouse can benefit greatly from budgeting consistently. As Ramsey says, "every dollar you make has a place in your budget."[17] Moreover, you and your spouse will need to agree on a budget to be able to develop a healthy habit of saving consistently.

Spend Wisely

According to CareerBuilder, "78 percent of U.S. workers live paycheck to paycheck to make ends meet."[18] Ramsey believes that most Americans live above their means and are not prepared for financial emergencies.[19] Additionally, "nearly 3 in 4 workers say they are in debt today - more than half think they will always be."[20] But, why are most people in debt and living from paycheck to paycheck? The answer might be multifaceted. It may include unemployment, unexpected medical expenses, poor spending habits, lack of financial management skills, lack of a budget, emotional spending, impulsive and compulsive shopping, and lack of long-term money-management goals.

It takes self-evaluation to detect unwise spending habits. Here is an example. When we lived in Texas, a man who owned a small carpet cleaning company came to clean our carpet. As he worked on cleaning the carpet, he shared that he and his wife had begun to pay attention to their spending habits, especially the habit of going out to eat with their family. He stated that they tracked their expenses and discovered that they had been spending thousands of dollars by eating out multiple times a week. As a result, he sought wise counsel and gained insight into his finances. Then, he and his wife made the decision to change their poor spending habits and, as expected, experienced tremendous financial gains. They even considered investing the money they saved to grow their family carpet cleaning business.

Unfortunately, many couples may come from families that provided them with little to no guidance about money management. Consequently, they entered adulthood and marriage without any proper training on how to manage their hard-earned dollars. The good news is that parents play an essential role in helping their children learn about money management. For instance, a study found that the involvement of parents in financial education training, such as workshops, is beneficial to the financial literacy for their children. Besides, a family's positive and open communication can enhance children's learning outcomes, including a better understanding of money.[21] We believe that it is the parents' responsibility to learn as much as they can about finances and, then, pass their financial knowledge and skills to their children. This is undoubtedly a tremendous legacy to leave to our children.

 It is wise to find a balance between enjoying the present without neglecting your financial preparation for the future.

Our spending habits are usually a reflection of our physical and mental conditions. For instance, when we go grocery shopping while hungry, we tend to buy more than we intended. Similarly, when we are sad, stressed, or bored, we may try to cheer ourselves up by engaging in emotional spending. Thus, for some people, shopping can become a way of coping with their feelings and life issues.

In the counseling field, counselors use the term *self-medication* to refer to behaviors people engage in to cope with stress, trauma, and painful physical or emotional issues as an attempt to experience emotional relief. For example, a person may use drugs, over the counter medication, alcohol, or even impulsive shopping to self-medicate. The problem is that self-medication simply adds to the problem and, often, creates additional financial issues. Using emotional shopping as self-medication exacerbates financial problems. Notably, impulsive buyers tend to pay more attention to products and, thus, are more easily enticed to buy them.[22] Consequently, they feed the unwise shopping cycle.

Avoid Debt at All Cost

Many Christian financial advisors use the verse "the borrower is slave to the lender" (Prov. 22:7 NIV) to support the principle that people should avoid debt. They believe that borrowing money creates a dynamic in which the lender gains tremendous amounts of power over the borrower, and, in turn, the borrower stays at the mercy of the lender. Besides, borrowing money may signal that people are presuming upon the future (James 4:13-15) and potentially preventing God from providing for their needs (Phil. 4:19).[23] You may be one of the 42 million Americans who have student loans.[24] This is indeed a heavy burden to carry in marriage. Our prayer is that you will be able to develop an effective plan to pay off your student loan debt quickly.

Christian financial advisors agree that borrowing money to buy a house is acceptable. However, they may have different guidelines on how to go about getting a house mortgage. For example, Ramsey recommends only a 15-year mortgage.[25] Nevertheless, the bottom line is that learning to live within our means helps us prevent debt. Living within our means requires self-control to avoid making impulsive purchases, including even buying a house. Therefore, having a budget becomes an essential part of living a debt-free lifestyle, even when you have a mortgage.

Invest Prudently

Investing in the future is a way to support a vision for your marriage. When you and your spouse know what type of marriage you want to have, and what kind of life you want to live as a couple, then you start considering the financial implications and investing in the future more intentionally. As mentioned previously, we are not to presume upon the future. Therefore, starting retirement planning at an early age is essential. In fact, it is never too early to plan for and invest in your retirement. Unfortunately, most Americans are not prepared nor preparing for retirement. According to a GOBankingRanks 2019 survey,

> When asked to estimate how much money they had in retirement savings, close to half of all respondents — 45% — claimed they had no money put aside for retirement, while 19% said they'll retire with less than $10,000 to their name. If these trends hold, that means 64% of all Americans will essentially retire broke. Twenty percent will retire with anywhere from $10,000 to $100,000.[26]

This shows that people are probably focusing on the present and are not setting money aside for the future. Hence, it is essential to meet with a Christian financial advisor and set SMART financial goals that include some long-term investments. We recommend that you find the balance between enjoying the present without neglecting your financial preparation for the future.

Give Generously

Paul called us to be "imitators of God" (Eph. 5:1 NASB). Therefore, we are to align our hearts with God's heart. Since God is the greatest giver, it would then be natural for us to become givers as well. We are called not only to give to support God's work through the church (Mal. 3:10; 2 Cor. 9:7), but also to give to meet human needs (Prov. 3:27-28). As clearly seen in the Bible, giving also helps us deal with the issue of loving money (1 Tim 6:6-10). David Alcorn in his book *Money, Possessions, and Eternity*, asserts that the New Testament guidelines for giving involves giving generously, regularly, deliberately, voluntarily, sacrificially, excellently, cheerfully, worshipfully, proportionally, and quietly.[27]

The Bible teaches us that we need to have a positive attitude about giving and give generously and cheerfully (2 Cor. 9:7). We want to encourage you to develop a giver mentality. We cannot be like a pond where the water (God's resources) becomes stagnant. Instead, we need to be a river that allows God's blessings and resources to flow into the ocean of people around us. We believe in the biblical teaching of giving to the local church and in giving above and beyond the tithing. However, when giving to individuals, we believe that it is vital to have a policy of giving, rather than just lending money. Keep in mind that giving to others can be an investment in God's kingdom and an opportunity to participate in what God is doing in other people's lives. Above all, the act of giving to others can be an act of worship and a way of thanking God for what He has given us.

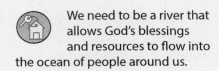

We need to be a river that allows God's blessings and resources to flow into the ocean of people around us.

Christian Money-Management Approaches

In this section, we briefly review three approaches to money management that have become popular within Christian circles. We focus on the main concepts proposed by Christian experts and organizations, namely Dave Ramsey, Crown Financial Ministry, and Ron Blue. The goal is to help you make your own educated decision regarding which approach you may want to use to manage your finances well. You may already follow one of them or even another method.

Dave Ramsey – Financial Peace University

Ramsey is the host of the radio show *The Dave Ramsey Show*, a very popular Christian radio program, and best-selling author of the book *The Total Money Makeover*.[28] He is also the creator of the *7 Baby Steps* approach to personal finance and the *Financial Peace University*, a program used in thousands of churches across America. Through his writings, teaching, and radio show, he helps people manage their finances and become debt-free. More recently, Ramsey started *EntreLeadership* to help business owners improve their leadership skills.

Ramsey uses the same biblical principle that Burkett taught for many years based on the verse "The rich rule over the poor, and the borrower is slave to the lender" (Prov.22:7 NIV). Ramsey is against debt and emphasizes that "debt creates enough risk to offset any possible advantage. Given time—a lifetime—risk will destroy any possible returns."[29] He believes most Americans have been deceived to go into debt to live a lifestyle they cannot afford. Hence, he offers his *7 Baby Steps* approach as a tool to help people live debt free. The *7 Baby Steps* includes having an emergency fund, eliminating existing debt, increasing the emergency fund, investing in retirement, starting a college fund, paying mortgage faster, and building wealth and giving.[30]

Going beyond the *7 Baby Steps* approach, Ramsey and his team developed many tools, such as the *everydollar* App, and books to address many aspects of financial management so people can find financial freedom. For instance, Chris Hogan, a retirement expert and a member of Ramsey's team, wrote the book *Retire Inspired* to provide sound advice on retirement. Hogan believes that "Retirement isn't an age. It's a financial number."[31] He provides a retirement calculator on his website along with assessment tools and a plan to help people retire inspired.[32] More recently, Hogan also wrote the book *Every Day Millionaires* based on research conducted by his team with over 10,000 millionaires across the U.S. He provides a summary of his book on his website and describes how millionaires think and act toward money. He highlights that millionaires take personal responsibility, practice intentionality, and are goal-oriented and consistent. He describes the steps on how to become a millionaire and the characteristics of millionaires, which include being out of debt, living on a budget, saving 15% of gross income, spreading money around, protecting investments, and meeting with a financial advisor regularly.[33]

Crown Financial Ministry – Money Life Planner

Crown was founded over 40 years ago by the late Larry Burkett, a pioneer in Christian financial management. Crown is now "a global ministry with resources translated into more than 120 languages in 104 countries."[34] In addition, Crown is strongly committed to providing financial principles based on the Bible. Crown has developed the MoneyLife Personal Finance Study, an online biblically based course for managing personal finances with easy-to-follow practical steps.[35] Crown also offers the *MoneyLife planner*, an online tool to help people assess where they are on their financial journey and develop a personal financial plan.[36]

In the book *Your Money Map: A Proven 7-Step Guide to True Financial Freedom*, Howard Dayton describes the principles that guide Crown Financial Ministry approach. Dayton points out that we are managers of God's resources, and our responsibility is to be faithful stewards, which includes working hard, giving generously, spending wisely, saving regularly, avoiding debt, investing steadily, training our children, and being completely honest when it comes to our finances.[37] Dayton eventually left Crown and created a new ministry, Compass—Finances God's Way.

Dayton's Money Map plan is very similar to Ramsey's *7 Baby Steps*. The plan has the following seven destinations:

- Destination 1: Saving for Emergencies and Your Spending Plan
- Destination 2: Credit Cards Paid Off
- Destination 3: Consumer Debt Paid Off
- Destination 4: Saving for Major Purchases
- Destination 5: Your Home and Paying Off, Investing
- Destination 6: Planning Your Estate
- Destination 7: True Financial Freedom[38]

Ron Blue – Four Hs of Financial Wisdom

Another Christian voice of wisdom in the financial world is Ron Blue. He authored and co-authored over 20 books on finances that range from giving generously to investing money wisely. He is well known in Christian circles and focuses on the application of biblical principles to finances to advance God's kingdom. The impact of his work is evident in the organizations he founded, such as the Ronald Blue & Co. and the Ron Blue Institute. Blue's wisdom is based on his strong commitment to the Lord and his family and rooted in his education and work experience as an entrepreneur. One of the hallmarks of Blue's work is to make money management a simple approach that anyone can understand. His goal is to help people in the process of decision-making, to apply biblical principles to money management, and to learn to be content.[39] We believe that contrary to Ramsey, Blue is less prescriptive and more principle oriented.

Blue summarizes his money-management philosophy and methodology in his latest work, *Simplifying the Money Conversation: Four Hs of Financial Wisdom*.[40] He identifies four areas of financial wisdom, which he calls *the four Hs*: Heart, Habits, Health, and Hope. The *Heart* represents the beliefs we hold about God's ownership over everything that exists, our access to His wisdom, our contentment with what He has given us, and our belief that we can express our faith by the way we handle our finances. The second H, *Habits*, emphasizes that our habits are, ultimately, guided by the principle of living according to our means, staying away from debt, establishing long-term goals, and giving generously to others. *Health* is the third area and addresses biblical principles on five priorities: live, give, owe debt, own taxes, and grow. Finally, *Hope* focuses on the reality that only through habit-changing actions, we can accomplish long-term goals and align the other three areas.[41] Blue provides several resources for the application of his approach on his website.[42]

We hope you have gained significant insights into a Christian perspective on money management. We must remind ourselves that in marriage, husband and wife agreement is key. It is only when couples agree on a financial plan that they can experience positive results and less financial conflict. Your home office, or the space where you handle your family's finances, can be an ordered place. It can be a place where your big dreams meet financial challenges and are celebrated as they are realized.

Check out the chapter video at: www.grtep.com

Now, let's walk to the laundry room.

Endnotes

1. "Top Three Special Function Rooms Homeowners Prefer," American Institute of Architects Press Release, accessed July 19, 2019, http://new.aia.org/press-releases/17506-top-three-special-function-rooms-homeowners-prefer.
2. "Workers with Advanced Degrees More Likely to Work at Home," United States Department of Labor, July 30, 2018, accessed August 25, 2019, https://www.bls.gov/opub/ted/2018/workers-with-advanced-degrees-more-likely-to-work-at-home.htm?view_full.
3. "Top Three Special Function Rooms Homeowners Prefer."
4. Ron Blue and Michael Blue, *Master Your Money: A Step-by-Step Plan for Experiencing Financial Contentment* (Chicago, IL: Moody Publishers, 2016), 23.
5. Kimberly Amadeo, "Average U.S. Credit Card Debt Statistics Is Your Credit Card Debt Higher Than Average?" *The Balance*, August 24, 2019, accessed June 15, 2019, https://www.thebalance.com/average-credit-card-debt-u-s-statistics-3305919.
6. "Happy Couples: How to Avoid Money Argument," American Psychology Association, accessed June 10, 2019, https://www.apa.org/helpcenter/money-conflict.
7. Jeffrey Dew, Sonya Britt, and Sandra Huston "Examining the Relationship Between Financial Issues and Divorce Family Relations," *Interdisciplinary of Applied Family Science* 61, no. 4 (September 4, 2012): 615, accessed July 12, 2019, doi:10.1111/j.1741-3729.2012.00715.x.
8. Lauren M. Papp, E. Mark Cummings, and Marcie C. Goeke-Morey, "For Richer, for Poorer: Money as a Topic of Marital Conflict in the Home," *Family Relations* 58, no. 1 (February, 2009): 91.

9. Catherine Rampell, "Money Fights Predict Divorce Rates," *Economix*, December 7, 2009, accessed June 11, 2019, https://economix.blogs.nytimes.com/2009/12/07/money-fights-predict-divorce-rates/.

10. Jeffrey P. Dew, "Two Sides of the Same Coin? The Differing Roles of Assets and Consumer Debt in Marriage," *Journal of Family and Economic Issues* 28, no. 1 (2007), 89–104; Jeffrey P. Dew, "The Relationship between Debt Change and Marital Satisfaction Change in Recently Married Couples," *Family Relations* 57, no. 1 (January 2008), 60–71.

11. "Money Ruining Marriages in America: A Ramsey Solutions Study," *Dave Ramsey Solutions*, February 7, 2018, accessed June 6, 2019, https://www.daveramsey.com/pr/money-ruining-marriages-in-america.

12. Dew, "Two Sides of the Same Coin?" 89–104; Dew, "The Relationship between Debt Change and Marital Satisfaction," 60–71.

13. Jason S. Carroll, Lukas R. Dean, Lindsey L. Call, and Dean M. Busby, "Materialism and Marriage: Couple Profiles of Congruent and Incongruent Spouses," *Journal of Couple & Relationship Therapy* 10, no. 4 (2011): 287, doi:10.1080/15332691.2011.613306.

14. Sonya L. Britt, et al., "Tightwads and Spenders: Predicting Financial Conflict in Couple Relationships," *Journal of Financial Planning* 30, no. 5 (May 2017): 36–42, accessed August 12, 2019, https://www.onefpa.org/journal/Pages/MAY17-Tightwads-and-Spenders-Predicting-Financial-Conflict-in-Couple-Relationships.aspx.

15. "Money Ruining Marriages in America."

16. Brian Kluth, *Experience God as Your Provider: Finding Financial Stability in Unstable Times* (Chicago, IL: Moody Publishers, 2010).

17. "Learn How to Budget," Dave Ramsey Solutions, accessed June 12, 2019, https://www.daveramsey.com/budgeting/how-to-budget.

18. "Living Paycheck to Paycheck is a Way of Life for Majority of U.S. Workers, According to New CareerBuilder Survey," Career Builder Press Room, accessed June 12, 2019, http://press.careerbuilder.com/2017-08-24-Living-Paycheck-to-Paycheck-is-a-Way-of-Life-for-Majority-of-U-S-Workers-According-to-New-CareerBuilder-Survey.

19. "Tired of Keeping up with the Joneses?" Dave Ramsey Solutions, accessed June 12, 2019, https://www.daveramsey.com/blog/tired-of-keeping-up-with-the-joneses.

20. "Living Paycheck to Paycheck."

21. Thomas A. Hanson and Peter M. Olson, "Financial Literacy and Family Communication Patterns," *Journal of Behavioral and Experimental Finance* 19 (2018): 64–71.

22. Oliver B. Büttner et al., "Hard to Ignore: Impulsive Buyers Show an Attentional Bias in Shopping Situations," *Social Psychological and Personality Science* 5, no. 3 (2014): 343–51, doi:10.1177/1948550613494024.

23. "Biblical Perspective on Debt," Focus on The Family, accessed June 17, 2019, https://www.focusonthefamily.com/family-q-and-a/life-challenges/biblical-perspective-on-debt.

24. "Student Debt: Lives on Hold," Consumer Reports, June 28, 2016, accessed June 28, 2019, https://www.consumerreports.org/student-loan-debt-crisis/lives-on-hold/.

25. "Why Dave's Against 30-Year Mortgages," Dave Ramsey Solutions, accessed September 20, 2019, https://www.daveramsey.com/blog/why-daves-against-30-year-mortgages.

26. Sean Dennison, "64% of Americans Aren't Prepared for Retirement and 48% Don't Care," Go Banking Rates, September 23, 2019, accessed September 28, 2019, https://www.gobankingrates.com/retirement/planning/why-americans-will-retire-broke/.

27. Randy Alcorn, *Money, Possessions, and Eternity* (Carol Stream, IL: Tyndale House Publishers, 2011).

28. Dave Ramsey, *The Total Money Makeover: A Proven Plan for Financial Fitness* (Nashville, TN: Nelson Books, 2013).

29. "Getting Out of Debt: The Truth about Debt," Dave Ramsey, accessed June 14, 2019, https://www.daveramsey.com/blog/the-truth-about-debt.

30. "Dave Ramsey's 7 Baby Steps," Dave Ramsey, accessed June 14, 2019, https://www.daveramsey.com/dave-ramsey-7-baby-steps.

31. Chris Hogan, "Create a Plan to Reach Your Retirement Dream," Ramsey Solutions, accessed June 14, 2019, https://www.chrishogan360.com/riq/.

32. Hogan, "Create a Plan to Reach Your Retirement Dream."

33. Chris Hogan, "How to Become an Everyday Millionaire," Ramsey Solutions, accessed June 14, 2019, https://www.chrishogan360.com/how-to-become-an-everyday-millionaire/.

34. "Crown's Story," Crown, accessed June 14, 2019, https://www.crown.org/about/.

35. "Pursue True Financial Freedom," Crown, accessed June 14, 2019, https://www.crown.org/personal-finance/.

36. "Money Life Planner," Crown, accessed June 14, 2019, https://planner.crown.org/.

37. Howard Dayton, *Your Money Map: A Proven 7-Step Guide to True Financial Freedom* (Chicago, IL: Moody Publishers, 2009), 49.

38. Dayton, *Your Money Map.*

39. Ron Blue and Karen Guess, *Never Enough? 3 Keys to Financial Contentment* (Nashville, TN: B&H Publishing Group, 2017); Blue and Blue, *Master Your Money.*

40. Ron Blue, *Simplifying the Money Conversation: Four Hs of Financial Wisdom* (Marion, IN: Ron Blue Institute, 2018).

41. Blue, *Simplifying the Money Conversation.*

42. "Tools and Links," Ron Blue Institute, accessed June 14, 2019, http://www.ronblueinstitute.com/tools.

CHAPTER 7

The Laundry Room: Cleaning up Conflict

> "Can two people walk together without
> agreeing on the direction?"
> Amos 3:3 (NLT)

According to the National Association of Home Builders (NAHB), a separate laundry room is the most sought-after home feature.[1] However, as one might expect, not all laundry rooms are designed the same way or located in the same area of a home. In some homes, the laundry room is a small closet tucked in a hidden side of the house or hallway. In other homes, the laundry room is located in the garage or even in the kitchen. Nevertheless, no matter what size or location of the laundry room, homebuyers appreciate the convenience of having a special place for them to store and wash their dirty laundry.

The popular metaphor of *dirty laundry* represents people's personal, private, and not-so-pretty issues or conflicts. In fact, "Don't air your dirty laundry in public" is an idiom that reminds us that some issues need to be kept private. So, dirty laundry refers to the conflicts you and your spouse may experience in your marriage. Unfortunately, many people tend to air their private problems and conflicts on social media, especially on Facebook. We do understand that sometimes couples need a third party, such as a counselor, to help them sort through and clean up their conflicts. However, just like dirty laundry, conflict, frustrations, and arguments that happen in marriage need to be dealt within the home as much as possible. After all, chances are that both of you may have contributed to creating the dirty laundry.

In this chapter, we use the metaphor of the laundry room and dirty laundry to discuss marital conflict. We examine conflict in marriage, provide a biblical perspective, and offer practical ways for you and your spouse to handle your conflicts. We believe that this chapter can help you identify unique factors in your marriage that cause unnecessary conflict and prevent you from building your dream home.

—— Understanding the Dimensions of Conflict in Marriage ——

Marital conflict may occur monthly, weekly, or even daily. Similar to your dirty laundry, not all conflicts are the same or happen with the same frequency. A laundry load can be big or small. Sometimes, the clothes are mainly sweaty, but other times, they may be filthy and muddy. The heavy loads may even need to stay in the washer longer and receive special treatment to remove stains. Here is an example of a conflict, or we should say dirty laundry.

It was a beautiful Sunday morning. Larry and Sally parked their car in the church parking lot on the same spot they usually did. However, that morning, it was not church as usual. While Sally regained her composure and got out of the car, Larry stayed in the car. He was furious and decided to sit in his car during the whole service. But, what was the problem? What prompted Larry to sit in the car and not go into the church building?

Interestingly, Larry and Sally seemed fine when they left their house. However, everything changed when Sally brought up an unresolved issue they had argued about intensely during the week. Their folly was to try to solve a complex and challenging problem on their way to church. As expected, the conversation went nowhere, and the conflict escalated. Criticism, blaming, personal attacks, and nasty looks were all thrown at each other. They soon realized that they had very little time to lower the tension and calm their emotions on a short ten-minute drive to the church. Inevitably, the conflict had escalated to levels beyond their control. When they parked their car, Larry was furious and frustrated, so he decided not to put on a happy face to walk into church. To his surprise, while he sat in the car frustrated, he watched as his wife made her way into church. At that point, he was not sure if she was going to air their dirty laundry to some of their friends and church members as a "prayer request."

This is one of many examples of conflict in marriage. As you can see, interpersonal conflict is multidimensional. Therefore, we need to understand the spiritual, relational, mental, and emotional dimensions of conflict.

Spiritual Dimension

According to the Bible, conflict occurs because of our sinful nature, selfish motives, and difference of opinions. When writing to the Christians at the church at Corinth, Paul asserts that the sinful nature is the root of conflict. He writes, "You are still worldly. For since there is jealousy and quarreling among you, are you not worldly? Are you not acting like mere humans?" (1 Cor. 3:3 NIV). Similarly, James indicates that selfish motives can be a catalyst for conflict. He states, "What causes fights and quarrels among you? Don't they come from your desires that battle within you?" (James 4:1 NIV). However, some conflicts arise simply because of differences in opinions. For instance, Paul and Barnabas, two strong Christians, "had such a sharp disagreement that they parted company" (Acts 15:39 NIV). Their disagreement was on whether they should take John Mark with them on a missionary trip (Acts 15:36–38). Unfortunately, two different opinions separated two church leaders who could not deal with their different opinions effectively.

The Bible provides solid guidance on how we can view and handle conflict effectively. In this section, we discuss three essential biblical principles for handling conflict in a healthy way. These principles include engaging in self-examination, having a Christ-like attitude, and promoting grace-filled interactions.

Engage in Self-Examination

Jesus taught that before we blame others, we should examine ourselves first. He states, "You hypocrite, first take the log out of your own eye, and then you will see clearly to take the speck out of your brother's eye" (Matt. 7:5 NASB). Jesus challenged his disciples, and He challenges us today to look at our lives first. As we know, it is easy for us to overlook our own major faults and wrongdoing while focusing on the smallest mistakes that other people make. During a marital conflict, couples may easily blame each other. To avoid this negative habit, we need to examine our thoughts and attitudes toward our spouse first before shifting the blame.

A practical technique is to look at yourself in the mirror, literally and figuratively. Then, ask yourself tough questions about where you may have failed in your relationship without defending or protecting your ego. This helps you become aware of your feelings and attitudes, and it empowers you to take the log out of your own eye first. It also helps you change your perceptions and take responsibility for your own dirty laundry. Additionally, it may help you see your spouse and your marriage from a different angle and with more clarity. Hopefully in the end, you will be able to see that what your spouse has done, in most cases, is minor or the action was not intended to offend you.

Have a Christ-Like Attitude

Sometimes our desire to be right and win an argument highlights how far we are from being Christ-like in how we relate to our spouse. Colossians 3:12 describes the Christ-like attitude we must have, "Therefore, as God's chosen people, holy and dearly loved, clothe yourselves with compassion, kindness, humility, gentleness and patience" (NIV). Similarly, Philippians 2:3–4 calls us to develop the same attitude of Christ as Paul says, "Do nothing out of selfish ambition or vain conceit. Rather, in humility value others above yourselves, not looking to your own interests but each of you to the interests of the others" (NIV). Jesus Christ set the example of humility when He, being God, humbled himself, lived among us, and died on the cross to bridge the gap between us and God (Phil. 2:7–8). Thus, in marriage, we need to be selfless and consider our spouse's point of view and interests with high regard. By doing so, we can help diffuse negative interactions that can escalate any conflict.

Ken Sande, in his book *The Peacemaker: A Biblical Guide to Resolving Personal Conflict*, describes two types of negotiation in conflict: competitive and cooperative negotiations. Competitive negotiation is self-centered and focuses on material issues. When people use the competitive approach, the focus is on defeating the opponent; consequently, they tend to use negative tactics such as intimidation and manipulation. As a result, they may damage their relationships. Sande recommends the use of cooperative negotiation, which focuses on people's concerns, perceptions, and feelings.[2] This approach goes along with Philippians 2:4 because it takes into consideration each spouse's interests. It also gives them the opportunity to take responsibility for their part in the conflict and work collaboratively as a team.

To develop a Christ-like attitude, we need to spend time with Christ and meditate on God's Word. There is no other path, so we want to encourage you to spend time studying the Bible and other Christian books to grow in knowledge and understanding of Christ. We also want to encourage you to spend time in prayer, asking God to fill you with the Holy Spirit. Only the Holy Spirit can make us capable of loving people unconditionally and living a life that reflects Christ's character.

Promote Grace-Filled Interactions

As Christians, we are to show grace to everyone, which is even more imperative in marriage. Paul writes in Colossians 3:13, "Bear with each other and forgive one another if any of you has a grievance against someone. Forgive as the Lord forgave you" (NIV). The term *bearing* in Greek means to endure, to have patience with,[3] and to put up with someone. This includes your spouse, a fallen and imperfect human being. Interestingly, this first part of the verse is not addressing major offenses or sinful actions, but the second part is. The word *grievances* in the Greek has been translated as "a complaint against"[4] or a "quarrel against."[5] Grievances refer to offenses that hurt and create separation. Such offenses need a different approach. They are not to be overlooked; instead, they need to be addressed directly, carefully, and thoughtfully. They call for forgiveness to restore the relationship (Col. 3:13).

The concept of bearing with each other in Colossians 3:13 also harmonizes with Proverbs 19:11, which emphasizes that it is honorable "to overlook an offense" (NIV). Overlooking an offense is a sign that you are a mature person who displays a Christ-like attitude and is willing to live in peace with others (Rom.12:18). It is a display of a deeper understanding of the mercy and grace you have received from God, which you can extend to others, including your spouse.

Relational Dimension

Every marital conflict is an interpersonal conflict, thus affecting the relational dimension of marriage. Interpersonal conflict is "an expressed struggle between at least two interdependent parties who perceive incompatible goals, scarce resources, and interference from others in achieving their goals."[6] We would like to highlight that perception is an essential aspect of this definition, particularly in marital conflict. For instance, when facing a financial conflict, the couple may perceive each other as having different financial goals. The husband may perceive that his wife is sabotaging their long-term goals by spending money to get immediate satisfaction. On the other hand, the wife may think that her husband is preventing them from enjoying

 As a team, husband and wife, need to tackle conflict together acknowledging their role and responsibility in the development and solution of the conflict.

life now. Since perception is subjective, the couple may not actually have different goals. The individual's interpretation of the situation prevails over reality; consequently, conflict arises. Thus, as a team, husband and wife need to tackle conflict together acknowledging their role and responsibility in the development and solution of the conflict.

Mental and Emotional Dimension

Marital conflict can be an intense and emotionally charged experience for couples. The emotional system of the brain is heightened and reactive during conflict. Strong emotions such as frustration and anger might be present and even escalate, making it a negative event for the couple. Researchers have studied physiological responses and reactivity during conflict. They point out that the body engages the fight or flight stress response, which involves the release of hormones such as adrenaline in the body, preparing it to face a threat by fighting or running away. In this case, the perceived threat is your spouse.

Researcher John Gottman calls physiological reaction *flooding*. He explains,

When we monitor couples for bodily changes during a tense discussion, we can see just how physically distressing flooding is. One of the most apparent of these physical reactions is that the heart speeds up-pounding away at more than 100 beats per minute-even as high as 165 (In contrast a typical heart rate for a man who is 30 is 76, and for a woman the same age, 82). Hormonal changes occur, too, including the secretion of adrenaline, which kicks in the "flight or fight response." Blood pressure also mounts.[7]

Additional research by Amy Hooper and her colleagues on the Four Horsemen of the Apocalypse (criticism, defensiveness, contempt, and stonewalling) and emotional flooding has provided important findings. They point out that "stonewalling [has] the greatest negative impact on relationship satisfaction and found that the longer participants were married, the less likely that they were to experience emotional flooding."[8]

People experience emotional flooding as the conflict escalates. Therefore, couples need to learn how to handle and express their anger constructively because anger is associated with cardiovascular disease and hypertension, among other negative physical health outcomes.[9] Undoubtedly, "negative daily moods like anger, anxiety, stress, and sadness [are] associated with more severe marital disagreements."[10] Susan A. David, author of the book *Emotional Agility*, teaches that "Emotional agility – being flexible with your thoughts and feelings so that you can respond optimally to everyday situations – is key to well-being and success."[11] This is a sound approach to monitor and regulate your emotions. Marriage researcher Gottman calls "self-soothing" the process to control the emotional flooding.[12] For instance, self-soothing activities may involve breathing exercises, prayer, and meditation to calm the body. So, learning to calm yourself down during a conflict will be essential for your physical, mental, and emotional health.

What Causes Conflict in Marriage?

According to researchers, intrinsic and extrinsic factors can cause conflict in marriage.[13] Intrinsic factors include poor communication skills, unrealistic expectations, and personality types, whereas extrinsic factors include financial management style, relationship with in-laws, and pornography use, to name a few. Next, we highlight and briefly discuss a few of these factors.

Poor Communication Skills

Research indicates that communication issues, such as poor communication or a breakdown in communication, are among the top reasons couples seek counseling.[14] Criticism, defensiveness, contempt, and stonewalling are negative communication habits and patterns that are predictors of divorce.[15] Thus, it is wise to learn how to use the active listening skills we discussed in Chapter 4 to prevent these habits from developing. It is also beneficial to show appreciation to your spouse and monitor your tone of voice and body language since they can directly affect the harmony in the communication process.

Unrealistic Expectations

When you thought about getting married, you probably began to develop your expectations of what your marriage would be like. Perhaps you imagined how your spouse would treat you, how often you would visit your in-laws, or the frequency of your sexual activity in marriage. There is nothing wrong with having expectations. However, the main issue with expectations is that couples tend to develop unrealistic expectations based on Hollywood movies and social media. Having unrealistic expectations will lead to unnecessary disappointment and frustration. Interestingly, a study found that "exposure of common myths or unrealistic expectations about one's partner and relationship may decrease the real–ideal discrepancy and increase marital satisfaction, thus increasing the likelihood of relationship longevity."[16] In other words, discussing your expectations with each other, especially in some type of marital counseling, can help you identify unrealistic expectations. Additionally, couples can develop more realistic expectations as their marriage matures.[17]

Sources of Conflict in Marriage

Poor Communication
Unrealistic Expectations
Unmet Needs
Personality
Culture
Finances
In-Laws
Parenting Styles
Lack of Intimacy
Pornography

Unmet Needs

Willard Harley, in his famous book *His Needs Her Needs*, discussed the primary needs of men and women. According to Harley, sexual fulfillment, recreational companionship, an attractive spouse, domestic support, and admiration are men's top needs. Women's needs, on the other hand, include affection, conversation, honesty, openness, financial commitment, and family commitment. When couples have unmet needs, they may feel frustrated and give up on the relationship.[18] Meeting each other's needs helps you have an affair-proof marriage. Besides, having a spouse who is in tune with your physical and emotional needs can make your marriage an exciting experience.[19]

We acknowledge that, sometimes, your spouse may have a need that is difficult for you to meet. For example, your spouse may frequently desire non-sexual physical touch, but showing affection may not come naturally to you. Therefore, you will have to make an effort to step out of your comfort zone to meet your spouse's need.

Personality

It seems that there are as many definitions of personality as there are people who attempt to define it. In short, personality is what helps us predict how people will behave in a given situation. It is the enduring and predictable part of ourselves that determines how we will respond and act in certain situations. Overall, personality includes characteristics that remain somewhat stable throughout our lives.[20]

Research shows that our personality traits usually dictate how we solve conflict.[21]In marriage, personality differences can be a double-edged sword; they can help create balance in the relationship, but they can also create and exacerbate conflict. A wife who is outgoing and outspoken will probably be more vocal during a conflict, while the husband might be more introspective and prefer to avoid discussing the issue or use fewer words to express his ideas and feelings. For this reason, couples need to develop healthy relationship skills so that they can deal with conflict in a way that promotes marital satisfaction, especially in the first five years of marriage.[22]

Studying your personality type may help you understand how you respond to conflict. For instance, you may fill out a personality inventory such as the Myers-Briggs Type Indicator (MBTI) free of charge online (https://www.16personalities.com/free-personality-test). Then, you and your spouse can explore your profile results and read the explanations available on the website to gain insights into each other's personalities. You may also want to discuss your profile results with a trained professional who is an expert on the MBTI. As you become more aware of your and your spouse's personality types and tendencies, you will understand each other better and minimize conflict.

Culture

Marriage is the intersection of two cultures, even for those who have the same cultural or ethnic background. After all, you come from different families with different structures and dynamics, which have shaped you into the person you are. However, it is essential to acknowledge and understand the unique dynamics present in interracial/interethnic marriages and how these cultural differences and dynamics may create or even exacerbate conflict.[23] For instance, a Hispanic or Latino male married to a White or Caucasian female may experience conflict because of different cultural values, norms, family of origin expectations, and even language. Thus, cultural differences, language fluency, and communication styles may have the potential to create conflict in marital relationships.[24] However, they also have the power to enhance the marriage in exciting ways.

Finances

In Chapter 6, we addressed the topic of finances and pointed out that couples who frequently argue about their finances are more likely to divorce.[25] This finding highlights the seriousness of marriage conflict over finances. For instance, a couple may need to buy a car. However, one of the spouses may want a new car as a boost to their status in the community, whereas the other spouse may be frugal and believe that a used car would be best for them. Thus, how couples handle their differences in money-management styles can determine if finances become a source of conflict in their marriage.

In-Laws

In the early years of marriage, the couple is working toward building their couple identity and creating a healthy separation or independence from their family of origin, especially their parents. However, some couples may have difficulty accomplishing this task early on in marriage, especially if they depend significantly on financial and emotional support from their parents and in-laws. We must keep in mind that culture may also play a role in how the in-laws are involved in the couple's life. In some cultures, in-laws have significant input in the couple's relationships ranging from where they should live and how many children they should have. However, even in more individualistic cultures, in-laws can become a source of conflict before and after marriage if the couple does not set appropriate boundaries and if the couple's relationship is weak.[26]

Different Parenting Styles

Often, couples experience conflict due to having different parenting styles or philosophies.[27] If you have children, especially preschool or school-aged children, you probably have started disciplining them. As a result, you may have already experienced disagreements on strategies to discipline your children. If you do not have children yet, sharing your thoughts with your spouse about parenting and gaining knowledge about child rearing is a wise step to take. We discuss parenting in Chapter 10.

Lack of Sexual Intimacy

Unfortunately, even newly married couples get overly busy with the many life's responsibilities. Such busyness may lead to fatigue and limit the time couples spend with one another. Also, due to exhaustion, a spouse may not be psychologically and emotionally present for sexual intimacy. Additionally, different levels of sexual desire may affect the dynamics of the relationship. We discuss these issues in-depth in Chapter 8.

Pornography

Statistics about pornography use are alarming. Sadly, this problem affects many couples, including a high number of Christians. According to *Covenant Eyes*, a Christian internet company that promotes accountability and protection against pornography and sex trafficking, "56 percent of divorce cases involved a partner's obsessive interest in porn sites. In addition, 64 percent of Christian men and 15 percent of Christian women report watching porn at least once a month."[28] If you or your spouse struggle with pornography, we encourage you to seek help from a Christian counselor who specializes in helping people deal with this issue.

In this section, we described briefly several factors that may create conflict in your marriage. You can probably add many other factors to the list. However, the key is to be aware of how these factors affect your marriage and develop healthy strategies to handle them. Next, we discuss different ways couples try to resolve their conflicts and the importance of forgiveness.

Conflict Management Styles

Unresolved conflict creates a separation between you and your spouse. Each negative interaction adds dirty laundry to the hamper or basket. If the dirty laundry is not addressed, you become distant and disconnected emotionally. We believe that a reasonable and realistic conflict management approach is necessary for you to deal with your dirty laundry effectively. Therefore, we hope that by the end of this chapter, you will be able to identify and address the issues affecting your relationship. You may begin by working on a big load, more hurtful and severe problems, or by focusing on smaller, less hurtful issues. The bottom line is that you have dirty laundry, that is, unresolved conflict, waiting for you and your spouse. We recommend that you consider your conflict management style and work as a team to tackle your dirty laundry and clean it up quickly and effectively.

Source: Elias and Denise Moitinho, adapted from the Thomas-Kilmann model

What is your conflict management style? According to the Thomas–Kilmann model, people typically handle conflict in one of five common ways. You will probably relate to one of them.[29]

Competing = I Win, You Lose

This is an adversarial approach in which a person wants to force his or her will and preferred outcome on others. It carries the attitude that communicates, "I am right and my way is better than yours." Consequently, spouses who use the competing style may be forceful or even aggressive, leaving the other spouse feeling hurt and coerced.

Accommodating = I Lose, You Win

This model is usually used by those who are people-pleasers. This person views conflict as disruptive and wants to seek harmony and peace at all costs, even if it means giving up his or her opinion and rights. Being accommodating in marriage means that a spouse will always agree with the other. Although the accommodating spouse will give the other spouse the satisfaction of winning an argument or conflict, he or she will end up yielding and losing.

Avoiding = I Lose, You Lose

This approach is used by people who view conflict as emotionally draining. They do not believe it is worth putting the effort and energy to present his or her side of the situation. For this person, it is easier to ignore conflict and pretend everything is fine. When couples ignore conflict, they lose because the problem or situation will be unresolved and will affect their relationship negatively.

Compromising = We Win Some, We Lose Some

People who use this approach have the attitude that one cannot win all the time; "you win some and lose some." They tend to negotiate and find a middle ground. Couples who use this model may feel satisfied realizing that each spouse can get their way at times.

Collaborating = I Win, You Win

Experts agree that a collaborative problem-solving approach is the ideal way to deal with conflict. This happens when both parties are committed to working together to resolve the conflict and find a solution that meets each other's needs. When couples use this model, they work as a team toward what is best for their marriage. Both end up feeling valued and cared for.

———— Forgiveness: Cleaning Up the Stains of Conflict ————

Conflict can certainly create an emotional separation, but couples can learn and grow through conflict. Conflict, like a pile of dirty laundry, can stand between you and your spouse unless you tackle it and clean it up. Forgiveness is an essential element in dealing with conflict in marriage. It is the cleaning agent that can help treat and remove the stain of past hurts in your marriage. Therefore, we will spend some time examining what forgiveness is and how you can continue to implement it in your marriage.

Understanding Forgiveness

Forgiveness is the catalyst that restores a marriage during conflict. As previously stated, conflict is the dirty laundry in your relationship. You will need to tackle it together as a couple with a forgiving heart. You will also need to have a clear understanding of what forgiveness is. Many people say they cannot forgive their offenders or even their spouses because they are angry and do not feel like forgiving. Other people believe they will always remember the offense and the hurt; therefore, they believe they cannot forgive. We acknowledge that when people feel hurt, they do not have the emotional desire to forgive. However, feeling hurt and desiring the pain to go away can be a motivation to forgive.

The first reason why you should forgive is obedience to the biblical command to forgive (Mark 11:25). Second, forgiveness creates the opportunity for reconciliation in your marriage. Third, forgiveness also alleviates your own hurt and helps you deal with painful memories in a healthy way that brings emotional healing to your life and marriage. Forgiveness is not forgetting, so do not expect that once you forgive, you will forget the event. You will continue to remember the hurtful events because they simply cannot be erased from your mind. However, expect to experience peace, a renewed sense of well-being, and the joy of breaking a negative cycle of interaction between you and your spouse.

Forgiveness Is a Multidimensional Process

Forgiveness is multidimensional by nature. It involves the mental, emotional, relational, and spiritual areas of our lives. From a Christian perspective, the word forgiveness means that our debt has been canceled.[30] It means that God through His grace and compassionate love forgave our offenses, so that we can continue to enjoy a relationship with Him. Moreover, when we consider God's forgiveness toward us, we cannot help but forgive others, including our spouses.

Mental (Your Mind)

Forgiveness is a cognitive, rational process. In other words, it involves your mind, and it is an act of the will. Therefore, it is not based on feelings since you have to make a conscious decision to forgive. Everett Worthington, a well-known researcher on forgiveness, explains that decisional forgiveness hap-

Forgiveness Is Multidimensional

Mental (Your Mind)
Emotional (Your Heart)
Relational (Your Connection)
Spiritual (Your Soul)

pens before emotional forgiveness. People make a decision to forgive, and once they verbalize their forgiveness, their emotions will begin to change.[31] Basically, you have to make the volitional choice to forgive, saying, "I forgive you" which means "I choose not to hold this offense against you." Along with this decision comes the next step, which involves not mentioning the offense to your spouse over and over again.

Emotional (Your Heart)

Forgiveness is also an emotional process that involves your feelings and, consequently, brings healing to your heart. You will need to let go of the negative emotions. When you make a decision to forgive, eventually, your feelings will begin to change. Of course, it takes time for the feelings of anger, resentment, and bitterness to subside and go away. However, forgiveness will help you deal with the emotional hurt and pain. Even though you have painful memories, you can choose to remind yourself that you made a decision to forgive and that you actually forgave. For this reason, Worthington recommends replacing negative emotions with empathy.[32]

A counseling technique we believe can be helpful to deal with the emotional aspect of forgiveness is the *bag of rocks* activity. Many counselors have used different variations of this technique. Here is our recommendation. Gather a few rocks to represent your spouse's offenses against you. You may choose different sizes of rocks or stones to represent smaller and larger offenses. If possible, write down the offenses on the rocks and place them in a bag. As you work on forgiving your spouse, each day lift the bag to feel its weight. Hopefully, this will help you realize that you have been carrying a heavy emotional load. Once you forgive your spouse, take your bag of rocks to a pond, lake, or river. Pray to God, acknowledging that you have forgiven your spouse for each of the offenses.

Then, throw the rocks in the water, one by one. This action will serve as a powerful symbol and reminder of your act of forgiveness. Whenever a painful memory comes back; remind yourself of your action and of the biblical truth that Agape love "does not hold grudges" (1 Cor. 13:5 TLB).

Relational (Your Connection)

Forgiveness creates an opportunity for reconciliation. Therefore, you must verbalize your forgiveness to your spouse by saying the powerful words, "I forgive you." Forgiveness does not demand or require reconciliation. However, forgiveness is essential for reconciliation to take place and connections to be restored, especially in marriage, because forgiveness eliminates relational barriers. However, forgiveness does not remove consequences for misbehavior in marriage. You may have to set boundaries or put some type of consequence in place, depending on the type of offense. For instance, if your spouse was contacting an ex-girlfriend or an ex-boyfriend on Facebook, a boundary or consequence may be that your spouse needs to unfriend the person on Facebook. Nevertheless, forgiveness with boundaries will bring peace to your home.

Spiritual (Your Soul)

Forgiveness is a spiritual activity because it involves God in the process. How we relate to people, in this case our spouse, affects our relationship to God. Jesus said, "For if you forgive other people when they sin against you, your heavenly Father will also forgive you. But if you do not forgive others their sins, your Father will not forgive your sins" (Matt. 6:14–15 NIV). Therefore, unforgiveness will affect your relationship with God as well.

Forgiveness is a central element in the Christian faith. In fact, God commands us to forgive. He gives us the example of how to forgive as Paul states, "Be kind and compassionate to one another, forgiving each other, just as in Christ God forgave you" (Eph. 4:32 NIV). God's forgiveness means that the guilt has been removed. In addition, forgiveness is costly and sacrificial because Christ suffered on the cross for our sins. It is the essence of Agape love since Agape love "keeps no record of wrongs" (1 Cor. 13:5 NIV). Forgiveness within a marriage creates the opportunity to restore trust and intimacy, and it allows for a second chance and a new beginning. So, pray for your spouse, and show kindness to him or her.

A Conflict Resolution Model

As you and your spouse acknowledge that you have some dirty laundry, you need to take care of it right away. You cannot allow it to sit there because it will eventually disrupt your whole home life. Similarly, unresolved conflict will affect your marriage and spread to other areas of your life. So, you need a plan. You need to be able to de-escalate the conflict and engage in a respectful, collaborative approach. When spouses are angry and experiencing a breakdown in communication, it is next to impossible to participate in a problem-solving approach to address the issue or problem at hand. As already discussed, due to the emotional flooding, couples tend do overreact. Thus, the first thing they need to do is to focus on emotion regulation which, in biblical terminology, means that they need to regain and maintain self-control.

Step 1: Self-Control

When you have a conflict with your spouse, you probably experience many negative emotions, which may lead to destructive patterns of communication. These patterns may include personal attacks, blaming, and insults, or any of the Four Horsemen of the Apocalypse. You may even raise your voices, initiating a complete breakdown in communication and a negative downward spiral that needs to stop. Therefore, we recommend that you and your spouse implement the Time-Out technique as described here. Remember that Scripture says "Better to be patient than powerful; better to have self-control" (Prov. 16:32 NLT).

You or your spouse may need to request a Time-Out to protect the relationship and de-escalate the conflict.[33] Taking a Time-Out simply means requesting a short break from interacting to allow time for each partner to return to a calm state of mind. If you are the one who needs to request the Time-Out, share with your spouse that you need a Time-Out. Then, explain that you are very frustrated and angry, and that it is not a good time for you to try to resolve the conflict. You may say, "I do not want to say anything that may hurt you even more. I need time to cool off. We can meet again this evening at 6 pm to talk about this issue." By setting up a specific time to address the issue, you are communicating that you are not using the Time-Out as an avoidance. Rather, you are ensuring that you and your spouse will deal with the conflict later when you are calm.

What you do during the Time-Out is vital for your emotion regulation. You need to engage in self-soothing activities that can help calm you down. We recommend that you do any of the following:

- Take a walk.
- Do some breathing exercises to relax the body (Inhale 3–4 seconds and exhale 6–7 seconds).
- Change your angry and negative thoughts by thinking of positive memories with your spouse.
- Listen to some relaxing music.
- Find a quiet place and pray.

Keep in mind that during a Time-Out, you need to work on changing your thoughts that feed the anger. Otherwise, you may come back from the Time-Out feeling even angrier. You may need to pray and reflect on the positive things you want to see or already have in your marriage. The goal is to come back with a Christ-like attitude as discussed earlier. Once you and your spouse have calmed down and are ready to address the problem, come together at the designated time and start step 2.

Step 2: Communication

In this step, you will express your feelings and thoughts without attacking your spouse. You will listen to your spouse with empathy. Before you engage in problem-solving, which is a cognitive/rational approach (the head), you need to deal with your emotions (the heart). You and your spouse are feeling hurt because of the conflict. By allowing each other to express thoughts and feelings and listening to each other, hopefully, both of you will feel understood.

We recommend that you use the "I" statement technique from Chapter 4 to express your emotions and thoughts. Both of you will have an opportunity to express your thoughts and feelings and will listen to each other respectfully and with empathy. For instance, you may say, "I feel *frustrated* (feeling), when you *make big purchases without talking with me* (behavior) because *it affects our budget* (tangible consequence)." Again, you must start with how you are feeling and avoid blaming or criticizing.

Next, listen to your spouse with empathy. At this point, an agreement or solution is not the goal. The goal is to understand your spouse's pain and point of view. You also need to show care, concern, and empathy. When you listen, use some active listening techniques, such as paraphrasing and reflecting feelings, and the Speaker-Listener Technique that you learned in Chapter 4. Once both of you have expressed your thoughts and emotions and have listened to each other with empathy, you will probably feel understood and cared for. Then, you are in a position to engage in problem-solving.

Step 3: Problem-Solving

Multiple collaborative problem-solving approaches exist. The model that we will describe now is a combination of some of these models.[34] We recommend that you start the problem-solving with prayer. You can pray individually or together. Even a short prayer asking God to guide you through the process will be helpful.

- **Set a time and place for the problem-solving**
  - Select a quiet and private setting
  - Turn off phones
- **Define the problem – in terms of needs, not solutions**
  - Do not state your preferred solution
  - State the need. For example, "we need to get out of debt"
- **Brainstorm a list of possible solutions**
  - Write down as many ideas as possible
  - Do not evaluate the ideas at this point
- **Discuss each suggested solution**
  - Think through how realistic each suggestion is
  - Do not think "this is my suggestion" or "this is your idea"
- **Agree on one "win-win" solution**
  - Discuss what is best for the marriage
  - Be willing to be flexible
- **Decide on who is going to do what (be specific)**
  - Determine the action each spouse will take
  - Be willing to make sacrifices
- **Evaluate the progress**
  - Set a specific date and time to meet again
  - Evaluate and adjust action steps
- **Celebrate your hard work**
  - Praise each other for the effort
  - Do something fun together

Congratulations! You have started the hard work of solving your conflict. However, according to marriage researcher Gottman, about 70 percent of marital conflict cannot be solved completely; he calls these ongoing conflicts perpetual problems.[35] He believes that having perpetual problems does not necessarily mean that couples have an unhappy marriage. He also proposes that an effective way of handling perpetual problems is to engage in a respectful dialogue, promote acceptance of the spouse, and avoid a communication gridlock.[36] So, choose your battles, and realize that at times, the wiser approach is to overlook an offense (Prov. 19:11).

The Do's and Don'ts of Handling Marriage Conflict

 Do's = Healthy Ways

1. Take Time-Out if needed
2. Make time to address the conflict
3. Be calm and respectful
4. Work collaboratively as a team
5. Focus on one issue
6. Attack the problem
7. Take personal responsibility
8. Be solution-oriented
9. Pray and seek God's wisdom
10. Look for the best in your spouse
11. Take care of the dirty laundry at home

 Don'ts = Unhealthy Ways

1. Don't pressure your spouse
2. Don't avoid addressing the conflict
3. Don't be verbally aggressive
4. Don't be selfish or self-centered
5. Don't bring up many issues
6. Don't attack your spouse
7. Don't blame your spouse
8. Don't be problem-focused
9. Don't ignore God's wisdom
10. Don't look for the worst in your spouse
11. Don't air dirty laundry on social media

Now, let us go back to Larry and Sally's conflict. How could they have handled their conflict, or dirty laundry, positively and effectively? We believe that they could have used some of the tips we shared in this chapter. For instance, while in the car, one of them could have requested a Time-Out to protect the relationship and set a time later on in the afternoon to address the conflict. We believe such action would have prevented the escalation. For instance, that afternoon during the meeting, they could have used step 2 to communicate clearly, share their thoughts and feelings, and listen to each other with empathy. Then, they could engage in step 3 to resolve their conflict constructively.

If your conflict is too severe and involves major issues such as pornography, infidelity, or substance abuse, we recommend that you seek the help of a

Check out the chapter video at: www.grtep.com

pastoral counselor or a professional Christian counselor. Remember, there is hope!

Now, let's walk to the master bedroom.

Endnotes

1. "Production Homes," National Association of Home Builders, accessed July 1, 2019, https://www.nahb.org/consumers/home-buying/types-of-home-construction/types-of-construction-production-homes.aspx.

2. Ken Sande, *The Peacemaker: A Biblical Guide to Resolving Personal Conflict* (Grand Rapids, MI: BakerBooks, 2004).

3. Stephen D. Renn, ed., *Expository Dictionary of Bible Words: Word Studies for Key English Bible Words Based on the Hebrew and Greek Texts* (Peabody, MA: Hendrickson Publishers, 2005).

4. Renn, ed., "*Expository Dictionary of Bible Words,*" 201.

5. Martin H. Manser, ed. *W. E. Vine's New Testament Word Pictures: Romans to Revelation: A Commentary Drawn from the Original Language* (Nashville, TN: Thomas Nelson, 2015), 588.

6. William W. Wilmot and Joyce L. Hocker, *Interpersonal Conflict*, 9th ed. (New York: McGraw-Hill, 2014), 13.

7. John Gottman and Nan Silver, *The Seven Principles for Making Marriage Work: Practical Guide for the Country's Foremost Relationship Expert* (New York: Harmony Books, 2015), 41.

8. Amy Hooper et al., "Revisiting the Basics: Understanding Potential Demographic Differences with John Gottman's Four Horsemen and Emotional Flooding," *The Family Journal* 25, no. 3 (June 22, 2017): 227, accessed July 10, 2019, https://doi-org.ezproxy.liberty.edu/10.1177/1066480717710650.

9. David E. Cox et al., "The Effect of Anger Expression Style on Cardiovascular Responses to Lateralized Cognitive Stressors," *Brain Informatics* 4, no. 4 (May 15, 2017): 231–39, doi:10.1007/s40708-017-0068-4.

10. Meghan P. McCormick et al., "Moods, Stressors, and Severity of Marital Conflict: A Daily Diary Study of Low-Income Families," *Family Relations* 66, no. 3, (July 2017): 435, doi:10.1111/fare.12258.

11. Susan A. David, *Emotional Agility: Get Unstuck, Embrace Change, and Thrive in Work and Life* (New York: Penguin Random House, 2016), 5.

12. Gottman and Silver, *The Seven Principles for Making Marriage Work*, 181.

13. Tommy M. Phillips, Joe D. Wilmoth, Loren D. Marks, "Challenges and Conflicts... Strengths and Supports: A Study of Enduring African American Marriages," *Journal of Black Studies* 43, no. 8 (November 2012): 936–52, accessed July 19, 2019, https://www.jstor.org/stable/23414682.

14. Brian. D. Doss, Lorelei. E. Simpson, and Andrew Christensen, "Why Do Couples Seek Marital Therapy?" *Professional Psychology: Research and Practice* 35, no. 6, (2004): 608–14, doi:10.1037/0735-7028.35.6.608.

15. John M. Gottman, Julie Schwartz Gottman, and Joan DeClaire, *Ten Lessons to Transform Your Marriage* (New York: Three Rivers Press, 2006).

16. Bettina J. Casad, Marissa M. Salazar, and Veronica Macina, "The Real Versus the Ideal: Predicting Relationship Satisfaction and Well-Being from Endorsement of Marriage Myths and Benevolent Sexism," *Psychology of Women Quarterly*, 39, no. 1 (March 2015): 119, doi:10.1177/0361684314528304.

17. J. Mitchell Vaterlaus et al., "Marital Expectations in Strong African American Marriages," *Family Process* 56, no. 4 (December 2017): 883–89, doi:10.1111/famp.12263.

18. Harley Willard F., *His Needs, Her Needs: Building an Affair-Proof Marriage* (Grand Rapids, MI: Baker Publishing Book, 2011).

19. Jennifer S. Kirby, Donald H. Baucom, and Michael A. Peterman, "An Investigation of Unmet Intimacy Needs in Marital Relationships," *Journal of Marital and Family Therapy* 31, no. 4 (October 2005): 313–25, doi:10.1111/j.1752-0606.2005.tb01573.x.

20. Duane P. Schultz and Sydney Ellen Schultz, *Theories of Personality*, 11th ed. (United States: Cengage Learning, 2017).

21. Happiness Ihuoma Igbo, Awopetu Ronke Grace, Ekoja Okwori Christiana, "Relationship between Duration of Marriage, Personality Trait, Gender and Conflict Resolution Strategies of Spouses," *Procedia-Social and Behavioral Sciences* 190 (May 2015): 490–96, doi:10.1016/j.sbspro.2015.05.032.

22. Klaus A. Schneewind and Anna-Katharina Gerhard, "Relationship Personality, Conflict Resolution, and Marital Satisfaction in the First 5 Years of Marriage," *Family Relations* 51, no. 1 (January 2002): 63–71, doi:10.1111/j.1741-3729.2002.00063.x.

23. Elias Moitinho et al., "Encouraging a More Perfect Union: Strategies for Counseling Clients in Interracial/Interethnic Marriages," *American Mental Health Counselors Association (AMHCA) The Advocate Magazine* (Fall 2018): 34–37.

24. Tiffany R. Tili and Gina G. Barker, "Communication in Intercultural Marriages: Managing Cultural Differences and Conflicts," *Southern Communication Journal* 80, no. 3 (May 2015): 189–210, doi:10.1080/1041794X.2015.1023826.

25. Jessica Halliday Hardie and Amy Lucas, "Economic Factors and Relationship Quality among Young Couples: Comparing Cohabitation and Marriage," *Journal*

of *Marriage and Family* 72, no. 5 (October 2010): 1141–54; Catherine Rampell, "Money Fights Predict Divorce," accessed June 11, 2019, https://economix.blogs. nytimes.com/2009/12/07/money-fights-predict-divorce-rates/.

26. Julie E. Artis and Martha Martinez, "Cohabitation, Marriage and Relationships with 'Parents-in-law'," *Families, Relationships, and Societies* 5, no. 1 (March 2016): 3–22, doi:10.1332/204674314X14164923149780.

27. Tanya Tavassolie et al., "Differences in Perceived Parenting Style Between Mothers and Fathers: Implications for Child Outcomes and Marital Conflict," *Journal of Child and Family Studies* 25, no. 6 (2016): 2055–68, doi:10.1007/s10826-016-0376-y.

28. Manny Alvarez, "Porn Addiction: Why Americans Are in More Danger Than Ever" *Fox News–Mental Health*, January 16, 2019, accessed July 2, 2019, https://www.fox-news.com/health/porn-addiction-why-americans-are-in-more-danger-than-ever.

29. "An Overview of the Thomas Kilmann Conflict Mode Instrument TKI," accessed August 20, 2019, https://kilmanndiagnostics.com/ overview-thomas-kilmann-conflict-mode-instrument-tki/.

30. Isaac K. Mbabazi, *The Significance of Interpersonal Forgiveness in the Gospel of Matthew* (Eugene, OR: Pickwick Publications, 2013), 177.

31. Everett L. Worthington, Jr., *Forgiveness and Reconciliation: Theory and Application* (New York: Routledge, 2013).

32. Everett L. Worthington, Jr., *Hope-Focused Marriage Counseling: A Guide to Brief Therapy*, 2nd ed. (Downers Grove, IL: IVP Academic, 2005).

33. Scott M. Stanley et al., *A Lasting Promise: The Christian Guide to Fighting for Your Marriage*, New and Revised Edition (San Francisco, CA: Jossey-Bass, 2014).

34. Robert Bolton, *People Skills: How to Assert Yourself, Listen to Others, and Resolve Conflict* (New York, NY: Simon & Schuster, Inc., 2011); David H. Olson and Amy K. Olson, *PREPARE/ENRICH Program: Version 2000*; Ken Sande, *The Peacemaker: A Biblical Guide to Resolving Personal Conflict* (Grand Rapids, MI: BakerBooks, 2004).

35. Gottman and Silver, *The Seven Principles for Making Marriage Work*, 138.

36. Gottman and Silver, *The Seven Principles for Making Marriage Work*, 138.

CHAPTER 8

The Master Bedroom: Keeping Intimacy and Passion Alive

"And they were both naked, the man and his wife,
and were not ashamed."
Genesis 2:25 (NKJV)

© Andy Dean Photography/Shutterstock.com

Many television shows and home décor websites describe the master bedroom as a stylish and private oasis that provides relief to couples at the end of a long and stressful day. Indeed, the master bedroom can be a magical place where the couple expresses their love, passion, and desire for each other. The layout and décor of the master bedroom can create a perfect environment for this to happen.

A well-planned and luxurious master bedroom may include a sitting or reading area, a spacious walk-in closet, and a large bathroom with double vanity sinks, and even a soaking tub. It may also include a multi-showerhead system along with large mirrors to add to the romance and adventure. Although not all master bedrooms fit this description, they generally provide privacy, so that the couple can experience intimate moments as they celebrate becoming one flesh (Gen. 2:24).

In this chapter, we use the master bedroom as a metaphor to discuss intimacy as intended by God. We address marital intimacy from a multidimensional perspective, consider the biblical design for intimacy, and explore the multisensory nature of sexual intimacy in marriage. Our goal is that you take time to evaluate your levels of intimacy from a multidimensional perspective, implement some of the ideas in this chapter, and continue to create an environment in your dream home where intimacy can flourish and thrive.

Reflecting on Your Overall Sexual Intimacy

EXCITING Meaningful LIVELY
Disconnected **FRUSTRATING**
Boring
Passionate Empty
creative
Predictable Romantic
Superficial *Surprising* **Routine**

Source: Elias and Denise Moitinho

Before we explore the master bedroom metaphor, we invite you to reflect on your sexual intimacy in your marriage. As you read the descriptive words in the box, identify the ones that, in your opinion, best describe how you currently view or feel about your overall sexual intimacy in your marriage.

Now that you are thinking about sexual intimacy with your spouse, we invite you to dive into this exciting chapter.

Understanding God's Design for Sexual Intimacy

 Sex is not the result of the Fall . . . but rather a good gift from God.

In a time when our secular society has redefined marriage and gender, Christian couples need to develop a clear understanding of the biblical view of sexuality and intimacy. This is important since how a husband and wife view human sexuality and intimacy influences how they behave toward each other sexually. Additionally, gaining knowledge of what the Bible says about sex and intimacy can help dispel myths and distorted ideas that are pervasive in our society. So, we will look at some essential elements that are part of a biblical worldview on sexuality by focusing on selected Bible passages. If you are interested in a more in-depth examination of this topic, please look at the endnotes in this chapter.

Sexuality Is Part of God's Creation

Human sexuality is a beautiful component of God's creation (Gen. 1:27–28; 2:24–25). In fact, God created Adam and Eve, the crowning glory of His creation, as sexual beings capable of experiencing sexual desire and arousal, engaging in sexual activity, and reproducing (Gen. 1:27–28). God even gave them the command to "be fruitful and multiply" (Gen. 1:28 NKJV) and declared that what He had created was "very good" (Gen. 1:31 NKJV). Hence, sex is not the result of the Fall or a necessary evil; it is not something dirty, but rather a good gift from God.[1]

God Created Male and Female

In God's economy, there are only two genders, male and female (Gen. 1:27–28). The Bible is clear regarding this aspect of creation. Sex was created for the union of a husband and a wife (Gen. 2:24–25). Köstenberger and Jones note that "God's creation of Eve demonstrates that God's plan for Adam's marriage, as well as all subsequent marriages, involves a *monogamous heterosexual* relationship. God only made one "suitable helper" for Adam, and she was a *female*."[2] In the New Testament, more specifically in Matthew 19:5, Jesus also quotes Genesis 2:24 emphasizing God's original plan for marriage.

Every Person Is Created in the Image of God (*Imago Dei*)

A Christian worldview teaches that every person is God's masterpiece and has dignity and intrinsic worth (Gen. 1:27–28; Ps. 139:14; Eph. 2:10). According to theologians, being created in the *Imago Dei* means that human beings are rational, relational, and spiritual beings.[3] However, the Fall damaged the image of God and created a separation between God and His creation. Nevertheless, God loved His creation so much that He sent Jesus Christ to be the Savior of the world (John 3:16). Once we accept Christ's love, we are transformed to live in a new way and become more like Him in our character, thoughts, and behaviors. Although we are still imperfect, the Holy Spirit empowers us to express more clearly the image of God in the way we relate to our spouse. Thus, husbands and wives need to affirm each other's God-given worth and encourage each other to live a life that showcases the restored *Imago Dei* through salvation in Christ. When we affirm our spouse, we are affirming the image of God since our spouse bears the image of God. On the other hand, when we belittle our spouse we grieve God's heart.

Sin Has Distorted the Expression of Sexuality

When Adam and Eve disobeyed God, sin came into the world and affected all aspects of life, including our sexuality. The image of God in humanity was marred and distorted; however, it was not eliminated or lost.[4] Throughout Scriptures, one can see examples of how sin distorted sexuality and how God condemns activities such as sexual immorality, rape, and adultery, to name a few (Rom. 1:18–27; 1 Thess. 4:1–7).

Restored Sexuality

God's plan of salvation includes restoring and transforming the whole person (John 3:16; Col. 3:9–11). Therefore, when a person is saved and becomes part of God's kingdom, he or she starts the process of becoming a new person (2 Cor. 5:17). The godly transformation requires new standards for living, which includes leading a life of purity and avoidance of sexual immorality (1 Thess. 4:1–7). This does not imply living a legalistic lifestyle, but rather using the freedom we have in Christ to honor Him in all areas of life, including sexual intimacy in marriage.

The Purposes of Sexuality and Sex

There are multiple purposes for sex and sexuality. Procreation is not the only one or the primary purpose of sexuality. Procreational sex is undoubtedly one of God's first commands to Adam and Eve (Gen. 1:28). Interestingly, while the Catholic Church has traditionally taught that procreation is the primary purpose of sexual relationship in marriage,[5] evangelicals, on the other hand, have embraced and taught the concepts of companionship, consummation, and sexual pleasure within marriage. This shift began to occur after the Reformation. Remarkably, since the 1980s, several Christian authors have written books affirming the blessings of sexual pleasure in the marital relationship.[6]

The idea that sex is a mutually pleasurable and intimate experience for married couples is expressed throughout Scripture. For instance, in the Old Testament, Solomon proclaims that a husband may find enjoyment in his wife. He states, "May your fountain be blessed, and may you rejoice in the wife of your youth. A loving doe, a graceful deer – may her breasts satisfy you always, may you ever be intoxicated with her love" (Prov. 5: 18–19 NIV). In the New Testament, the apostle Paul provides a discussion on the mutual responsibility that husbands and wives have to meet each other's sexual needs. He states, "The husband should fulfill his wife's sexual needs, and the wife should fulfill her husband's needs" (1 Cor. 7:3–5 NLT). Hence, exciting, thrilling, and joyful sexual fulfillment is biblical, and it is for married couples.

God's Guidelines and Boundaries

God has established some guidelines for us to express our sexuality in marriage. God's guidelines and boundaries are for our protection and safety. Below are a few of these guidelines revealed in Scriptures:

 God's guidelines and boundaries for sexuality are for our protection and safety.

- Sexual pleasure is to be enjoyed in the context of heterosexual marriage (Gen. 2:24–25; Ex. 20:14; Heb. 13:4).

Genesis 2:24 is the classical passage frequently read in many Christian weddings. This verse affirms that God's original design for marriage includes a man and a woman, "Therefore a man shall leave his father and mother and be joined to his wife, and they shall become one flesh" (Gen. 2:24 NKJV). The term "one flesh" refers to the consummation of the sexual relationship between the man and the woman.

- Sexual expression involves mutual responsibility and respect for the spouse

  "The husband should fulfill his wife's sexual needs, and the wife should fulfill her husband's needs. The wife gives authority over her body to her husband, and the husband gives authority over his body to his wife. Do not deprive each other of sexual relations, unless you both agree to refrain from sexual intimacy for a limited time so you can give yourselves more completely to prayer. Afterward, you should come together again so that Satan won't be able to tempt you because of your lack of self-control" (1 Cor. 7:3–5 NLT).

The apostle Paul wrote these verses to help Christians at Corinth to understand God's perspective on marriage and sexuality. Corinth had become a prosperous city during the New Testament times. However, it was also a place full of idolatry where the temple of the goddess Aphrodite had about a thousand prostitutes. Corinth was known for its sexual immorality, so much so that people used the verb *to corinthianize* to describe sexual immorality at that time.[7] Paul emphasizes that providing sexual pleasure is a mutual responsibility. Christian married couples need to be on the alert because Satan can tempt them in the sexual area of their marriages. Especially if they are not meeting each other's sexual needs.

- Married couples must protect purity in their sexual relationship.

The author of Hebrews highlights that couples need to value and respect marriage. "Marriage should be honored by all, and the marriage bed kept pure, for God will judge the adulterer and all the sexually immoral" (Heb. 13:4 NIV). The term marriage bed is the Greek word *koité*,[8] which refers to "sexual intercourse within marriage, meaning husbands and wives should remain sexually faithful to one another and to their marriage vows."[9] Therefore, Christian couples need to focus on creating an affair-proof marriage.

Intimacy Is a Multidimensional Experience

Intimacy is a holistic experience that involves all areas of a person's life (Gen. 1:27–28; Prov. 5:18–19; Song of Songs). It is an experience that needs to be synchronized and harmonized emotionally, mentally, spiritually, and physically for couples to experience a more profound overall level of intimacy. However, we must keep in mind that emotional intimacy precedes physical intimacy. We expand on this paramount concept in the next section.

——————————— Multidimensional Intimacy ———————————

Multidimensional intimacy is a sublime connection of a couple's hearts, minds, bodies, and souls.

In the 1980s, Shaefer and Olson developed the PAIR inventory (Personal Assessment of Intimacy in Relationships) and identified five types of intimacy: emotional, social, sexual, intellectual, and recreational.[10] As you probably have noted, their model does not include spiritual intimacy. However, since then, many Christians and secular authors alike have explained intimacy as a multidimensional experience that encompasses all areas of our lives. In fact, Christian authors tend to highlight the spiritual component of intimacy.[11]

Intimacy is incredibly complex and multifaceted. As we mentioned in Chapter 4, intimacy is to know and to be known. It requires self-disclosure, vulnerability, trust, acceptance, and kindness. For instance, when you give yourself to your spouse intimately, you are opening your whole being, and in your nakedness, becoming vulnerable. As you engage in sexual activity, you trust that your spouse will embrace you with acceptance and tender love. Consequently, intimacy involves at least four aspects of our lives: heart, mind, body, and soul.

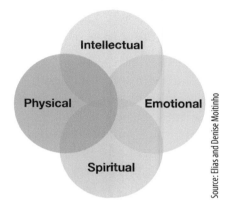

Source: Elias and Denise Moitinho

Emotional Intimacy – Share Your Heart

Emotional intimacy is a connection of the hearts. As you and your spouse engage in a deeper level of communication, you will share your feelings and your true selves. This more profound sharing involves not only authenticity and vulnerability, but it also requires no fear of rejection. Moreover, emotional intimacy produces a sense of closeness and creates a growing emotional bonding.

Susan Johnson, who developed emotionally focused therapy (EFT), an attachment-based counseling model, asserts that spouses are emotionally attached and dependent on each other in a way that is similar to the attachment of a child to a parent.[12] We agree with Johnson and believe that you as a couple need to connect emotionally by sharing your feelings and listening to each other with empathy. You also need to guard your hearts against lust and negative emotions and be authentic in your interactions with each other. In this way, you will have a better chance of developing and maintaining emotional intimacy.

Intellectual Intimacy – Share Your Mind

You and your spouse have unique minds with different thoughts, ideas, and opinions about life issues. You also have personal vision, goals, and aspirations. Sharing them with each other creates a connection of your minds. It stimulates and challenges each other's thinking and allows you to show respect for your spouse's intellect. Besides, it allows you to encourage your spouse's mental growth and show appreciation for his or her beautiful mind. Creating a shared vision and mission for your marriage, as discussed in Chapter 1, leads to intellectual intimacy.

Physical Intimacy – Share Your Body

Physical intimacy is a multisensory experience that involves several neurobiological reactions. All senses, including vision, smell, touch, taste, and hearing, contribute to the married couple's physical pleasure. Research shows that when couples engage in physical intimacy, their bodies react and respond with a biochemical cascade. For example, the brain releases *dopamine*, the neurotransmitter that produces a sense of excitement and intense exhilaration, *oxytocin*, which is a hormone that promotes bonding and trust,[13] and the adrenal glands release *adrenaline*, which increases heart rate, muscle strength, and blood pressure, among many other neurochemicals and hormones. Thus, couples need to learn ways to enhance their multisensory experience before, during, and after physical intimacy. Taking care of your own body, and affirming and appreciating your spouse's body can also strengthen your sexual intimacy. Perhaps investing in aromatherapy, linens, romantic music, and lighting is a clever way to enhance your multisensory experience. Obviously, it would be wise to consider your spouse's sensory preferences to maximize your sexual encounter.

Spiritual – Share Your Soul

Christian couples may have the privilege of sharing the same faith and attending church together at least once a week. However, attending church together does not mean they share their souls. For the purpose of this discussion, sharing your soul means that you engage in spiritual conversations and practice spiritual disciplines as a couple. Prayer, worship, fasting, Scriptural meditation, Bible reading, Bible study, disciple-making, confession, service to others, and fellowship are some of the spiritual disciplines practiced within the Christian faith. Therefore, we encourage you to engage in some of the spiritual disciplines. By doing so, you are investing in your spiritual intimacy with God and with each other. We acknowledge that you may be married to someone who is not a believer. If this is the case, we encourage you to continue to grow in your faith and live a life that may draw your spouse to Christ (1 Pet. 3:1).

Sexual Response

Multiple changes happen in the body during the sexual relationship. In this section, we provide a brief overview of a widely used linear model developed by William Masters and Virginia Johnson in 1966, which helps us understand some of these changes. Their well-known four-phase model of the sexual response of men and women includes excitement, plateau, orgasm, and resolution. This model focuses on physiological changes that happen during the sexual act.[14]

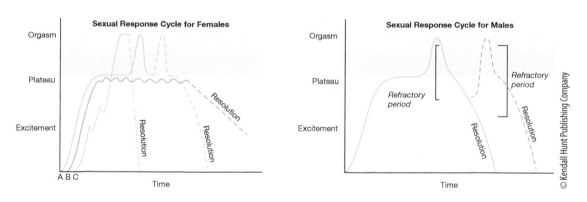

The Excitement phase refers to physiological changes that happen as a result of arousal. It includes the engorgement of the genitals, which occurs in both men and women. As a result, the man experiences an erection of the penis whereas the woman's clitoris swells and her vagina lubricates. In the Plateau phase, other physiological changes occur, such as increased breathing, heart rate, and blood pressure. The Orgasmic phase represents the climax of sexual interaction when a man and a woman experience orgasm. The Resolution phase is the process of the body returning to the normal levels of functioning prior to the Excitement phase.[15] While men experience the refractory period, in which they are physiologically unable to have another orgasm, women are physiologically capable of having multiple orgasms.[16]

As expected, there is the potential for sexual problems or dysfunctions in any phase of the sexual act to occur. For instance, in the Excitement and Plateau phases, men and women may experience low desire and lack of arousal, and men may suffer from erectile disorder. In the Plateau and Orgasmic phase, men may experience premature or delayed ejaculation while women may experience orgasmic disorder or pain during penetration.[17] Moreover, in the Resolution phase, a couple may experience conflict or emotional issues based on how the sexual act went or how they responded to each other.

We would like to emphasize that while men and women may have similar responses, they also tend to differ in some of the way they respond sexually. Therefore, couples will need to take time to learn how their spouses respond uniquely during the sexual act, and be mindful that their responses may vary in each sexual encounter. It takes time to learn and adjust to each other's sexual patterns of responses. Being patient, loving, and kind will enhance the opportunity for an optimal orgasmic experience. It is important to note that other models that seek to explain the sexual act from different perspectives exist. Couples will benefit from learning as much as they can from the experts as well as from each other.

Multifaceted Factors of Sexual Intimacy

Multiple factors may influence sexual intimacy in marriage positively and negatively.[18] A couple's lack of information or misinformation about human anatomy, ignorance of the physiological and neurobiological responses of the body to sexual stimuli, and lack of knowledge about the sexual response cycle can affect their sexual experience in marriage. Additionally, issues related to physical and mental health, medication side effects, pornography, and infidelity, among many others, can sabotage a couple's sex life. Thus, couples will benefit from learning as much as they can about these factors. We will discuss some of these factors here.

Physical Health

A couple's physical health can definitely play a major role in their sexual intimacy. Generally, couples tend to have more enjoyable overall sexual satisfaction when they are in good physical health than when they exhibit poor health. For instance, studies show that people who suffer from chronic diseases, such as heart disease, cancer, diabetes, and arthritis often encounter unique challenges, such as shortness of breath and low-sex drive.[19] It is important to note that though chronic diseases tend to appear later in life, some couples may experience them earlier in marriage.[20] These chronic diseases may bring new challenges to couples, such as erectile dysfunction and low sexual interest or arousal disorders. These challenges may also be exacerbated by the side effects of medications. The Diagnostic and Statistical Manual of Mental Disorders (DSM–5), used by psychiatrists and counselors to diagnose mental disorders, includes sexual dysfunctions that affect both men and women.[21] Many of these sexual dysfunctions present physical symptoms; however, the underlying cause of the symptoms may be psychological as well as physical.

DSM-5 Sexual Dysfunction Diagnoses

Male	Female
Hypoactive sexual desire disorder	Sexual interest arousal disorder
Erectile disorder	Orgasmic disorder
Premature (early) ejaculation	Genito-pelvic pain/penetration disorder
Delayed ejaculation	Substance/medication-induced sexual dysfunction
Substance/medication-induced sexual dysfunction	

Source: Stephen B. Levine, "Sexual Dysfunction: The Role of Clinical Psychiatry," *Psychiatric Times*, March 20, 2017. https://www.psychiatrictimes.com/cme/sexual-dysfunction-role-clinical-psychiatry/page/0/4

Mental Health

An individual's mental health will affect his or her sex life positively or negatively. Obviously, a person who is in good mental health, exhibiting a positive sense of well-being, will probably experience a positive impact on his or her sexual intimacy. Unfortunately, a large number of people are suffering from mental disorders. In fact, the prevalence of depression and anxiety disorders in the U.S. is high. According to the Centers for Disease Control and Prevention (CDC), "During 2013–2016, 8.1% of American adults aged 20 and over had depression in a given 2-week period [and] women (10.4%) were almost twice as likely as were men (5.5%) to have had depression."[22] In addition, according to the National

Institute of Mental Health (NIMH), in a 2017 report, "An estimated 19.1% of U.S. adults had any anxiety disorder in the [previous] year . . . [In 2016, the] prevalence of any anxiety disorder was higher for females (23.4%) than for males (14.3%)."[23]

Depression and anxiety can affect the sex life of couples in many ways. The spouse affected by depression or anxiety may have low sexual desire or may be too anxious about his or her sexual performance. While struggling with mental health issues, the spouse may be overly worried about himself or herself and, consequently, show little interest in romantic interaction or any interaction at all. Moreover, for the non-depressed spouse, a challenge is to be patient and committed to the relationship, in sickness and in health. During these times of significant sexual challenges, couples need to stick together and seek professional help to solve or alleviate mental health problems. Perhaps we need to consider that a spouse's mental health issue can become an issue for the couple.

Medication Side Effects

Sometimes, individuals may be unaware of the possible adverse sexual side effects of prescription medications. A spouse may misunderstand his or her spouse's lack of sexual interest as a sign of rejection or that he or she is running out of love. The spouse may also think that he or she is no longer attractive enough to arouse the spouse. However, the truth is that many medications can have side effects that may interfere with sexual functioning. A spouse who feels tired, drowsy, bloated, or dizzy regularly due to medication side effects may not feel excited about having sex. In fact, some medications for depression and anxiety may lower the sex drive.[24] For instance, a study shows that many couples try different strategies to cope with the side effects that interfere with their sex life.[25] For this reason, couples need to consult with their physicians when side effects interfere with the quality and frequency of their sexual life. Most physicians will adjust medication so that couples can continue to enjoy the gift of sex without having to deal with unnecessary medication side effects.

Body Image and Self-Esteem

How a husband and wife perceive, like, or dislike parts of their bodies influence their sexual intimacy. For instance, a study focusing on male body image found that "more negative body attitudes toward muscularity, body fat, height, and genitals [are] significantly related to greater sexual dissatisfaction."[26] The authors also highlight that men's insecurity or sense of confidence about their bodies is closely related to how they view their sexual organs.[27] Another study focusing on female body image found that women who have poor body image tend to experience lower levels of sexual functioning.[28] In addition, women who have survived breast cancer face many challenges related to body image, which can affect their sexual functioning.[29] Unfortunately, many adults struggle with poor body image.[30] Thus, couples need to affirm and praise each other's physical appearance frequently since their body image satisfaction and attitude influence their sexual intimacy.

Couples are in a great position to help each other enhance body image satisfaction. Couples can affirm and praise each other's beauty. For instance, instead of merely making a general statement such as "you look beautiful" or "you are gorgeous," couples may follow the example given by Solomon and the Shulamite in the Song of Songs. They praised and affirmed each other's body by being specific and focusing on each part of the body (Song of Songs 4:1–7; Song of Songs 5:10–16). For instance, Solomon praised her eyes, hair, teeth, smile, lips, cheeks, neck, and breasts and concluded that she was completely beautiful. The Shulamite, in turn, praised his skin, hair, eyes, cheeks, lips, arms, body, legs, posture, and mouth. She concluded that he was very attractive and desirable.

Traumatic Past Experiences

Past experiences shape our worldview, including our understanding and beliefs about the sexual relationship in marriage. Experts note that sexual, physical, and psychological abuse, violence in the family, and bullying are cumulative adverse childhood experiences that can lead to complex symptoms in a person's life.[31] Research shows that women who have been victims of sexual trauma often face challenges regarding sexual intimacy and marital satisfaction.[32] Furthermore, individuals who experienced maltreatment in childhood and view their spouses as less empathetic toward them may feel less validated and satisfied with their marriage relationship.[33] Consequently, couples need to exercise wisdom when facing sexual intimacy challenges derived from their own or their spouse's past traumatic experiences. We recommend consulting with a marriage counselor or a certified sex therapist for professional help.

All Rooms Affect the Bedroom

The smell of food from the kitchen can invade every nook and cranny of the house. For example, on Thanksgiving Day, we enjoy the smell of roasted Turkey, mouth-watering casseroles, and decadent pecan pies. During the Christmas season, we enjoy the smells of the fresh pine scent from our Christmas décor, childhood favorite gingerbread cookies, and creamy hot chocolate. These scents can even create a positive atmosphere that reminds us of our love for our family. On the other hand, a messy and dirty kitchen reminds us that our lives may have become extremely busy and disorganized. Figuratively, the kitchen and dining room represent how we take care of our body, mind, soul, and relationships. The living room reminds us to focus on positive communication. The laundry room calls us to work on resolving conflicts. The office invites us to keep the finances in check, and so forth. Therefore, all areas of our lives affect our intimacy in the bedroom, in other words, all rooms influence the master bedroom.

An older female friend once made the comment that, often, husbands neglect their wives' emotional needs during the day, but expect sexual intimacy at night. Then, she added, "they are not going to get it." The truth is that a sexual relationship between husband and wife does not happen in isolation. Instead, it is the reflection of what is happening in their relationship as a whole. As a result, experts recommend treating sexual desire problems holistically.[34] Since intimacy is multidimensional, all areas of the marital relationship affect the couple's physical intimacy. For instance, unresolved conflict and unforgiveness create negative emotions that may decrease sexual desire. The good news is that research shows that forgiving oneself and a partner can lead to greater relationship satisfaction.[35] Besides, our view of our spouse creates feelings that can draw us emotionally closer or away from them. As a result, maintaining a healthy sexual relationship means that we must cultivate emotional intimacy because it precedes physical intimacy. Since it takes two to tango, couples need to cultivate a climate of love and kindness in each room of their dream home. By doing so, they will enrich their experience in the master bedroom.

 Emotional intimacy precedes physical intimacy.

Busy Schedules

Our 21st-century fast-paced lifestyle creates busy schedules and, consequently, exhausted bodies. As we know, fatigue and sex do not go well together. However, how can couples find time for quality sex when work, school, household chores, parenting, and other demanding activities place their lives in a constant rat-race? According to research, parents of young children reported a lower level of interest in having sex.[36] Also, couples tend to experience higher levels of marital satisfaction and life satisfaction in the early years of marriage before the parenting years.[37] This might be due to the multiple demands of parenting that may create a child-centered marriage, in which the husband–wife relationship may be neglected. Besides, experts note that parenthood does not seem to affect men's desire for sex in the same way it does women.[38] Therefore, we recommend that couples manage their daily schedule wisely to minimize negative interferences with their sex life.

Communication

Communication can make or break a relationship. When couples engage in negative patterns of communication, such as criticism, contempt, defensiveness, and stonewalling, their relationship suffers. As we discussed in Chapter 4, effective communication is key to building intimacy. In fact, a study found that "greater amounts of sexual communication were associated with increased orgasm frequency in women and greater relationship and sexual satisfaction in both sexes."[39] So, if your communication with your spouse has not been constructive lately, it is time to consider how you can improve it for the sake of your sexual intimacy.

Pornography and Affairs

As mentioned in Chapter 7, unfortunately, a large number of Christians view pornography. Current research shows that religious individuals who use pornography often experience mental health issues and distress.[40] This makes sense because most Christians believe that the Bible condemns sexual immorality and that they are supposed to live a pure life. So, when they are caught in the sin of using pornography, many Christians experience high levels of guilt, anxiety, and mental distress because their behavior is incongruent with their faith. From a Christian perspective, viewing pornography violates the biblical principles previously discussed in this chapter. Fortunately, many Christian ministries and resources are available to help Christian men and women deal with their pornography issues.

Marital unfaithfulness is the most destructive factor in a couple's intimacy, even after forgiveness. Unfortunately, some Christian couples may go through an experience in which one of the spouses engages in an extramarital affair. Social media, specifically Facebook, has created an environment that facilitates emotional as well as sexual affairs.[41] David Carder in his book, *Torn Asunder*, conceptualized affairs into four types: The *one-night stand* is usually a short-term relationship without commitment. The *entangled affair* develops gradually and meets some relational needs not being met in the marriage. The *sexual addiction* includes several relationships with multiple partners and compulsive behaviors. The *add-on affair* is a type of affair that involves having commonalities with a lover that do not exist in the marriage.[42] Carder asserts that the *entangled affair* and the *add-on affair* "are the most problematic and common form of infidelity and some of the most stubborn to rehabilitate due to the extensive emotional involvement."[43]

Sexual Behaviors in Marriage

Often times, Christian couples wonder about what sexual behaviors are biblically acceptable in Christian marriage. However, the purpose of this section is not to provide a list of do's and don'ts regarding what specific behaviors or sexual activities are acceptable for Christian married couples. Our main goal is to provide some guidance on how you can think about this issue and engage in a God-honoring decision-making process with your spouse. Keep in mind that the Apostle Paul says, "Everything is permissible, but not everything is helpful. Everything is permissible, but not everything builds up" (1 Cor. 10:23 HCSB). Review the chart "A Couple's Guide to Analyzing Sexual Behaviors in Marriage" on the next page and discuss it with your spouse.

Keeping Passion and Intimacy Alive

Most of us agree that our spouses deserve our best. However, the busyness of life, including work schedules, parenting, and household chores, causes fatigue that can prevent us from giving our very best to our spouse, emotionally and sexually. For instance, getting home exhausted after a long stressful day at work or feeling drained after countless hours dealing with a sick or defiant child can decrease the possibility of sexual intimacy. Demanding and stressful activities during the day can deprive us of the physical and emotional energy needed for quality sex. Thus, when negative patterns develop affecting the frequency and quality of our sexual encounters, we need to become proactive and intentional to keep passion and intimacy alive in marriage.

A Couple's Guide to Analyzing Sexual Behaviors in Marriage

- **The Behavior**
  - How did you or your spouse learn about this behavior?
  - What aspects of this behavior are healthy or unhealthy physically, emotionally, mentally, and spiritually?
- **The Bible**
  - What are some biblical principles that may directly or indirectly relate to this behavior?
  - What are some biblical principles that may support or discourage this behavior directly or indirectly?
- **The Spouse**
  - What does your spouse think about this behavior?
  - What does your spouse believe, prefer, like, or dislike about this behavior?
- **The Couple**
  - How will this behavior enhance marital connection?
  - How will the behavior impact marital intimacy?
- **The Context**
  - Is this behavior going to be practiced within the marriage?
  - Are you engaging in this behavior together, or is it done by one spouse alone?
- **The Motivation**
  - What is your motivation for engaging or not in this behavior?
  - What is your spouse's motivation for engaging or not in this behavior?
- **The Purpose**
  - What do you or your spouse hope to get by engaging in this behavior?
  - What need are you or your spouse trying to meet through this behavior?
- **The Biology/The Anatomy**
  - What are some scientific or medical views about this behavior?
  - How does this behavior affect the body?
- **Agape Love**
  - How do you express Agape love through this behavior?
  - Do you or your spouse consider this behavior selfish or self-seeking rather than an expression of Agape love (1 Cor. 13:4-7)?

Give Your Best, Not Leftovers

Making intimacy a priority is essential to a healthy marriage. You may want to consider making necessary changes to your lifestyle, such as managing work schedules, organizing schoolwork, and decreasing children's after-school activities. Perhaps, you may even need to hire a baby sitter more regularly to alleviate the load so that you can have more time alone with your spouse. Some experts even recommend that couples schedule a specific time for intimacy. They believe that if the time for intimacy is not prioritized, it will not happen. However, not everybody believes that scheduling time for sex is a good idea. Some think that scheduling intimacy can make sexual experiences too artificial or mechanic. Nevertheless, to some, scheduling intimacy may create a sense of anticipation and excitement and allow spouses to give their best to each other.

Communicate Openly before, during, and after Sexual Intimacy

Effective communication is vital for the couple to engage in and enjoy meaningful sexual intimacy. This intentional communication needs to occur before, during, and after sex.

Before – Heartfelt intimacy starts when a new day begins. All your daily interactions with your spouse contribute to your sexual intimacy. So, it is a good idea to appreciate and affirm your spouse first thing in the morning. Share your expectations and desires throughout the day and not assume that your spouse knows what you want. Obviously, as the years go by, you and your spouse will develop your unique verbal and non-verbal patterns of communication that facilitate your sexual encounters. Effective communication will also help you and your spouse deal with the initiation of the sexual intimacy and the times when one of you may not be in the mood and does not want to have sex.

During – You and your spouse will need to communicate during sex to let each other know what is bringing the most pleasure and what may be an annoyance. Again, such communication can be verbal or non-verbal. A spouse may also communicate how aroused he or she is and perhaps, even guide the other spouse gently. We recommend that you avoid making assumptions and clarify miscommunication with a great deal of kindness, understanding, and grace. Your negative actions, thoughts, and words during the sexual act can affect the moment negatively and decrease desire and passion, frustrating the overall experience.

After – What follows after the sexual encounter will depend on the time of the day and how tired you and your spouse may feel. Perhaps the only communication after having sex during the night will be non-verbal such as caressing, hugging, and kissing as you fall asleep at the sound of "That was amazing! I love you." However, it is important to realize that physiologically women tend to be more energized by the hormone oxytocin, whereas men become more tired, even

sleepy, due to the release of oxytocin after having sex. Louann Brizendine, a neu-
ropsychiatrist, in her book *The Male Brain*, explains that for women, the release
of oxytocin and dopamine creates in women a desire to cuddle and engage in
communication. On the other hand, for men the release of oxytocin makes them
sleepy. Consequently, women may feel neglected and disconnected with their
husbands even after sex.[44]

Showing kindness, love, and affection consistently after the sexual encounter needs to continue and not cease once the sexual need has been met. Such
consistency can potentially create a positive pattern. However, when the sexual
experience does not meet the couple's expectations, it is wise for the couple to
think of ways to reshape the next encounter. Therefore, communicating positively after any experience of unfulfilling sex is essential. Displaying patience and
affirmation will be critical to help address what happened during the sexual act
and create a sense of expectation for the next encounter.

Express Agape Love Daily

Agape love is selfless and other-serving. Consequently, to show Agape love,
consider letting go of a self-centered and self-serving attitude. In other words,
instead of mentally asking, "What is in it for me?" or "What will he/she do
for me?" you need to ask, "What can I do for my spouse?" or "Honey, what
do you need from me today?" To express Agape love, you need to become
aware of the areas in your marriage in which you tend to be self-centered.
Your Agape-love-filled interactions will set the stage for a joy-filled sexual
encounter with your spouse because emotional interaction precedes sexual
interaction.

We believe that an outpouring of Agape love can revolutionize any marriage. For example, if your spouse is having a stressful day, and shows anger and
frustration, keep in mind that these are only secondary emotions. The primary
emotion that your spouse is experiencing below the surface is hurt. Sometimes,
your spouse has emotional needs that only you can meet; hence, a wise action
step would be to comfort your spouse. You may ask your spouse to share what
is bothering him or her. Then, you can use active listening skills to validate your
spouse's feelings by empathizing with him or her. This is not the moment to try
to fix the situation, but to show concern and support. Therefore, you may even
ask your spouse what he or she needs from you at that moment. Your spouse
may simply need your listening ear and a hug.

Agape Love in Action

- At the start your day, you may ask yourself these questions:
  - How can I show love, care, and concern for my spouse?
  - How can I encourage and build up my spouse today?
  - How can I bless my spouse and meet my spouse's needs today?

As you answer the questions, decide on something specific you can do for your spouse and do it.

- Throughout the day, express your love to your spouse:
  - You may email, text, or call your spouse to give a word of affirmation and encouragement.
  - You may offer to help your spouse with household chores and errands.
  - You may ask, "How may I help you today?"
- At the end of the day, set a positive pace for the evening:
  - Pray for the evening and choose to be a blessing to your spouse.
  - Have a positive attitude. You may say the following to yourself: "I will not focus on myself, my needs, and my desires. Rather, I will focus on my spouse, and seek to meet my spouse's needs and desires."

Catch Your Spouse Doing Something Good

Couples frequently develop the habit of noticing and focusing on the faults and mistakes their spouses make. Instead, we need to look for the good things our spouse does. You may start by making a list of the good things or actions that you see your spouse perform for you no matter how small they might be.[45] Keep in mind that the Devil wants you to focus on the negative elements of your marriage, so resist him (James 4:7), and focus on the positive things your spouse does. Set a time each week to share your list with your spouse and to talk about the positive things you caught your spouse doing. By acknowledging and giving your spouse credit for his or her actions, you will help the relationship flourish and bring more love to the master bedroom.

—— Evaluating Your Multidimensional Intimacy ——

Now that we have finished our discussion on multidimensional intimacy, we would like to invite you to rate your overall marriage intimacy in the four areas.

Consider the descriptive statements below and choose the appropriate adverbs that best describe your experience. We believe this exercise will help you to continue to grow in your intimacy. By the way, the questions below start with the word "we" to reflect the idea of oneness in the marriage relationship.

1 – Never   2 – Seldom   3 – Sometimes   4 – Often   5 – Always

Emotional
- _____ We have open communication
- _____ We give each other our undivided attention
- _____ We seek to discover and meet each other's needs
- _____ We share our feelings and feel validated
- _____ We practice honest confession followed by genuine forgiveness

Intellectual
- _____ We support and encourage each other's educational journey
- _____ We respect each other's thoughts and opinions
- _____ When we disagree with each other, we discuss issues respectfully
- _____ We admire and respect each other's intelligence and wisdom
- _____ We agree on our vision, mission, and goals for our marriage

Physical
- _____ We enjoy the frequency and intensity of our sexual relationship
- _____ We are satisfied with each other's sensitivity in meeting our sexual needs
- _____ We believe that our sex life is improving
- _____ We like the way we approach each other sexually
- _____ We love passionately

Spiritual
- _____ We support and encourage each other's spiritual growth
- _____ We worship, pray, and study the Bible together
- _____ We serve God together
- _____ We are growing closer to God together
- _____ We count our blessings together

Now, let's check out the walk-in closet.

Check out the chapter video at:
www.grtep.com

Endnotes

1. Clifford Penner and Joyce J. Penner, *The Gift of Sex: A Guide to Sexual Fulfillment* (Nashville, TN: Thomas Nelson, 2003).

2. Andreas J. Köstenberger, *God, Marriage, and Family: Rebuilding the Biblical Foundation*, 2nd ed. (Wheaton, IL: Crossway Books, 2010), 25.

3. James Leo Garrett, *Systematic Theology: Biblical, Historical and Evangelical*, vol. 1 (Grand Rapids, MI: William B. Eerdmans, 1990).

4. Wayne Grudem, *Systematic Theology: An Introduction to Biblical Doctrine* (Grand Rapids, MI: Zondervan, 1994).

5. Robert Obach, *The Catholic Church on Marital Intercourse: From St. Paul to Pope John Paul II* (New York, NY: Lexington Books, 2008).

6. Penner and Penner, *The Gift of Sex*; Douglas E. Rosenau, *A Celebration of Sex: A Guide to Enjoying God's Gift of Sexual Intimacy* (Nashville, TN: Thomas Nelson, 2002); Douglas Rosenau and Deborah Neel, *Total Intimacy: A Guide to Loving by Color* (United States: Amazon Digital Services LLC, 2014); Christopher McCluskey and Rachel McCluskey, *When Two Become One: Enhancing Sexual Intimacy in Marriage* (Grand Rapids, MI: Fleming H. Revell, 2006); Ed Wheat and Gaye Wheat, *Intended for Pleasure: Sex Technique and Sexual Fulfillment in Christian Marriage*, revised (Grand Rapids, MI: Fleming H. Revell, 2010).

7. Kennedy L. Barker and John R. Kohlenberger III, *The Expositor's Bible Commentary: New Testament*, Abridged Ed. (Grand Rapids, MI: Zondervan, 1994).

8. The NAS New Testament Greek Lexicon, "Koite," accessed August 3, 2019, https://www.biblestudytools.com/lexicons/greek/nas/koite.html.

9. David L. Allen, *New International Version–The New American Commentary: An Exegetical and Theological Exposition of Holy Scripture, Hebrews* (Nashville, TN: B&H Publishing Group, 2010), 609, 35.

10. Mark T. Schaefer and David H. Olson, "Assessing Intimacy: The PAIR Inventory," *Journal of Marital and Family Therapy*, 1 (1981), 47–60.

11. Scott M. Stanley, Daniel Trathen, Savana McCain, and Milt Bryan, *A Lasting Promise: The Christian Guide to Fighting for Your Marriage*, New and Revised ed. (San Francisco, CA: Jossey-Bass, 2014).

12. Sue Johnson, *Hold Me Tight: Seven Conversations for a Lifetime of Love* (New York, NY: Little, Brown and Company, 2008).

13. Joe S. McIlhaney, Jr., and Freda McKissic Bush, *Hooked: The Brain Science on How Casual Sex Affects Human Development* (Chicago, IL: Moody Publishers, 2019).

14. Jerrold E. Greenberg, Clint E. Bruess, and Sara B. Oswalt, *Exploring the Dimensions of Human Sexuality*, 6th ed. (Burlington, MA: Jones and Bartlett Learning, 2016).

15. Greenberg, Bruess, and Oswalt, *Exploring the Dimensions of Human Sexuality*.

16. Greenberg, Bruess, and Oswalt, *Exploring the Dimensions of Human Sexuality*.

17. American Psychiatric Association (APA). *Diagnostic and Statistical Manual of Mental Disorders*, 5th ed. (Arlington, VA: American Psychiatric Publishing, 2013).

18. Maria del Mar Sánchez-Fuentes, Pablo Santos-Iglesias, and Juan C. Sierra. "A Systematic Review of Sexual Satisfaction," *International Journal of Clinical and Health Psychology* 14, no. 1 (2014): 67–75.

19. Dorota Kalka, "Sexual Satisfaction, Relationship Satisfaction, and Quality of Life in Individuals with Type 2 Diabetes: Evidence from Poland," *Sexuality and Disability* 36, no. 1 (March 2018): 69–86; Yasmin Hawkins et al., "Changes in Sexuality and Intimacy After the Diagnosis and Treatment of Cancer: The Experience of Partners in a Sexual Relationship with a Person with Cancer," *Cancer Nursing* 32, no. 4 (July/August 2009): 271–80; Elaine E. Steinke, Victoria Mosack, and Twyla J. Hill, "Change in Sexual Activity After a Cardiac Event: The Role of Medications, Comorbidity, and Psychosocial Factors," *Applied Nursing Research* 28 (2015): 244–55.

20. Yasmin Hawkins et al., "Changes in Sexuality and Intimacy," 271–80.

21. American Psychiatric Association (APA). *Diagnostic and Statistical Manual of Mental Disorders*.

22. Debra J. Brody, Laura A. Pratt, and Jeffery P. Hughes, "Prevalence of Depression Among Adults Aged 20 and Over: United States, 2013–2016," NCHS Data, no. 303 (February 2018): 1, accessed August 3, 2019, https://www.cdc.gov/nchs/products/databriefs/db303.htm.

23. National Institute of Mental Health, "Any Anxiety Disorder," accessed August 3, 2019, https://www.nimh.nih.gov/health/statistics/any-anxiety-disorder.shtml#part_155094.

24. Julie Corliss, "When an SSRI Medication Impacts Your Sex Life," *Harvard Health Publishing* (May 2017), accessed August 4, 2019, https://www.health.harvard.edu/womens-health/when-an-ssri-medication-impacts-your-sex-life.

25. Cathy O'Mullan et al., "Women's Experiences of Coping with the Sexual Side Effects of Antidepressant Medication," *Psychology and Health* 29, no.12 (2014): 1388–406.

26. Femke van den Brink et al., "Negative Body Attitudes and Sexual Dissatisfaction in Men: The Mediating Role of Body Self-Consciousness During Physical Intimacy," *Archives of Sexual Behavior* 47, no. 3, (April 2018): 697.

27. Brink et al., "Negative Body Attitudes and Sexual Dissatisfaction," 693–701.

28. Angela D. Weaver and E. Sandra Byers, "The Relationship among Body Image, Body Mass Index, Exercise, and Sexual Functioning in Heterosexual Women," *Psychology of Women Quarterly* 30, no. 4 (December 2006), 333–39.

29. Virginia M. Boquiren et al., "Sexual Functioning in Breast Cancer Survivors Experiencing Body Image Disturbance," *Journal of the Psychological, Social and Behavioral Dimensions of Cancer* 21, no. 1 (January 2016): 66–76.

30. Elizabeth A. Fallon, Brandonn S. Harris, and Paige Johnson, "Prevalence of Body Dissatisfaction among a United States Adult Sample" *Eating Behaviors* 15, no. 1 (January 2014): 151–58.

31. Noémie Bigras et al., "Cumulative Adverse Childhood Experiences and Sexual Satisfaction in Sex Therapy Patients: What Role for Symptom Complexity?" *The Journal of Sexual Medicine* 14, no. 3 (March 2017): 444–54.

32. Belle Liang, Linda M. Williams, and Jane A. Siegel, "Relational Outcomes of Childhood Sexual Trauma in Female Survivors: A Longitudinal Study," *Journal of Interpersonal Violence* 21, no. 1 (January 1, 2006): 42–57.

33. Marie-Pier, and Vaillancourt-Morel et al., "Intimacy Mediates the Relation Between Maltreatment in Childhood and Sexual and Relationship Satisfaction in Adulthood: A Dyadic Longitudinal Analysis," *Archives of Sexual Behavior* 48 (2019):803–14.

34. Cynthia A. Gram et al., "What Factors Are Associated with Reporting Lacking Interest in Sex and How do These Vary by Gender? Findings from the Third British National Survey on Sexual Attitudes and Lifestyles," *BMJ Open* 7, no. 9 (September 2017): 1–22.

35. Chance A. Bell and Frank D. Fincham, "Humility, Forgiveness, and Emerging Adult Female Romantic Relationships," *Journal of Marital and Family Therapy* 45, no. 1 (October 2017): 149–60.

36. Cynthia A. Gram et al., "What Factors Are Associated with Reporting Lacking Interest in Sex," 1–22.

37. James K. McNulty, Carolyn A. Wenner, and Terri D. Fisher, "Longitudinal Associations among Relationship Satisfaction, Sexual Satisfaction, and Frequency of Sex in Early Marriage," *Archives of Sexual Behavior* 45, no. 1 (January 2016): 85–97.

38. Cynthia A. Gram et al., "What Factors Are Associated with Reporting Lacking Interest in Sex," 1–22.

39. Adam C. Jones, W. David Robinson, and Ryan B. Seedall, "The Role of Sexual Communication in Couples' Sexual Outcomes: A Dyadic Path Analysis," *Journal of Marital and Family Therapy* 44, no. 4 (October 2018), 606–23.

40. Joshua B. Grubbs et al., "Pornography Problems Due to Moral Incongruence: An Integrative Model with a Systematic Review and Meta-Analysis," *Archives of Sexual Behavior* 48, no. 2 (2019): 397–415; S. L. Perry, and A. L. Whitehead, "Only Bad for Believers? Religion, Pornography Use, and Sexual Satisfaction among American Men," *Journal of Sex Research* 56, no. 1 (January 2018): 50–61.

41. Zackery A. Carter, "Married and Previously Married Men and Women's Perceptions of Communication on Facebook with the Opposite Sex: How Communicating

through Facebook Can Be Damaging to Marriages," *Journal of Divorce and Remarriage* 57, no. 1 (January 2016): 36–55.

42. Dave Carder, *Torn Asunder: Recovering from an Extramarital Affair* (Chicago, IL: Moody Publishers, 2010).

43. Carder, *Torn Asunder*, 53.

44. Louann Brizendine, *The Male Brain: A Breakthrough Understanding of How Men and Boys Think* (New York, NY: Three Rivers Press, 2010).

45. Gary M. Schultheis et al., *Couples Therapy Homework Planner* (Hoboken, NJ: John Wiley & Sons, 2010).

"...enter into [your] closet...and pray"
Matthew 6:6 (KJV)

A closet can be a multifunctional space. It can be much more than a place to store clothes, valuable items, and sentimental knickknacks. It can also be a place where people go to hide their intense emotions from others after an argument with a spouse, a family member, or a friend. However, for many Christians, the closet also has a powerful spiritual meaning related to prayer, as Jesus states, "enter into [your] closet...and pray" (Matt. 6:6 KJV).

© EPSTOCK/Shutterstock.com

Your master bedroom closet is a private place. You probably do not invite your guests into your master bedroom closet, do you? The closet is, for the most part, off-limits. Of course, unless there is a unique reason for you to invite someone there. Let us explain. Perhaps you have heard of or watched the Christian movie *War Room*.[1] In this movie, Priscilla Shirer, a popular Christian author and speaker, plays the role of a realtor, Elizabeth Jordan, who is experiencing marital struggles. In the movie, Elizabeth meets Miss Clara, an older woman who is selling her house. Miss Clara gives Elizabeth a house tour and shows her the closet she uses as a prayer room, or what she calls, *war room*. Throughout the movie, Miss Clara, a spiritually mature Christian, mentors Elizabeth on the importance of prayer and spiritual growth in the life of the believer. As you may have guessed, Elizabeth starts her own prayer closet and, through fervent prayer in her closet, experiences a transformation in her marriage with God's help.

All of this was possible because someone, namely Miss Clara, invited her into her prayer closet.

Jesus says, "But you, when you pray, go into your room [closet], and when you have shut your door, pray to your Father who *is* in the secret *place;* and your Father who sees in secret will reward you openly" (Matt. 6:6 NKJV). Reflecting on Jesus' words and on the closet metaphor as displayed in the movie *War Room,* we identify four central truths. First, we need to protect and prioritize our personal time of spiritual devotion to God. Second, growing in our intimacy with God is a privilege we have as children of God. Third, we are called to pray for our family, community, country, and the whole world regularly. Fourth, a consistent, private prayer life can have a powerful impact, including on your own marriage.

In this chapter, we use the closet metaphor to represent a couple's spiritual growth. We discuss how people view religion and spirituality in the U.S. Then, we explore spiritual growth, spiritual formation, spiritual disciplines, and different ways couples can grow together in their spiritual life. We conclude that success in marriage and life is birthed, ignited, and sustained by our spiritual growth in the closet.

Religion and Spirituality

Religion and spirituality are not the same things. In general, the term religion represents people's attempt to reach the divine. It can also refer to a structured or organized belief system and practices that a group of people uses to understand or relate to the divine or the supernatural. The word religion has its roots in two Latin words: *religare,* which implies binding, and *relegere,* which refers to observing.[2] In this sense, religion implies a set of regulations and standards a person must live by or a systematic way of practicing one's faith. In other words, religion is humanity's attempt to connect with the divine by observing laws and regulations and fulfilling expectations believed to be required to gain access to and please the divine.

Spirituality is more complicated to define since people approach it from multiple perspectives. Spirituality in the U.S. includes religious syncretism, which is a blending of many beliefs and practices from various religions. Consequently, individuals tend to engage in a process of customizing their spirituality by adopting spiritual practices they prefer from various faith traditions, thus creating a personalized spirituality.

When researchers look at spirituality, they focus on four key aspects: belief, practice, awareness, and experience.[3] For instance, the Public Religion Research Institute (PRRI), "measured spirituality using self-reported experiences of being connected to something larger than oneself . . . [and] religiosity using frequency of religious attendance and the personal importance of religion."[4] Interestingly, Americans fell into the following four categories:

- 29% [were] both spiritual and religious;
- 18% [were] spiritual but not religious;
- 22% [were] not spiritual but religious; and
- 31% [were] neither spiritual nor religious.[5]

In the same year, the Barna Group released a couple of reports about a survey among adults in the U.S. which identified two groups of individuals in relationship to Jesus, church, religion, and spirituality. The first group was labeled *love Jesus but not the church*[6] and the second group was labeled *spiritual but not religious*.[7] The first group *love Jesus but not the church* includes people who identify themselves as Christians and consider their faith as an important part of their life; however, they reject the church as an institution. These individuals may have decided no longer to attend church because they experienced church wounds, or because they believe they do not need the church to have a relationship with God.[8] The second group *spiritual but not religious* is made up of people who view themselves as religious, but do not consider their religious faith as an important element in their life, or may not have any religion at all. They may even create their own spirituality by engaging in a selective blending of beliefs and practices from different religions.[9] Thus, in light of this current context in our country, our focus will be on spiritual growth and Christian spirituality from a biblical perspective.

Contrary to an individualized spirituality, Christian spirituality is richly rooted in the Bible and in Christian history. It has several unique features. First, it is Trinitarian with an emphasis on the Father, the Son, and the Holy Spirit. Second, it is Christological or Christ-centered because it emphasizes the saving work of Christ on the cross.

 Christian Spirituality

- It is Trinitarian.
- It focuses on the saving work of Christ.
- It teaches that the Holy Spirit indwells Christians.

Third, Christian spirituality is Holy Spirit-filled because it asserts that the Holy Spirit indwells believers and empowers them to live the Christian life.[10] Thus, Christian spirituality is distinct from a customized, personalized, or secularized spirituality.

——— Defining Spiritual Growth and Spiritual Formation ———

As we mentioned in Chapter 5, spiritual growth is the process of becoming more like Jesus in character, attitude, and behavior. Therefore, it is a transformational process that does not happen automatically or quickly. Spiritual growth is the result of an intentional relationship with the Lord. Other terms used for spiritual growth are spiritual formation and sanctification. Spiritual formation is the process in which "God spiritually forms the believers into the image of Christ."[11] Sanctification is a theological term that refers to the work of God in the lives of believers through the Holy Spirit empowering them to become holy and grow in the likeness of Christ.[12] Spiritual growth happens when you enter into your closet metaphorically.

A growing relationship with the Lord involves practicing spiritual disciplines consistently. Spiritual disciplines are "practices found in Scripture that promote spiritual growth among believers in the gospel of Jesus Christ."[13] Interestingly, popular author and pastor John Ortberg in his book, *The Life You've Always Wanted*, goes a step further and states that a spiritual discipline is "any activity that can help [Christians] gain power to live life as Jesus taught and modeled it."[14] We agree with Ortberg and believe that engaging in practices exemplified by Christ such as worship, prayer, meditation on Scriptures, fasting, and serving people, among others, is part of the pursuit of growing in godliness (1 Tim. 4:7). As a result, these practices lead us to know God more intimately and to live a life that pleases Him through the power of the Holy Spirit.

It is not surprising that God is interested in our attitude when we engage in spiritual practices. A checklist of behaviors cannot measure true spiritual growth because God looks at our hearts. In fact, we may attend church, but if we are not worshipping in "spirit and in truth" (John 4:24 NKJV), then the experience is simply an activity that gets a checkmark. Therefore, we must be fully focused, devoted, and engaged with the Lord through the spiritual disciplines. As the Lord says through prophet Isaiah, "These people come near to me with their mouth and honor me with their lips, but their hearts are far from me. Their worship of me is based on merely human rules they have been taught" (Isa. 29:13 NIV).

Christian Spirituality: Issues and Extremes

You may have heard various opinions or positions on spiritual growth. They may range from a prescriptive approach that can lead to a legalistic faith or to a permissive approach that leads to viewing God's grace almost as a license to do whatever people want without any consequences.[15] You may also have heard people say that the church is full of hypocrites. Usually, the person who makes such a remark is using it as an excuse for not attending church. As we know, the word hypocrite refers to someone who does not live by the faith he or she professes. For example, in Matthew 23, Jesus condemned the Pharisees and called them hypocrites multiple times. Jesus' main charge against the Pharisees was that they focused on outward behavioral practices, rather than inward soul change. Since we do not want to be hypocrites, we must continue to ask God to help us live lives that are congruent with what we believe.

The accurate measure of spiritual growth needs to be how we display the fruit of the Spirit in our daily interactions with our spouse and others. The "fruit of the Spirit is love, joy, peace, patience, kindness, goodness, faithfulness, gentleness, self-control" (Gal. 5:22–23 NASB). Dave Earley in the book *Spiritual Formation Is...: How to Grow in Jesus with Passion and Confidence* states that "as the life of Jesus streams through the disciple, the personality of Jesus will be formed in the disciple. The more of Jesus that flows through you, the more like Jesus you will be."[16] Similarly, Ortberg explains spiritual formation as having a "well-ordered heart"[17] or a well-ordered soul. He says,

> God designed us so that our choices, our thoughts and desires, and our behavior would be in perfect harmony with each other and would be powered by an unbroken connection with God, in perfect harmony with him and with all of his creation. That's a well-ordered soul.[18]

Imagine you and your spouse, as Jesus stated, entering in your closet and growing spiritually together. As you and your spouse experience inner changes, your attitude and behaviors toward each other and people will also change and reveal the Christian virtues that, ultimately, reflect the character of Christ. When this happens, real spiritual growth takes place.

Becoming Spiritually Mature and Wise

All Christians are called to grow in the Lord (2 Pet. 3:18). Growing spiritually will lead you to become mature and wise. Let us think for a moment about what it means to be a wise person. According to scholars, *hokmâh*, the Hebrew word most often translated as wisdom, has a broad meaning that includes intellectual ability, wise judgments, discernment, trade skills, and discretion in speech and behavior.[19] A central feature of wisdom in the Old Testament includes knowing how to live well or the ability to live skillfully. Consequently, to be wise does not merely mean to accumulate knowledge, though having knowledge is an essential part of being wise. To sum up succinctly, to be mature and wise means "living a day-to-day godly life in a complicated world."[20]

 As a Christian, obedience and the practice of the spiritual disciplines become more natural as we follow the prompting of the Holy Spirit who dwells in us.

The Bible clearly teaches that God is the ultimate source of wisdom and that He grants wisdom to those who trust Him (Prov. 2:6). James writes, "If any of you lacks wisdom, let him ask of God, who gives to all liberally and without reproach, and it will be given to him" (James 1:5 NKJV). For instance, God granted Solomon vast and comprehensive wisdom (1 Kings 4:29–30). Moreover, it is reassuring to know that we can ask and receive wisdom from God. However, becoming wise or mature involves various factors, rather than a one-time miraculous experience like we see in Solomon's life.

According to Scriptures, becoming wise starts with the fear of the Lord (Prov. 9:10). Once this fear or reverence for God is in place, we see other factors emerging and interacting with each other to manifest wisdom in the life of the person (Exod. 31:1–5; Dan. 5:11–12). We also note that these factors do not come together in a structured order. As Christians, obedience and a desire to practice the spiritual disciplines become more natural as we follow the prompting of the Holy Spirit who dwells in us.

The synergy of our biblical knowledge along with our knowledge in other areas of life helps us make sense of the spiritual and material worlds. Consequently, wisdom becomes the evidence of Christ living in us. Once we allow the Holy Spirit to take control of our lives, we will have an intrinsic desire to obey God and practice the spiritual disciplines.

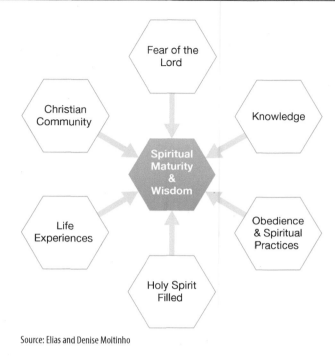

Source: Elias and Denise Moitinho

Spiritual Maturity and Wisdom Start with God

"The fear of the Lord is the beginning of wisdom" (Prov. 9:10 NIV) is a message that carries the idea of engaging in a reverent relationship with God. Fear is respect, acknowledgment of God's authority and sovereignty. It is not the type of fear that makes us want to be away from Him; on the contrary, it helps us realize who we are and who God is. It brings us to our knees in adoration.

Spiritual Maturity and Wisdom Require Knowledge

To be wise, in general, we need knowledge about specific areas of life. For instance, when we are making a decision to buy a house, we will need knowledge about the neighborhood, the house, and the mortgage loan, among other things, to make the correct decision. A prudent person makes decisions based on knowledge (Prov. 13:16). Also, in terms of spiritual growth, we gain knowledge from the Lord about His character and His will. As we read about

God in the Bible, listen to sermons, and participate in Bible studies, the Holy Spirit teaches us and helps us grow in understanding God, His creation, and ourselves.

Spiritual Maturity and Wisdom Require Obedience

Once we hear from God, the next step is to obey, to put into practice what we have learned. As we mentioned in Chapter 2, Jesus concluded his sermon on the mount with the statement that the wise person is one who hears His teaching and puts it into practice (Matt. 7:24).

Spiritual Maturity and Wisdom Call for a Life Filled with the Holy Spirit

As believers, we need to embrace the presence of God in our lives and the truth that we are now a temple of the Holy Spirit (1 Cor. 6:19). We are jars of clay holding an amazing treasure in us (2 Cor. 4:7); *Immanuel*, which means "God with us," is a reality in our lives (Matt.1:23 NIV).

Spiritual Maturity and Wisdom Include Learning from Life Experiences

Reflecting on our life experiences helps us grow (Prov. 24:30–24). For instance, Solomon says, "When I saw, I reflected upon it; I looked, and received instruction" (Prov. 24:32 NASB). So, when we observe life events and circumstances, and reflect upon them, we gain insights and learn from them. Additionally, the Holy Spirit living in us helps us connect the dots and find meaning that transcends the temporal level. We also gain insight into life as we walk with wise people (Prov. 13:20).

Spiritual Maturity and Wisdom Are Cultivated in the Christian Community

Church attendance and church participation may fill our calendar, but they do not automatically lead to spiritual growth. Similarly, a person may have been a Christian for a long time, but may not necessarily be spiritually mature. It is only when church attendance and participation translate into a meaningful relationship with God and others that spiritual growth and wisdom can flourish. Gordon Johnston, in his chapter in the book *Foundations of Spiritual Formation*, reminds us that the Christian community creates the context for wise interactions, character building, meaningful accountability, and a strong support system.[21] Thus, being actively engaged in the body of Christ is essential for spiritual maturity and wisdom.

Discovering Your Approach to Spiritual Growth

We agree with Ortberg when he says that, "spiritual transformation cannot be orchestrated or controlled, but neither is it a random adventure.... We need a plan."[22] Christians can use a variety of plans or strategies for their spiritual growth. However, the most important thing is that these strategies are Christ-centered. Therefore, entering into the closet (Matt. 6:6) to experience God and pursue spiritual growth may look different for each person.

As a couple, you and your spouse may have different personalities and possibly different learning styles. So, it is normal for you to prefer and use different strategies for spiritual growth. For instance, you may prefer to pray in the morning, whereas your spouse may prefer to pray in the evening. You may enjoy reading the Bible daily; your spouse may enjoy reading Christian devotional books. Still, your spouse may find encouragement listening to Christian music, while you may feel empowered when listening to sermons, and so forth. Sometimes you will engage in these activities with your spouse or other Christians, and sometimes you will engage them by yourself.

Let us consider a few more examples. You may prefer memorizing Bible verses because memorization comes easily to you. However, your spouse may have difficulty memorizing Bible verses. You may have the habit of getting up at 5:00 am to pray, but your spouse may not, and may prefer to be in prayer throughout the day. You and your spouse may not engage in a prolonged fast, but you both may engage in partial fasting. As you can see, there are multiple ways to connect with God. The main point is to be connected with Him in spirit and truth.

All spiritual practices mentioned in the Bible are ways to draw us near to God. Again, some people prefer to engage in spiritual activities in groups such as worship in church or Bible study groups, while others may prefer to have a devotional time and moments of solitude with God. So, the bottom line is that we must consider the intent and motivation. The intent must be to connect with our Heavenly Father and experience change in our lives, to abandon sin, and to live a Christ-centered life. The motivation needs to be intrinsic within our soul.

For instance, as a couple, you may also feel the prompting of the Holy Spirit to engage in a specific spiritual discipline such as fasting.

From Stressed to Blessed

Everyone wants to live his or her life to its fullest (John 10:10) and experience success. Unfortunately, many couples are overwhelmed by stress in their attempt to win at life in the areas they deem relevant to them. In their effort to climb the corporate ladder or keep up with the Joneses, they may end up neglecting each other emotionally, physically, and even spiritually. Notably, the Bible speaks numerous times about the importance of walking with God and meditating on His word to live a blessed and successful life.

In the Bible, a blessed person is a successful person. In fact, at the beginning of Psalm 1, King David describes the blessed person as a godly person who "does not walk in step with the wicked or stand in the way that sinners take or sit in the company of mockers" (Ps. 1:1 NIV). Indeed, this person displays God-honoring ethical conduct. David adds that this person delights in God's Word and meditates on it day and night. As a result, the person "is like a tree planted by streams of water, which yields its fruit in season and whose leaf does not wither — whatever they do prospers" (Ps. 1:3 NIV). Undoubtedly, this is the most profound picture of productivity, resilience, and real success.

Psalm 1 also provides a vivid picture that to be blessed is to be productive. To be highly productive means, "to succeed beyond standard norms, consistently over the long term."[23] The blessed person is *highly productive*. He or she is like a tree planted in the right resourceful spot, that is, by streams of water and for this reason, it always gets the nourishment it needs for growth. Additionally, the blessed person meditates on the Word of God and can grow to the point of producing good fruit. This fruit means engaging in God-honoring behaviors and activities. So, we encourage you to ask yourself what kind of fruit or results you want to see in your life and marriage.

Next, Psalm 1 implies that to be blessed means to be an *energetic and resilient* person. This resilience is exemplified by the fact that the leaf does not wither, it does not lose its color, and it does not dry out. Think about it. The popular phrase *rise and grind* means that you get up and overwork, but we believe that having a strong work-ethic does not need to make you wither. When you are meditating on God's Word, you are not going to lose spiritual stamina and vitality. On the contrary, you are going to enrich your life spiritually, mentally, relationally, and emotionally. You become energetic and resilient and ready to face life's challenges together with your spouse. Moreover, meditating on God's Word needs to be a part of your self-care plan, as discussed in Chapter 5.

Finally, Psalm 1 reveals that you can become a *successful person*. As we know, society's definition of success inevitably includes money, fame, and popularity. However, in the Bible, success means being faithful and obe-

 Growing spiritually together does not happen by chance. It involves a certain level of intentionality.

dient to God in fulfilling your God-given purpose and mission (Matt. 25:23). Ultimately, it does not necessarily imply financial blessings or worldly success. The verse says that "whatever" the blessed person does prospers. The word "whatever" includes a multitude of activities from holding a job to building a family. The word "prosper" evokes words such as excel, expand, succeed, and even surpass. Interestingly, this is the same message that God gave Joshua when he replaced Moses as the leader of Israel. "Keep this Book of the Law always on your lips; meditate on it day and night, so that you may be careful to do everything written in it. Then you will be prosperous and successful" (Jos.1:8 NIV). The same Joshua proclaimed, "But as for me and my family, we will serve the Lord" (Jos. 24:15 TLB). Accordingly, the path to success in life and in marriage certainly includes meditating and being grounded upon the Word of God.

We believe you can go from stressed to blessed as you allow God to make you a productive, energetic, resilient, and successful person. By placing your relationship with your spouse under God's care, you can grow, thrive, flourish, and excel in building your dream marriage. We encourage you to continue to meditate on God's Word and allow Him to plant you by living streams of water.

Growing Spiritually as a Couple

Growing spiritually together does not happen by chance. It involves a certain level of intentionality. For us, this experience started over 30 years ago at the very beginning of our relationship as a couple. When we first met, I (Elias) was involved in the children's ministry of the International Baptist Church in Rio de Janeiro, Brazil. Then, Denise gladly joined me. Some years later, we moved to the U.S. to study at a seminary. As soon as we arrived in Texas, together we volunteered with the youth ministry of a local church. A few years later, I (Elias) became the interim pastor and then the pastor of a church in Ennis, Texas, and we found ourselves serving together again. Next, during the time I (Elias) was working as an assistant professor at Southwestern Baptist Theological Seminary, Denise was the Mother's Day Out program director at a local church. We intentionally served together in the children's ministry and family ministry of our church. Eventually, we moved to Lynchburg, and together we have led family ministry in our church. Notice that we purposefully used the word *together* multiple times in this paragraph. We found that serving together has been key to our spiritual intimacy.

As we reflect on these 30 years of serving the Lord together as a couple, we want to share with you a few words of encouragement and tips. We hope they will inspire you to continue growing in your intimacy with God and with each other.

Source: Elias and Denise Moitinho

Growing Together through Bible Study

Several years ago, a popular marketing campaign asked a simple question, "Got Milk?" The goal of the campaign was to emphasize the nutritional value of milk and, obviously, to encourage more people to buy and drink milk. As we know, milk is vital to our diet and growth since it provides many essential nutrients to our bodies. Peter, inspired by the Holy Spirit, uses the metaphor of milk to represent the Word of God (1 Pet. 1:23–2:1–3). He challenges Christians to be like newborn babies and crave spiritual milk or the Word of God to grow and mature. As you may know, a newborn wants milk every 2 hours. Similarly, Peter admonishes Christians to have an intense and eager desire to read, study, and meditate on God's Word regularly.

Tips
- Protect your individual and couple daily devotional time with God.
- Be consistent in your Bible reading and worship.
- Share with your spouse what you are learning from your Bible study.
- Encourage your spouse with scriptures. You may want to text your spouse a Bible verse.
- Choose a Christian devotional book to study together.

Growing Together through Worship

We believe that worship is an encounter with God in which we acknowledge and praise Him for who He is, what He has done, and what He will do for us. In worship, we also acknowledge who we are: sinners in need of forgiveness. This definition certainly has a biblical foundation.

When we think of the vision prophet Isaiah had of God's throne room (Isa. 6:1–8), we see worship unfolding. The prophet Isaiah saw God's majesty and heard the angels praising God "Holy, holy, holy is the Lord Almighty" (Isa. 6:3 NIV). During his vision of the transcendent God, he realized the greatness and the personal character of God. When he was in God's presence, he experienced the conviction of his own sin. He realized he was unworthy to be in the presence of such a holy God. However, in God's presence, he experienced forgiveness and cleansing. Isaiah's experience ended with his response to God's call of service. This is indeed a true picture of worship.

In our house, we have a 6-inch reflector telescope that allows us to see a glimpse of the majestic and magnificent universe. From our backyard, we see the craters on the moon, Saturn with the rings, and even Jupiter, though these planets appear very tiny in our telescope. However, when we think of the Hubble telescope that has been exploring the vastness of the Universe and taking astonishing pictures of amazing galaxies, we recognize the greatness and the majesty of our God. Therefore, through worship we can witness God's greatness, majesty, and holiness while simultaneously becoming aware of our finiteness, brokenness, and sinfulness. The beautiful thing is that you and your spouse can worship God together and enjoy this beautiful experience as a couple.

Tips
- Sing with all your heart every time you and your spouse gather for worship (much like the angels).
- Examine your personal life and confess your sin to God.
- Practice confessing your sins to one another, in this case, your spouse.
- Share with your spouse what you heard from God through worship.
- Respond to God when He speaks to you as individuals and as a couple.

Growing Together through Prayer

Prayer is communicating with God, our heavenly Father. According to the Pew Research Center, "More than half (55%) of Americans say they pray every day,"[24] although it is not clear to whom they are praying. As Christians, we pray to God in the name of Jesus. While petition is the most common type of prayer, we cannot reduce prayer to merely asking God for blessings. Prayer is more than asking God to meet our needs and wants. Unfortunately, many Christians view prayer as a last resort or as a means to ask God to provide for their needs. Nevertheless, many other types of prayer exist, such as praise, thanksgiving, intercession, and confession. These types of prayer need to be part of a couple's prayer life as well.

We cannot pass the opportunity to encourage you to make time to pray together as a couple. We understand that if you do not have the habit of praying together in your home, it may feel a little awkward and even artificial the first time. The most important thing is to start. Our experience is that God always shows up (Matt. 18:20). At first, you may start with short prayers. Eventually, as you and your spouse get more involved in the practice of praying together, you can pray for various issues and areas of your lives. Consider praying for each other, your children, members of the extended family, your church leaders, friends, neighbors, co-workers, and government leaders. As you can see, the list can grow very quickly.

Throughout our marriage, we have grown spiritually together through prayer. We remember when we had been waiting for a final answer regarding our coming to the U.S. to study. We remember being inspired by the story of King Hezekiah's prayer when he presented a letter before the Lord (2 Kings 19:14). Similarly, we both sat on our bed, and held the U.S. school paperwork in our hands, presented it to God in prayer together. I (Denise) remember feeling an intense presence of God in the room. We knew we were not alone. God miraculously opened the way for us to study at Southwestern Baptist Theological Seminary.

Tips
- Invite your spouse to pray together with you.
- Be consistent and make praying together a daily habit.
- Decide on the best time for you and your spouse to pray together.
- Send your spouse a voice message with a prayer.
- Text a prayer to your spouse.

Growing Together through Service to the Church

A Bible story that helps us see the need to be involved in Christian ministry is the story of the four men who brought a paralyzed friend to Jesus (Mark 2:12; Luke 5:17–26). Interestingly, the four men became aware of the physical need of the paralyzed man, but Jesus addressed the man's spiritual need for forgiveness first before he healed him. You can clearly see that these men recognized and believed that Jesus was the answer to the paralyzed friend's physical problem. Finally, their compassion for him resulted in creative action to take him to Jesus. Thus, we see three foundational principles in this story. We call them the ABC's of real ministry. *A* stands for awareness of the needs in our community and in the world. *B* reminds us that Jesus is the only answer to sin and the hurt and pain in the world. *C* emphasizes compassion in action.

We believe that all Christians have the responsibility to serve the Lord. Couples can serve together. In fact, that has been what we have done throughout our marriage. Serving the Lord together has brought us closer because it allows us to have multiple conversations about the needs we see around us

ABC's of Real Ministry

A - Awareness of the needs in our community and in the world
B - Belief that Jesus is the only answer
C - Compassion in action

and how Jesus can meet those needs. It also helps us brainstorm ways that we can become part of the solution by serving through our church or other ministries.

Tips
- Talk with your spouse about the needs you see in your neighborhood, community at large, and even in the world.
- Pray together and ask God to show you and your spouse how as a couple you can join Him in what He is already doing.
- Put your compassion in action by becoming involved as a couple in ministries through your church or Christian organizations.
- Pray together for a ministry that God has for you as a couple.
- Get out of your comfort zone and invite your spouse to serve together.

Growing Together through Spiritual Conversations

We enjoy having what we call "spiritual or theological conversations." Doing so does not mean that we are more spiritual than other Christian couples. In fact, we believe that we need to grow spiritually each and every day. During our spiritual conversations, we talk about how we understand God's purpose for our lives as a couple so that we do not "run aimlessly" as Paul says (2 Cor. 9:26 NIV). We want to be focused on the purpose God has for our lives and not waste any precious time. For example, the idea of writing this book happened as a result of multiple spiritual conversations while going for walks in our neighborhood. Similarly, many other ministries that we have been involved through our local church or Christian organizations have been the result of our spiritual conversations. We realize that you and your spouse may be at different places in your spiritual location in relationship to God. However, we encourage you and your spouse to continue engaging or start engaging in these types of conversations.

Tips
- Start spiritual conversations with your spouse without having the pressure to come up with goals, plans, or solutions.
- Talk about how you and your spouse see God moving in and through your lives.
- Talk about the needs (physical, material, emotional, relational, etc.) that you and your spouse have become aware of recently.
- Talk about your vision and mission statements for your marriage (Chapter 1).
- Listen to your spouse attentively and make spiritual connections.

Growing Together through Spiritual Warfare

Being a Christian in a world that is hostile to God and His word is challenging. Christians deal with all sorts of temptations and face daily life challenges like anyone else in the world. However, thankfully, living the Christian life is not something we do alone and much less on our own strength and power. The Bible encourages us to be strong through complete reliance on the power of God (Eph. 6:10). The reality is that every Christian is engaged in an invisible war in which Satan has plans to attack him or her (Eph. 6:11). We need to be careful and avoid extremes. On one end, some people see the devil in everything; in other words, they over-spiritualize life's challenges and dilute personal responsibility. Consequently, they have an attitude that conveys "the devil made me do it" message. On the other end, there is the extreme of complete ignorance, denial, or even rejection of the biblical teaching regarding the reality of spiritual warfare. Therefore, you must take a biblical perspective and consider Paul's words that we must "Put on the full armor of God, so that you will be able to stand firm against the schemes of the devil" (Eph. 6:11 NASB). God wants you and your spouse to be strong in the Lord, be aware of this invisible reality, be fully armored, and ready for battle.

Tips
- Read about spiritual warfare and discuss it with your spouse.
- Be part of a prayer group.
- Invite your spouse to listen to testimonies on spiritual warfare together.
- Participate in prayer walks with your spouse.
- Ask God to help you understand that your fight is not against flesh and blood, but against the enemy of your soul.

The closet can indeed become a powerful place in your dream home. When you and your spouse make time to be with the Lord and engage the various spiritual disciplines, you can experience God's love and grace in a meaningful way. As a result, you not only grow closer to God, but also closer to each other.

Now, let's check out the kids' room.

Endnotes

1. *War Room*, directed by Alex Kendrick, produced by Stephen Kendrick (Affirm Films, 2015), DVD (Sony pictures, 2015).

2. Harvey J. Sindima, *Introduction to Religious Studies* (Lanham, MA: University Press of America, 2009), 157.

3. Michael B. King and Harold G. Koenig, "Conceptualising Spirituality for Medical Research and Health Service Provision," *BMC Health Services Research* 9, no. 116 (2009): 1–7.

4. Art Raney, Daniel Cox, Robert P. Jones, "Searching for Spirituality in the U.S.: A New Look at the Spiritual but Not Religious," *PRRI* (2017), accessed September 26, 2019, https://www.prri.org/research/religiosity-and-spirituality-in-america/.

5. Raney, Cox, Jones, "Searching for Spirituality in the U.S."

6. Barna Group, "Meet Those Who Love Jesus but Not the Church," 2017, accessed August 31, 2019, https://www.barna.com/research/meet-love-jesus-not-church/.

7. Barna Group, "Meet the Spiritual but Not Religious," 2017, accessed August 31, 2019, https://www.barna.com/research/meet-spiritual-not-religious/.

8. Barna Group, "Meet Those Who Love Jesus but Not the Church."

9. Barna Group "Meet the Spiritual but Not Religious."

10. Bruce A. Demarest, ed., *Four Views on Christian Spirituality* (Grand Rapids, MI: Zondervan, 2012).

11. Paul Pettit, ed., *Foundations of Spiritual Formation: A Community Approach to Becoming Like Christ* (Grand Rapids, MI: Kregel Publications, 2008), 44.

12. Millard J. Erickson, *Christian Theology*, 3rd ed. (Grand Rapids, MI: Baker Academics, 2013).

13. Donald S. Whitney, *Spiritual Disciplines for the Christian Life* (Colorado Springs, CO: NavPress, 2014), 4.

14. John Ortberg, *The Life You've Always Wanted: Spiritual Disciplines for Ordinary People* (Grand Rapids, MI: Zondervan, 2002).

15. Kenneth Boa, *Conformed to His Image: Biblical and Practical Approaches to Spiritual Formation* (Grand Rapids, MI: Zondervan, 2001), 503–507.

16. Rod Dempsey and Dave Earley, *Spiritual Formation Is...: How to Grow in Jesus with Passion and Confidence* (Nashville, TN: B&H Publishing Group, 2018).

17. John Ortberg, *Soul Keeping: Caring for the Most Important Part of You* (Grand Rapids, MI: Zondervan, 2014), 66.

18. Ortberg, *Soul Keeping*, 66.

19. Donald K. Berry, *An Introduction to Wisdom and Poetry of the Old Testament.* (Nashville, TN: Broadman and Holman Publishers, 1995); Dianne Bergant, *Israel's Wisdom Literature: A Liberation-Critical Reading* (Minneapolis, MN: Fortress Press, 1997); Thomas B. Maston, *Words of Wisdom* (Nashville, TN: Broadman Press, 1984).

20. J. Scott Duvall and J. Daniel Hays, *Grasping God's Word: A Hands-on Approach to Reading, Interpreting, & Applying the Bible*, 2nd ed. (Grand Rapids, MI: Zondervan, 2005), 389.

21. Pettit, ed., *Foundations of Spiritual Formation*, 71–102.

22. Ortberg, *The Life You've Always Wanted*, 200.

23. Brendon Burchard, *High Performance Habits: How Extraordinary People Become That Way* (Carlsbad, CA: Hay House: 2017), 14.

24. Michael Lipka, "Five Facts About Prayer," *Pew Research Center* (2016), accessed August 31, 2019, http://www.pewresearch.org/fact-tank/2016/05/04/5-facts-about-prayer/.

CHAPTER 10

The Kids' Room: Parenting with Purpose

"Rules without relationship lead to rebellion."
Josh McDowell

© Yuganov Konstantin/Shutterstock.com

The kids' room is often a magical and fun place filled with toys, child-size furniture, and colorful cartoon characters. As children grow older, super-heroes, famous athletes, or singers may replace the cartoon characters. Nevertheless, no matter how the kids' room is decorated, it is an essential place where young children take naps, play, and, hopefully, sleep all night.

Even couples who do not have children may often consider having a room they can transform into a kids' room someday. They understand that this room is not only for their children to sleep and keep their belongings, but also a place where they can spend meaningful time interacting, playing, and talking with their children.

The kids' room is also a place where children learn how to share their space and toys with their siblings. It is a place where preteens and teenagers create their own private world. Some teenagers even post a "do not enter" sign on their bedroom door as a way of marking their territory. Sadly, research shows that as children get older, parents tend to spend less time with them.[1]

In this chapter, we use the kids' room as a metaphor for parenting, and we draw from the behavioral sciences and biblical principles to discuss how to parent with purpose. Even if you are not a parent yet, we encourage you to continue reading to gain valuable insights. We briefly describe child development and share ways for you to connect with your child meaningfully. Then, we explore a biblical perspective on parenting, address parenting styles, and discuss some challenges children and families may face. We conclude with a description of intentional and relational parenting as the key to parenting with purpose.

Life with Children and Marital Happiness

Children are a tremendous blessing from God (Ps.127:3), and they indeed enrich a marriage. However, they may also become a source of stress in the couple's lives. Research suggests that marital satisfaction tends to decline during the parenting years.[2] For instance, research shows that both the U-shaped curve of marital happiness and the U-shaped curve of life satisfaction indicate that couples experience higher levels of marital satisfaction at the beginning of their marriage before having children. Then, during the child-raising years and midlife, their marital happiness and life satisfaction tend to be lower, and eventually, they increase again.[3] Obviously, this is not every couple's experience. However, studies seem to show this pattern consistently over the years.

Our goal is not to present the parenting years only as difficult times. Instead, we want to ensure that you are fully aware of the possible challenges ahead when you start having children. Therefore, if you are already facing tough parenting issues, we hope this chapter will provide you with encouragement and hope. Unfortunately, many couples neglect their marital relationship while raising their children because they make their children the center of their affection. Therefore, we encourage you to avoid having a child-centered marriage, a marriage in which the spouses' primary focus is on raising their children while neglecting the marital relationship.

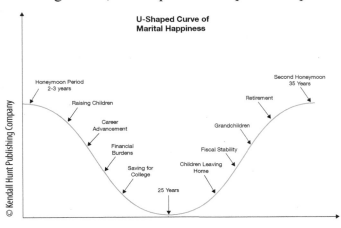

———————— ## Understanding Your Child's Development ————————

When our children were growing up, we developed the habit of recording their height (physical growth) on the doorposts of their bedrooms. From time to time, we would have them stand with their backs to the doorpost, and we would methodically draw a line above their heads and date it. Then we would proudly celebrate with them each inch they had grown.

It is not an exaggeration to say that to us, our children's growth happened in a blink of an eye. It seems that it was yesterday when we were spoon-feeding them or watching them learn how to crawl and walk. Together, as a couple, we went through many significant milestones in their lives. Obviously, besides growing physically, they were also growing psychologically, socially, and spiritually. These areas of growth were all significant to our family.

Since children are precious like a multifaceted diamond, we use the biopsychosocial-spiritual approach to discuss a few essential developmental characteristics of children. You may recall that we discussed this model in Chapters 1 and 5. We use this holistic approach here as well because we believe parents need to be aware of what is happening with their children in all developmental areas. Parents need to have realistic expectations and use age-appropriate teaching and discipline methods. Interestingly, the Bible describes Jesus' development holistically when it says, "Jesus grew in wisdom and stature, and in favor with God and man" Luke 2:52 (NIV). Therefore, we can see that Jesus grew in these four areas: physical (stature), psychological (wisdom), social (in favor with man), and spiritual (in favor with God). Considering this is not a textbook on child development, our discussion will be brief.

Physical Development

Children experience a significant growth spurt during infancy and puberty. Since the normal physical development of children happens quite fast, parents need to be in tune with the different phases of physiological transformation that children experience. Children's dramatic growth influences all the other areas of their lives, including their interaction with parents. In fact, positive interaction in the early months and the first couple of years of a child's life is essential to help shape the child's developing brain. Research shows that in the early years, the brain makes intricate and complex connections and creates pathways with each interaction.[4]

Most parents enjoy looking at developmental charts to see if their children have reached any new developmental milestones. These milestones involve the mastering of gross and fine motor skills, the appearance of first teeth, and the pronunciation of first words to name a few. The ability to speak and have a more extensive vocabulary empowers children to interact with others verbally and express their ideas more clearly. As expected, when puberty comes, it marks the beginning of adolescence, which is a period of intense and rapid physical growth accompanied by psychological and social development. Thus, metaphorically and literally, when you spend time in the kids' room you witness the achievement of a variety of milestones in your children's lives.

Psychological Development

John Bowlby and Mary Ainsworth's research on attachment theory helps us understand that generally, during infancy, babies develop an attachment or strong bond with their parents or caregivers, which affects them for the rest of their lives. However, this attachment varies depending on the relationship exchange between the child and the parents or caregivers. Researchers have identified four types of attachment: secure, disorganized, ambivalent, and avoidant.[5]

Children who display secure attachment to their caregivers tend to have higher self-esteem, be more outgoing, and develop more trusting relationships throughout life. As expected, children who have a disorganized attachment may show avoidance and resistance. They may also have difficulty controlling their emotions and maintaining strong and meaningful relationships throughout life. On the other hand, children who show ambivalent attachment may be unenthusiastic about developing emotional intimacy with others, have difficulty in letting go of a relationship, and may doubt people's love for them. Finally, children with avoidant attachment style are not willing to invest emotionally in relationships because they fear they will have their feelings hurt.[6]

Children learn how to trust parents and caregivers at an early age. That initial trust can help children perceive the world as a safe place, regulate their emotions, and be more confident in their abilities to interact with the environment and others. Erik Erikson, a developmental psychologist, created the well-known psychosocial theory of human development that focuses on both a psychological and a social perspective (see the chart). He emphasized that as people grow and develop, they go through eight stages of development, and each stage is marked by a crisis. These crises can have a positive or negative impact on the individual.[7]

Life Stage	Approximate Age	Psychosocial Crisis	Key Events	Outcomes
Infancy	Birth–1 ½	Trust vs Mistrust	Feeding	Children develop trust when their needs are met by parents or caregivers consistently. Neglect leads to mistrust.
Toddlerhood	1 ½–3	Autonomy vs Shame and Doubt	Toilet training	Children develop independence and self-control. Negative experiences lead to shame and doubt.
Preschool	3–6	Initiative vs Guilt	Exploration and play	Children develop a sense of purpose and self-confidence. Disapproval leads to guilt.
School Age	7–12	Industry vs Inferiority	School	Children develop competence and confidence in their abilities. Negative experiences lead to a sense of inferiority.
Adolescence	12–18	Identity vs Role Confusion	Social relationships	Adolescents develop a sense of self-identity. Negative outcome is a weak self-identity.
Young Adulthood	19–40	Intimacy vs Isolation	Intimate relationships	Young adults form strong relationships, experience love, and commit to a long-term relationship. Negative outcome is loneliness.

(Continued)

(Continued)

Life Stage	Approximate Age	Psychosocial Crisis	Key Events	Outcomes
Adulthood	40–65	Generativity vs Stagnation	Work and parenting	Adults contribute to the next generation though parenting and to the world through work, or they are superficial.
Mature Adulthood	65+	Integrity vs Despair	Life review	Older adults reflect on how they lived their lives. They may experience wisdom and peace, or a sense of despair.

It is important to note that children also develop their thinking or cognitive abilities. Jean Piaget, a Swiss psychologist, was a pioneer in studying children's intellectual development and described how children's thought process develops. Therefore, awareness of your children's mental development will help you engage them appropriately at each stage of their cognitive development.

Awareness of the attachment styles, psychosocial and cognitive development, and possible outcomes helps us understand the importance of investing in positive and loving interactions with our children from the time they are born. However, it also helps us evaluate our own upbringing and ask ourselves about the way we were raised. Hope is possible if we are willing to enter a relationship that transcends any other relationship we had before, that is, a relationship with the living God through Jesus Christ. This can transform us into a more secure person and, in turn, change the way we parent our children.[8]

Social Development

The social development of children depends significantly on the quality of their interactions with parents and caregivers. Parents' interactions with their children in the kids' room allow children to respond to social stimuli as they assign meaning to their parents' facial expressions. As we know, children tend to imitate their parents and caregivers. They also imitate others, including friends and television characters. This can be clearly seen in the way children engage in parallel and collaborative play.

Social development also influences children's moral development. Children learn from their parents and others what is appropriate and acceptable behaviors, including right and wrong choices. As expected, during the teenage years, children become more independent and some tend to value their peers' opinions more than their parents'. Thus, time spent with your children in the kids' room early on will be foundational for your children's positive social behavior as they grow and develop.

Spiritual Development

We believe that parents have the primary responsibility for teaching their children about God. However, the decision to believe in Jesus as personal Savior must be made by the child alone and not by his or her parents. Here, we will not engage in the theological debate about the so-called age-of-accountability or at what age a child can or cannot understand the plan of salvation to be saved. Rather, we want to emphasize that sharing Bible stories and biblical concepts with your children at an early age is biblical and a wise approach to help your children develop spiritually.

Children are spiritual beings and their spiritual development is as important as their physical, emotional, and mental development. Few scientific studies exist on the spiritual development of children compared to other facets of life; however, parents often witness and report on how their children process and speak of spiritual matters. Usually, a child's ability to make a logical connection between something mundane with something spiritual happens as the child participates in religious activities and interact with others. This means that children may gain spiritual insight by learning Bible stories and going to church.

God commands us to share our faith with our children and teach them to know Him (Deut. 6:4–7). Our curriculum needs to be focused on teaching our children about God, Jesus, the Holy Spirit, the church, people, and the world. For instance, as a couple, we taught our children about God by reading Bible stories, teaching Bible verses, and singing Christian songs to them. In addition, we took our children to church so that they could learn about God and engage in age-appropriate church activities. If we are filled with God and our interactions with our children point to the reality of a God who sent a savior, Jesus, to the world, then chances are our children will see that in us and through us.

Connecting with Your Child

Successful parenting happens when parents can enter their children's world, or should we say, their kids' room and connect with them. We agree with Ross Campbell, a former associate clinical professor of pediatrics and psychiatry at the University of Tennessee College of Medicine, author of the best-selling books *How to Really Love Your Child* and *How to Really Love your Teenager*, when he shares that parents can show love to their children through appropriate eye contact, physical contact, and focused attention.[9]

When it comes to making appropriate eye contact with your child, you need to put your phone away, turn off the television, walk away from your computer, sit down, or even kneel down to be in an eye-level position with your child. Perhaps you need to get into the habit of looking at your child in the eye when he or she is talking to ensure that you are paying attention. If your child is a baby or toddler, you can hold your child's face gently and kindly toward you, so you and your child can lock eyes, which according to research will put you in sync physiologically with your child.[10]

Physical contact is important at any age. Unfortunately, it seems that the older kids get, the less they are hugged by their parents. Please keep in mind that just because pre-teens or teenagers may avoid being hugged by parents in front of their friends, it does not mean they do not want you to hug them at home or at other places and occasions. When hugging takes place, the body releases oxytocin, a hormone that promotes bonding and generates several health benefits, including stress reduction and mood regulation.[11] In fact, research also shows that hugs have physical and emotional benefits, even to prematurely born babies in the newborn intensive care unit (NICU).[12] Thus, appropriate hugs can be a great way to communicate your love to your child.

Focused attention is essential to help parents connect with their children. Many times, television watching, phone calls, and web searching can prevent parents from paying attention to what their children are saying. It is not surprising that many times, parents and caregivers answer their children's questions without paying attention to what they are asking. Then, when they discipline their children, they soon realize that they have answered a *yes* to a question that should have been a *no*. This probably frustrates the children. Furthermore, parents need to remember that the same Bible that says children must obey their parents also says, "Fathers, do not provoke your children to anger by the way you treat them" (Eph. 6:4 NLT). Not listening appropriately to what their children are saying can create confusion and anger in their children's hearts and minds, as it may convey the message that what they are saying is unimportant.

The Purpose and Goal of Parenting: A Biblical Perspective

Christian parents must be purposeful regarding how they raise their children. In other words, they must have an ultimate goal or end in mind. Here are two essential purposes for parenting your children from a Christian perspective.

Raise Your Children to Love God and Love People

We believe that the first essential element of parenting is to pass down our Christian faith to our children (Deut. 6:4–7). When Jesus was asked about the greatest commandment, he replied, "'Love the Lord your God with all your heart and with all your soul and with all your mind.' This is the first and great-

 It is your God-given responsibility to teach and model your faith in God to your children. The church's role is not to replace parents, but to come alongside and support them in fulfilling their God-given task.

est commandment. And the second is like it, 'Love your neighbor as yourself'" (Matt. 22:37–39 NIV). Therefore, Christian parents have the primary responsibility not only to teach their children about God, but to teach them to love God as well. We understand that you cannot make or force your children to become Christians. However, it is your God-given responsibility to teach and model your faith in God to your children. The church's role is not to replace parents, but to come alongside and support them in fulfilling their God-given task. Unfortunately, many Christian parents think that their responsibility is only to take their children to church.

Deuteronomy 6:4–7 is a pivotal passage in Scriptures that addresses how parents need to teach their children about God. This passage is also known as the first part of the Shema, "the oldest fixed daily prayer in Judaism, recited morning and night since ancient times."[13] It means to hear God's Word with the intent of obedience:

Hear, O Israel: The Lord our God, the Lord is one. Love the Lord your God with all your heart and with all your soul and with all your strength. These commandments that I give you today are to be on your hearts.

Impress them on your children. Talk about them when you sit at home and when you walk along the road, when you lie down and when you get up (NIV).

These commandments have a significant meaning to Jews and Christians alike because they are the basis of the covenant relationship with God. In the

> You cannot give your children what you do not have.

book of Deuteronomy, we can read about Moses leading the people of Israel to renew their covenant with the Almighty. Based on God's commandments in the Law, the Israelites prepared to enter the Promised Land. Similarly, Jesus emphasizes that loving God involves believing, accepting, and internalizing His commandments (Matt. 22:37–39 NIV).

Moses also emphasizes the Israelite parents' responsibility to teach their faith to their children by impressing the commandments on their children (v. 7). Eugene Merrill, a Bible scholar, describes the role of parents in faith transmission eloquently. He writes:

> the covenant recipient must impress the words of covenant faith into the thinking of his children by inscribing them there with indelible sharpness . . . The image is that of an engraver of a monument who takes a hammer and chisel in hand and with a painstaking care etches a text into a solid slab of granite. The sheer labor of such a task is daunting indeed, but once done the message is there to stay.[14]

Thus, raising children is a challenging yet rewarding task.

In Deuteronomy 6:4–7, we receive guidance on how to accomplish the parenting task. According to verse 7, we must be intentional and diligent in teaching our children throughout the day by using formal and informal methods. Thus, raising our children requires commitment and consistency, and it must be a priority, not an inconvenience in our life.

5 W's and 1 H of Parenting

Passing on the Faith
(Deuteronomy 6:4-7)

Who?	Parents
What?	Love God and Teach their children
Where?	Everywhere At home and outside
When?	All the time
Why?	To share their faith
How?	Intentionally and consistently Formally and informally

Later on, in Deuteronomy 6:20, Moses warned the parents that, as the Israelite children would grow, they would question why they had to practice God's commandments. Moses reminded the Israelite parents that they were to answer their children's questions by retelling the story of the Exodus and God's mighty acts. This is supported by other Bible passages that emphasize that we should share with our children "things we have heard and known, things our ancestors have told us . . . we will tell the next generation the praiseworthy deeds of the Lord, his power, and the wonders he has done" (Ps. 78:3–4 NIV).

Raise Your Children to Be Influential Citizens in Society and in God's Kingdom

Although many intrinsic factors can affect children's behavior, the experiences they have with parents and other caregivers throughout life can help shape who they become as adults significantly. Here is an example very close to our hearts. The other day, our 22-year-old son told us that a customer at the store where he works told him that his parents raised him right. That made us very proud of him and of ourselves. The truth is that most parents feel good when they hear those words. Who does not want to have children who are mature adults who can regulate their emotions, show self-control, and interact respectfully and professionally with others? We all do, don't we?

Tony Evans in his book, *Raising Kingdom Kids*, asserts that there are three essential pillars for raising children following God's kingdom principles, namely encouragement, discipline, and instruction. He points out that "encouraging [our] children gives them an expectation of God's goodness and favor on both their todays and their tomorrows."[15] He also asserts that when parents discipline their children, it helps them develop their own self-discipline and wise decision-making process. Finally, he contends that it is the parents' responsibility to instruct their children to internalize and live out the message of Christ.[16] We agree with Evans and believe that this can place our children on the path to become good citizens who joyfully contribute to society and to God's Kingdom.

We would like to highlight Andy and Sandra Stanley's teaching on the Four Stages of Parenting.[17] This is another helpful and practical model for parenting. The first stage is the *Discipline years* and range from birth to 5 years old. Since children are young in this stage, they need a large amount of discipline. Next in the *Training years*, which range from ages 5 to 12, parents need to explain and reason with their children a little more than in the previous stage. Interestingly, in the *Coaching years*, as children become teenagers, they still need guidance, boundaries, and supervision. They also need more relationship-based discipline. In fact, parents' work during this stage can be compared to the work of coaches who stand by the sidelines providing significant encouragement and motivation to players. Finally, the *Friendship years* happen in adulthood. Although parents never cease being parents, their roles change to that of mentors who are always available to provide experiential wisdom to their adult children.

Parenting Styles

In the 1960s, psychologist Diana Baumrind developed a groundbreaking theory on parenting styles. She believed that four distinctive types of parenting styles, including Authoritative, Authoritarian, Permissive, and Neglectful influenced children's development and outcomes.[18] Below is a brief description of each style.

The Permissive Parenting Style – Parents who adopt this style tend to be more accepting and supportive of their children. They focus on promoting their children's self-esteem and independence. However, permissive parents do not control their children. Instead, they give them the freedom to decide what to do. This style is also known as *Laissez-faire* parenting. Children raised by permissive parents tend to have more behavioral problems and lack of self-control.

The Authoritarian Parenting Style – Parents who operate from this style, tend to focus on controlling their children's behaviors based on the parents' standards. These parents are demanding, strict, and inflexible. They focus on the rules and guidelines that the children must follow. This style reflects the popular *helicopter* parent who is always hovering over the children. Authoritarian parents try to control their children's world and even solve their problems, thus limiting their children's emotional, intellectual, and social development. Children raised by authoritarian parents tend to have emotional challenges and lack motivation.

The Authoritative Parenting Style – Researchers view this style as the ideal parenting style. It combines the positive elements of both authoritarian and permissive parenting styles, including a loving and supportive relationship with rules and appropriate discipline. Parents who embrace this style are firm and provide rules and guidelines for their children in a loving, accepting, and supportive relationship. They establish appropriate boundaries for their children and promote responsible independence with close parental supervision and guidance. According to research, children raised by both authoritative parents tend to have fewer behavioral and developmental problems and display emotional intelligence.[19]

Neglectful Parenting Style – When operating from this style, parents neglect their children's physical, mental, emotional, social, and spiritual needs. They do not provide rules and guidelines for the children's behaviors. They are uninvolved in the children's lives because they are overinvolved in their own world. Children raised by neglectful parents tend to have severe emotional and behavioral problems.

Many authors have built on Baumrind's work to understand the dynamics and factors involved in these parenting styles. A recent article in the USA today entitled *What type of parent are you? Lawnmower? Helicopter? Attachment? Tiger? Free-range?*[20] exemplifies the ongoing interest in this topic and the new emerging parenting styles. The article reviews these five popular parenting styles. For instance, the *lawnmower* parent is overinvolved and clears the path for their children by removing all perceived obstacles or challenges. The *tiger* parent emphasizes academic performance and consequently have their children spend more time engaged in school-related activities. The *helicopter* parent, as previously mentioned, is overly involved in the child's life even during the college years. The *attachment* parent focuses on activities that promote connection with their children and on positive discipline. The *free-range* parent is similar to the permissive or even neglectful parent as they grant their children free-range with minimum supervision.

Perhaps you are already familiar with the attachment and the parenting style theories and may find yourself operating based on one of these styles. Maybe you are unaware of your natural tendency to gravitate toward a particular style. We believe that parents who have an authoritative parenting style combined with a biblical perspective on parenting tend to be more successful in raising their children. Again, we cannot highlight enough the importance of listening to our children with our hearts and finding meaning in the words they say. As we approach our children with excitement, compassion, kindness, and patience, we allow them to see our love and God's love for them.

> We believe that parents who have an authoritative parenting style combined with a biblical perspective on parenting tend to be more successful in raising their children.

Childhood Issues and Challenges

The parenting years are not exempt from concerns since children face many challenges and issues as they grow and develop. Obviously, our children's challenges and issues will become ours as well. Thus, in this section, we discuss briefly some of the problems children and their families may face, such as childhood obesity, technology and social media use, friendships and peer pressure, and special needs.

Childhood Obesity

The prevalence of childhood obesity in our country has increased tremendously. According to the Centers for Disease Control and Prevention (CDC), "nearly 1 in 5 school age children and young people (6 to 19 years) in the United States has obesity."[21] Multiple factors contribute to obesity in children, including dietary intake, disordered eating, lack of physical activity, environment, sedentary lifestyle, health issues, and sleep.[22] Additionally, a recent study identified key caregiver's characteristics that contribute to the obesity problem in children. These characteristics range from insufficient understanding about healthy and unhealthy foods and inadequate time to prepare meals at home, which, in turn, affects the overall nutrition of their children.[23]

Childhood obesity can take an emotional toll on children since it affects their sense of self-esteem and self-worth negatively. Additionally, it affects their social life as well. Research shows that obese children have a higher chance of being bullied and have a poor relationship with peers. Researchers are not sure if social problems lead to obesity or if obesity prevents children from developing socially. Despite the dilemma, "obesity and impaired social competence often occur together and have serious implications for children's well-being."[24] Unfortunately, overweight and obese children are at high risk of developing serious health problems, including diabetes and cardiovascular disorders.[25]

10 Parenting Tips

Parents must be part of the solution to the child obesity problem.[26] Here are a few ways in which you can help prevent or address this problem:

- Promote and model healthy eating habits.
- Involve your child in meal preparation whenever possible.
- Engage your child in physical activities.

- Participate in 'walking for a cause' programs in your community.
- Monitor and control your child's screen time, including television, video gaming, computer, and cell phone time.
- Ensure that your child gets adequate amounts of sleep.
- Help your child deal with emotions in constructive ways.
- Avoid using food as a reward for good behavior.
- Learn about foods and proper nutrition with your child.
- Visit a farm together or a farmers' market to learn about fruits and vegetables.

Technology and Social Media

A large number of children and adolescents are using technology and engaging in social media multiple times and for multiple hours daily.[27] In fact, according to research, children and teenagers spend over six hours using their cell phones and computers daily.[28] Unfortunately, children may develop computer vision syndrome (CVS) and eyesight problems.[29]

According to the American Academy of Child & Adolescent Psychiatry (AACAP), online social networking has many risks for children, including cyberbullying, online harassment, inappropriate sharing of photos and videos, sexting, being vulnerable to predatory adults, exposure to age-inappropriate ads, identity theft, and having decreased physical activity.[30] The consequences of inappropriate use of technology and social media can be devastating to children in the long run. Thus, parental supervision and accountability combined with intentional guidance and education are crucial in this media-saturated age. This means that parents need to implement rules that protect their children and reinforce the idea that having a cell phone, for instance, is a privilege that can be taken away if rules are not followed.

Parents also need to be wise and cautious about *sharenting*, overposting pictures and information online about their own children. Stacey Steinberg, a legal skills professor at the University of Florida Levin College of Law, points out that while parents are ultimately responsible for protecting their children's privacy, they are creating their own "narrative" and "digital footprint" of their children by the social media posts. She highlights that as these children become adults, they may resent the disclosure that parents made through social media.[31] Furthermore, parents are responsible for monitoring their children's activity on social media, providing guidance, and ultimately protecting their children.

10 Parenting Tips

- Use apps to monitor your child's social media use.
- Use age-appropriate language to talk to your child about the positive and negative effects of technology use.
- Know your child's computer and cell phone passwords.
- Turn off phones during bedtime.
- Model wise technology use to your child by putting your phone away during meals and conversation time.
- Read age-appropriate books that teach about proper technology use.
- Engage in technology-free activities such as riding a bike, swimming, drawing, and painting.
- Be wise and sensitive regarding posts you make on social media about your child.
- Protect your child's best interest and privacy in your social media.
- Limit your child's daily use of phone and social media.

Friendships and Peer Pressure

From an early age, children need interaction with others to develop socially as they move from parallel to collaborative play. As they interact with others, they learn new vocabulary and imitate the behaviors displayed around them. They develop trust in others and initiate new friendships with children and adults. Unfortunately, as children get older, they may fall prey to peer pressure. However, by using age-appropriate tools and having positive interaction with your children, you can help them navigate the world of friendship and resist peer pressure. The more positive interactions you have with your children, the more they will internalize the values you want them to follow.

10 Parenting Tips

- Model healthy friendship to your child.
- Know your child's friends and their families whenever possible.
- Spend time listening to your child when he or she is talking about friends.
- Supervise your child when friends are around.
- Be cautious about sleepovers and slumber parties.
- Talk to your child about appropriate and inappropriate behavior from an early age.

- Read to your child age-appropriate books about friendships and peer pressure.
- Explain to your child that changes in friendships are a normal part of life.
- Help your child set healthy relationship boundaries.
- Make your home the center of activity for your child and friends.

Children with Special Needs

The terms "special needs" or "Special Health Care Needs" are umbrella terms that cover a variety of physical and intellectual diagnoses that children may have.[32] We are aware that the terms "special needs" or "disabilities" can be perceived as hurtful and offensive by some people. Having a child with special needs can be devastating to parents who have to deal with their own emotions and the special needs of their children simultaneously. They also need to deal with the effects of their child's unique needs on their marriage. Research confirms that many parents who have children with special needs face challenges due to the child's particular diagnosis and experience a higher rate of divorce than the general population.[33] It is vital for parents to know that children with special needs are entitled to specialized services in school under federal and state laws. Thus, "parents should always advocate for their child and take necessary steps to make sure their child receives appropriate services."[34]

10 Parenting Tips

- Be an advocate for your child in the school system and in your community.
- Celebrate your child's milestones and development.
- Join support groups for parents of special needs children.
- Practice self-care.
- Prioritize your daily activities.
- Accept help from family members and others.
- Revise your expectations for yourself, your child, and your family.
- Do not neglect your marriage and other family members. Make time for them as well.
- Make time for your spouse and talk about your relationship.
- Participate in "walks" to raise funds and awareness to issues affecting your child and family.

In addition to these issues, parents need to be aware of and informed about many other potential challenging problems for children such as substance abuse, high caffeine intake in the form of energy drinks, vaping, alcohol, marijuana, over the counter medication, and others. Parental supervision is key to prevent these issues.

Intentional and Relational Parenting

Parents need to be intentional and relational to parent with purpose. The term intentional parenting has become popular in recent years. We like the word intentional because it means deliberate, calculated, conscious, done on purpose, intended, planned, considered, studied, willful, and purposeful, among other meanings.[35] When you are intentional, you engage in a deliberate effort with a clear purpose or goal in mind. Thus, as a parent, you need to engage in intentional parenting and not expect that your children will lead the way. Again, this does not mean forcing your children to follow a particular career or professional path or trying to live your dreams through your children. You are responsible for guiding your children with appropriate guidelines and expectations for positive behaviors.

We want to emphasize that parents need to be intentional in developing a loving, caring, and supportive relationship with their children. Doing so will help them develop a secure attachment. Such attachment is foundational for a stable relationship to flourish. Several years ago, Ross Campbell wrote the book *Relational Parenting*, in which he emphasized that parents need to meet the emotional and nurturing needs that children have. Parents need to show love and acceptance to their children in a way that is meaningful to their children and avoid reactive parenting. He asserts, "Reactive parenting responds primarily to what kids do. Proactive parenting deals primarily with what kids need."[36] Therefore, we recommend that you focus on your children's emotional needs and meet those needs with love and acceptance.

We believe that intentionality is the key to becoming a positive influence in your child's life. As previously mentioned, the Bible says, "Fathers, do not provoke your children to anger by the way you treat them. Rather, bring them up with the discipline and instruction that comes from the Lord" (Eph. 6:4 NLT). This challenges parents to fulfill their role with excellence. First, parents need to avoid behaviors that will anger or embitter their children. Second, they need to engage, intentionally, in positive behaviors that will combine appropriate discipline and teaching.

Parents may anger their children actively or passively. Parents anger their children actively when they verbally abuse them by yelling and screaming, or by making fun of, or belittling them. Unfortunately, many parents send negative messages to their children, such as "you will never amount to anything," "you never do anything right," or "you should have known better." Other times, parents may anger their children by being emotionally reactive out of anger and frustration. Parents may also frustrate their children by not keeping their word, changing rules, comparing them to other children, using unfair punishment, punishing out of anger, or not explaining expectations. Unfortunately, some parents may also anger their children passively by neglecting, not being available, and ignoring them. We believe that learning how to become more sensitive and less reactive, more collaborative, and less prescriptive will enhance your relationship with your children and make parenting an easier task.

The ABC's of Parenting with Purpose: Being Intentional and Relational

Here are a few tips and insights that will help you be intentional and relational in your parenting experience.

A – Agreement

You and your spouse need to be on the same page regarding your parenting goals and discipline strategies. We encourage you to discuss with your spouse what you expect your children to become when they grow up. As some people say, start with the end in mind. Agree on the final picture. Again, we are not talking about living your dreams through your children. Rather, we are referring to character and values. What type of character do you want your children to have when they turn 18? What values do you want them to live by? Additionally, you and your spouse need to agree on how to discipline your

 The ABC's of Parenting with Purpose

A - Agreement = Agree with your spouse on parenting goals and discipline strategies

B - Being = Spend quantity and quality time with your children

C - Consistency = Be consistent in your interactions with your children and in how you discipline them

D - Doing = Have positive, fun, and enriching activities with your children daily

E - Expert = Become an expert on your children by observing them and learning about their development

F - Faith = Be responsible for the spiritual formation of your children

children. Doing so will minimize conflict and will prevent your children from pitting you against each other. We recommend that you agree to discipline your children promptly, consistently, calmly and lovingly.

B – Being

As previously mentioned, the neglectful parenting style is detrimental to a child's life. Unfortunately, many parents may be physically present but psychologically and emotionally distant. Multiple factors such as technology and media, and even work, may distract parents from engaging with their children. They may be in the kids' room, but not engaging or interacting meaningfully with their children. In this sense, *being* means spending quantity and quality time with your children and being available physically and mentally present with them. When you spend quantity and quality time with your children, you communicate that you love them and that they are important to you.

C – Consistency

We recommend that you and your spouse be consistent in your interactions with your children and in how you discipline and reward them. Having clear expectations for behavior and clear consequences for misbehavior is essential. Unfortunately, many parents discipline their children out of frustration and anger and reward their children's behavior based on the feelings and emotions they are experiencing at that moment. Doing so will create confusion in their children's minds. For this reason, you need to take into account that discipline needs to be not only consistent, but also age-appropriate. It needs to be beneficial, educational, and constructive and never with the intent to harm your child physically, emotionally, or mentally.

D – Doing

What are you doing with your children? Our popular culture and social media make parents believe that their children need big events and big vacations. Taking children to fun activities and on vacations can be a great and positive experience for them. However, many families get into debt when taking an extravagant vacation they cannot afford to keep up with their social media friends who are also taking expensive vacations. Therefore, we advocate for an emphasis on having positive, fun, and enriching activities with your children daily. These activities do not need to derail your budget. Keep in mind that positive daily interactions and creative activities with your children may be more precious than an expensive annual vacation. For example, when our children were little, we took them to the Fort Worth public library regularly and helped them find fun books. Sometimes, we would return home with over 30 books. We would sit in our living room and go through all the books with them. To this day, our children remember our visits to the library. As a result, they have become avid readers.

E – Expert

Parents need to become experts on their children. What do we mean? An expert is someone who has studied a subject or topic in-depth and has gained a lot of knowledge about it to the point of understanding it well. Becoming an expert requires time, dedication, commitment, and yes, love for the subject or topic. Similarly, we believe that you will need to become a student of your children. Besides observing your children and researching online about your children's development, we recommend that you and your spouse collaborate with the experts or doctors who treat and work with your children. For example, working collaboratively with your children's doctors and teachers will not only improve their services to your children, but it will also expand your understanding about your children.

F – Faith

We strongly believe that Christian parents have the primary responsibility to share God's love with their children and teach them biblical principles. Therefore, we believe that parents have a fundamental responsibility for the spiritual formation of their children. Parenting does not happen in a vacuum, and it does not need to be a repeating of behaviors and attitudes from our parents. Parenting can be creative and dynamic and take its own form as we intentionally position ourselves to learn the art of parenting from our Heavenly Father.

Now, let's walk to the guest room.

Endnotes

1. Chun Bun Lam, Susan M. McHale, and Ann C. Crouter, "Parent-Child Shared Time from Middle Childhood to Late Adolescence: Developmental Course and Adjustment Correlates," *Child Development* 83, no. 6 (November/December 2012): 2089–2103.

2. Erika Lawrence et al., "Marital Satisfaction Across the Transition to Parenthood," *Journal of Family Psychology* 22, no. 1 (2008): 41–50; Gilad Hirschberger et al., "Attachment, Marital Satisfaction, and Divorce During the First Fifteen Years of Parenthood," *Personal Relationships* 16, no. 3 (2009): 401–20.

3. Shawn Grover and John F. Helliwell, "How's Life at Home? New Evidence on Marriage and the Set Point for Happiness," *Journal of Happiness Studies* 20, no. 2 (February 2019): 373–90.

4. "Early Brain Development and Health," Centers for Disease Control and Prevention, accessed July 13, 2019, https://www.cdc.gov/ncbddd/childdevelopment/early-brain-development.html.

5. John Bowlby, *A Secure Base: Parent Child Attachment and Healthy Human Development* (London: Routledge, 1988).

6. Tim Clinton and Gary Sibcy, *Attachments: Why You Love, Feel, and Act the Way You Do* (Brentwood, TN: Integrity Publisher, 2002).

7. Erik H. Erikson, *The Life Cycle Completed* (New York, NY: W. W. & Norton, 1982).

8. Clinton and Sibcy, *Attachments*.

9. Ross Campbell, *How to Really Love Your Child* (Colorado Spring, CO: David C. Cook, 2004); Ross Campbell, How to Really Love Your Teen (Colorado Spring, CO: David C. Cook, 2004).

10. Laura Sanders, "Staring into a Baby's Eyes Puts Her Brain Waves and Yours in Sync," *Science News*, December 5, 2017, accessed July 12, 2019, https://www.sciencenews.org/blog/growth-curve/staring-baby-eyes-brain-waves-sync.

11. Stacey Colino, "The Health Benefits of Hugging: A Hug a Day Just Might Keep the Doctor Away," *U. S. News*, February 3, 2016, accessed July 7, 2019 https://health.usnews.com/health-news/health-wellness/articles/2016-02-03/the-health-benefits-of-hugging.

12. Lisette Hilton, "Hugging is Healing for NICU Babies," *Contemporary Pediatrics* 35, no. 5 (May 2018): 27–28, 30–31.

13. Tracey R. Rich, *Judaism 101* (2011), accessed July 9, 2019, http://www.jewfaq.org/shemaref.htm.

14. Merrill H. Eugene, *Deuteronomy: An Exegetical and Theological Exposition of Holy Scripture* (Nashville, TN: Broadman & Holman Publishing, 1994), 167.

15. Tony Evans, *Raising Kingdom Kids* (Carol Stream, IL: Tyndale House Publishers, 2016), 95.

16. Evans, *Raising Kingdom Kids*.

17. Sandra Stanley, "An Intentional Parenting Strategy for Andy Stanley and Sandra Stanley," *Focus on the Family*, accessed July 15, 2019, https://www.focusonthefamily.com/parenting/parenting-roles/parents-working-together/intentional-parenting-strategy; https://www.youtube.com/watch?v=mrg12LnQGUk.

18. Diana Baumrind, "Child Care Practices Anteceding Three Patterns of Preschool Behavior," *Genetic Psychology Monographs* 75, no. 1 (1967): 43–88.

19. Sofie Kuppens and Eva Ceulemans, "Parenting Styles: A Closer Look at a Well-Known Concept," *Journal of Child and Family Studies* 28, no. 1 (2019): 168–81; John Gottman and Joan DeClaire, *Raising an Emotionally Intelligent Child* (New York, NY: Simon & Schuster, 2011).

20. Sonja Haller, "What Type of Parent Are You? Lawnmower? Helicopter? Attachment? Tiger? Free-range?" *USA Today*, September 19, 2018, accessed July 8, 2019, https://www.usatoday.com/story/life/allthemoms/2018/09/19/parenting-terms-explained-lawnmower-helicopter-attachment-tiger-free-range-dolphin-elephant/1357612002/.

21. "Childhood Obesity Facts," Centers for Disease Control and Prevention, accessed July 8, 2019, https://www.cdc.gov/healthyschools/obesity/facts.htm

22. Michael I. Goran, ed., *Childhood Obesity: Causes, Consequences, and Intervention Approaches* (Boca Raton, FL: Taylor and Francis Group, 2017).

23. Melawhy L. Garcia et al., "Engaging Intergenerational Hispanics/Latinos to Examine Factors Influencing Childhood Obesity Using the PRECEDE–PROCEED Model," *Maternal and Child Health Journal* 23, no. 6 (2019): 802–810, accessed September 19, 2019, https://doi.org/10.1007/s10995-018-02696-y.

24. Sandra L. Jackson and Solveig A. Cunningham, "Social Competence and Obesity in Elementary School," *American Journal of Public Health* 105, no. 1 (January 2015): 153.

25. "BMI in Children," American Heart Association, accessed September 25, 2019, https://www.heart.org/en/healthy-living/healthy-eating/losing-weight/bmi-in-children

26. "Helping Your Child Who is Overweight," National Institute of Diabetes and Digestive and Kidney Diseases, accessed July 9, 2019, https://www.niddk.nih.gov/health-information/weight-management/helping-your-child-who-is-overweight; "Tips for Parents–Ideas to Help Children Maintain a Healthy Weight," Centers for Disease Control and Prevention, May 23, 2018, accessed July 9, 2019, https://www.cdc.gov/healthyweight/children/index.html.

27. Jenny Anderson, "Even Teens Are Worried They Spend Too Much Time on Their Phones," *Pew Research*, August 23, 2018, accessed July 9, 2019, https://qz.com/1367506/pew-research-teens-worried-they-spend-too-much-time-on-phones/.

28. Anderson, "Even Teens Are Worried."

29. "Computer Vision Syndrome," American Optometric Association, accessed September 25, 2019, https://www.aoa.org/patients-and-public/caring-for-your-vision/protecting-your-vision/computer-vision-syndrome.

30. "Social Networking and Children," American Academy of Child and Adolescent Psychiatry, February 2017, assessed July 8, 2019, https://www.aacap.org/AACAP/Families_

and_Youth/Facts_for_Families/FFF-Guide/Children-and-Social-Networking-100.aspx.

31. Stacey Steinberg, "Sharenting: Children's Privacy in the Age of Social Media," *Emory Law Journal* 66, no. 4 (2017): 839.

32. "Population Specific Fact Sheet-Child with Special Health Care Needs," National Disability Navigator Resource Collaborative, assessed July 9, 2019, https://nationaldisabilitynavigator.org/ndnrc-materials/fact-sheets/population-specific-fact-sheet-child-with-special-health-care-needs/.

33. H. Barry Waldman, Jeffrey Seiver, and Steven P. Pearlman, "Does a Child with a Disability = a Divorce?" *American Academy of Developmental Dentistry EP Magazine* (June 2019), 16–18; Daniel B. Pickar and Robert L. Kaufman, "Parenting Plans for Special Needs Children: Applying a Risk-Assessment Model," *Family Court Review* 53, no. 1 (January 2015): 113–33.

34. "School Services for Children with Special Needs: Know Your Rights," *The American Academy of Child and Adolescent Psychiatry (AACAP)* 83 (September 2016), accessed July 7, 2019, https://www.aacap.org/AACAP/Families_and_Youth/Facts_for_Families/FFF-Guide/Services-In-School-For-Children-With-Special-Needs-What-Parents-Need-To-Know-083.aspx.

35. The Merriam Webster Dictionary, s.v. "Intentional," accessed July 9, 2019, https://www.merriam-webster.com/dictionary/intentional

36. Ross Campbell, *Relational Parenting: Going Beyond Your Child's Behavior to Meet Their Deepest Needs* (Chicago, IL: Moody Press, 2000), 12.

CHAPTER 11

The Guest Room: Practicing Hospitality

"Offer hospitality to one another without grumbling."
1 Pet. 4:9 (NIV)

© BondRocketImages/Shutterstock.com

Many couples desire to have a guest bedroom so they can welcome family and friends into their home. For many of them, "a guest room should be a welcoming space that combines the amenities of a hotel with the intimacy and charm of a home."[1] However, no matter the design or the size of the guest bedroom, most of us agree that it needs to be a comfortable place where guests can keep their luggage, enjoy privacy, rest, and sleep well.

Hospitality involves at least two people, a guest, and a host or hostess. A guest is a person who needs to be hosted by someone, while the host or hostess is the person willing to share his or her space with a guest. You may have played both roles. As a couple, we have experienced the hospitality offered by several friends who provided us with not only a comfortable room but also opened their whole houses to us. Similarly, we have provided the gift of hospitality to multiple friends and even to their family members. In this process, we felt connected and learned about those who received us and about each other.

In this chapter, the guest bedroom serves as a metaphor to represent Christian hospitality. Since each room in the house contributes to the couple's overall intimacy, we explore the importance of hospitality in the lives of couples as a tool to build couple intimacy. We believe that hospitality allows you and your spouse to love others, and to witness each other's kindness toward family members, friends, and even strangers. Additionally, hospitality helps you learn about each other and gives you a picture of your spouse's commitment to becoming Christ-like.

Defining Hospitality

When we think of hospitality, it seems that many of us automatically think of words such as "entertainment" or "inconvenience" as if hospitality is only a one-way street in which we give something and receive nothing in return. Schnorrenberg explains that we have a tendency to equate hospitality to entertainment, and this, in turn, leads to a flood of illogical excuses grounded on a perfectionist view of home life.[2] We agree with Schnorrenberg that it is very easy to create a faulty understanding of hospitality and allow excuses to prevent us from practicing hospitable acts.

Sometimes, we mistakenly embrace the idea that we cannot practice hospitality for various reasons. We may say our house is not big enough or nice enough. We may believe we are exempt from engaging in hospitality if we are overly busy or perhaps often away from home. We may even think that only extroverted couples can host people in their homes. Additionally, we may consider that hospitality can only happen when our financial situation is optimal. However, it is conceivable that if we take into consideration the real goal and meaning of Christian hospitality, we will find creative ways to engage in hospitality.

Rosaria Butterfield in the book, *The Gospel Comes with a House Key*, indicates that hospitality is something radical and ordinary.[3] She contends that Christian hospitality is a radical idea because it moves strangers to the category of neighbors and affirms our understanding that people are created in God's image.[4] Hospitality is ordinary because it is centered on everyday interactions.[5] We agree with Butterfield and add that hospitality is also a state of mind, the result of our own understanding of who God is, who we are, and who our neighbor is. Furthermore, hospitality "is one of the simplest and most exciting ways to engage in God's mission."[6]

Intentionality is another aspect of hospitality that we need to consider. When we are intentional, all excuses we have to not engage in hospitality fall apart, leaving us with the naked reality that we have not been intentional enough. Intentionality also fosters creativity. When we are intentional, we tend to find a way to make something happen. In fact, this reminds us of our first visit to South Carolina.

When we were engaged and still living in Brazil, the South Carolina Baptist Convention had a partnership with the Carioca Baptist Convention in Rio de Janeiro. Through this partnership, groups of Americans from various Baptist churches in South Carolina traveled to Rio de Janeiro for weeklong mission trips. We were excited about this ministry and volunteered to serve as interpreters for many groups. As a result, we developed deep relationships with some of the Americans. Consequently, when we moved to Fort Worth, Texas, to study at Southwestern Baptist Theological Seminary, we made plans to visit our American friends during our first summer vacation. Since they lived in different cities in South Carolina, we went all over the state. First, we stayed with a lovely couple for a few days, and then they drove us to the next friend's house, and this pattern continued until the summer ended. Needless to say, we had a fantastic time as we sat with our friends and reminisced about their mission trips to Brazil. Some of them hosted us for a few hours, and others for a few days, but all of them were welcoming and friendly to us. We have sweet memories of their hospitality toward us in that summer of 1993.

During our adventure in South Carolina, one of our friends who invited us to stay with her owned a small business and, therefore, was free only on weekends. However, she really wanted us to stay at her house and meet her family. So, she arranged for one of her friends to spend time with us and take us on a beautiful scenic drive on the Blue Ridge Mountains during the week. That summer, we witnessed the epitome of hospitality. Our friends provided the kind of Christian hospitality that was indeed beyond the famous Southern hospitality.

Throughout the years, we have developed our own definition of hospitality and have come to the realization that hospitality is more than having people stay in our guest bedroom. We believe that hospitality is more than simply opening our homes; it is about Hospitality is more than having people stay in our guest bedroom. It goes beyond that… It is about intentionally opening our hearts and sharing our ordinary lives with others. intentionally opening our hearts and sharing our ordinary lives with others. Hospitality is about becoming approachable and opening ourselves up to receiving people in our world. In fact, every time we open our homes to others, we are reminded that hospitality transcends culture and languages. Thus, hospitality is about showing the same welcoming attitude to those we know, as well as to those whom we meet for the first time. It is indeed an attitude of the heart, and we believe this definition harmonizes with the goal of hospitality, which is "to mirror the loving welcome of Jesus Christ and live it out in tangible ways."[7]

Butterfield reminds us that we need to be able to separate authentic hospitality from counterfeit hospitality.[8] She believes that the core of counterfeit hospitality is to separate the "host and guest in a way that [allows] no blending of the two roles."[9] Counterfeit hospitality erroneously categorizes people in the relationship, placing the host on a higher pedestal than the guest, and it calls for payback, reward, and profit. Interestingly, although Butterfield acknowledges that counterfeit hospitality is necessary, such as the kind that happens in Airbnbs and coffee shops, our hospitality needs to go beyond that.[10] As we reflect on this understanding of hospitality, we conclude that the term *counterfeit* could be replaced with the term *secular* or *business*. Furthermore, we conclude that two types of hospitality exist: *secular or business hospitality* and *Christian hospitality*. Our goal in this chapter is to address Christian hospitality in the life of Christian couples.

Christian Hospitality

Christian hospitality is about loving and serving others. Several biblical principles support hospitality. For instance, Matthew 7:12 says, "So in everything, do to others what you would have them do to you, for this sums up the Law and the Prophets" (NIV). Galatians 5:14 states, "For the entire law is fulfilled in keeping this one command: "Love your neighbor as yourself" (NIV). Accordingly, Paul says, "Share with the Lord's people who are in need. Practice hospitality" (Rom. 12:13 NIV). The author of Hebrews writes, "Do not forget to show hospitality to strangers, for by so doing some people have shown hospitality to angels without knowing it" (Heb. 13:2 NIV). Finally, Peter states, "Offer hospitality to one another without grumbling"

 Christian hospitality stems from an understanding that all we have belongs to God and that we are simply managers of God's possessions.

(1 Pet. 4:9 NIV). In these selected verses, we can clearly see that hospitality needs to be offered to both those in the church and outside the church.

Christian hospitality is different from the act of purely entertaining guests at home. It has an additional layer, which involves ministering to others, offering encouragement, and providing emotional and physical comfort. Christian hospitality creates the optimal environment for us to carry each other's burdens

(Gal. 6:2), listen with empathy, and meet needs. The Bible says that we are the temple of the Holy Spirit (1 Cor. 6:19). Every temple has a door. We believe that when we are interacting with others, in our home or outside our home, we are allowing our guests, metaphorically, to enter this temple and see who we are as Christians. This broad understanding of hospitality implies that you will demonstrate the fruit of the Spirit as you host and interact with people in your personal world. A smile and a kind word can help open the doors of our lives so that anxious souls become willing to come in and share who they are. Perhaps through this exchange, they can see your transformed life and feel the urge to enter into spiritual conversations with you and eventually with God.

Christian hospitality stems from an understanding that all we have belongs to God and that we are simply managers of God's possessions. Rosaria emphasizes that practicing hospitality becomes difficult for those who value their belongings more than they value people.[11] Furthermore, Christian hospitality is making people feel welcome in our house by showing that we are not in a hurry for them to leave. It is conveying that we are glad to share with them the possessions God has entrusted to us.

Christian hospitality is missional. In this sense, it is "the secret weapon for gospel advancement."[12] Our home can be more than a place where we sleep, carry out daily activities, and interact with family members. It can be a place where we directly participate in missions. As a couple, we have seen people come to our home to visit. As the conversation flows, spiritual topics surface, and we are able to share our beliefs about God with them. As a result, the interaction flows into prayers, sharing, and even confessional moments. Then, we witness God hosting our guests with us and transforming their minds and hearts and giving them hope.

Following the Example of Others

Throughout decades, we have observed many Christian couples practicing hospitality with a deep understanding that God owns everything, even their house and possessions. We are thankful to be part of these couples' lives and witness their understanding that people are more important than things, and that we are managers of God's possessions. Looking at their example has helped us rethink the meaning of hospitality. It has also created in our hearts a desire to pay it forward and to become more intentional in engaging in hospitality as a couple. Let us share a few of these examples with you.

When we lived in Brazil, we attended the International Baptist Church of Rio de Janeiro, which was about one hour away from our house. We had to take a train and a bus to get to that church and we often stayed for both morning and evening services. Knowing that we lived far away from the church, the pastor and his wife, who were American missionaries, invited us and other church members to stay with them every Sunday after the morning service so we could have some lunch and fellowship. Eventually, they became our friends and mentors and their welcoming attitude continues to shape how we practice hospitality to this day.

We also met many hospitable people when we lived in Texas. It would be impossible to talk about all of them here in this book. Each one of them contributed to our hospitality experience and our desire to honor God and minister to others through the way they modeled hospitality to us. For instance, there was an older single lady who often invited us to her house for a Sunday meal. She would cook all kinds of dishes and always had people from the church at her home for lunch on Sundays. However, that was not all. She frequently had women who needed temporary housing to stay with her. Sometimes, it was a struggling family member. Sometimes it was a friend. Some were Christians, and some were not. It did not matter. Her attitude and desire to influence others through her ministry of hospitality was evident. Almost every Sunday, someone would come out of her car and cross the church parking lot with her.

We also recall another sweet couple in the church where we used to serve in Texas. They were very supportive of the church youth ministry. They often opened their home and backyard pool to the youth of our church. Kids from the other side of town would pack this sweet couple's backyard during the hot Texas summer through our youth min-

 All homes have implicit and explicit rules or boundaries either set by society, culture, or the family who lives in the house. As expected, hospitality involves the same basic rules or boundaries to protect our guests and us and our family.

istry. This couple did not fuss when the kids would accidentally come into their house with wet feet to use the restroom or when they became a little loud. They offered food and sodas to the kids and volunteers and often expressed how blessed they felt to be part of the church ministry to the community. The beautiful thing is that, through hospitality, this couple allowed children from broken and dysfunctional families to take a look into their lives and see them model Christian marriage and hospitability.

Sometimes a couple's reputation of being hospitable follows them wherever they go. We believe that was the case for a sweet Hispanic family in our church. They opened not only their home, but also their hearts to others. They continually hosted friends who needed a place to stay. They invested their time and energy into their lives and brought them to church. Like the other couples we mentioned in the previous paragraphs, they also lived and breathed hospitality. We remember on one occasion when one of our relatives was visiting us in Texas. This couple not only showed kindness to our relative but also shared the gospel with him. The moment they spent with our relative made an eternal imprint in his heart. Upon returning to Brazil, our relative made a decision to recommit his life to Christ and has been serving Him to this day.

Hospitality and Boundaries Issues

Mi Casa es Su Casa is a saying in Spanish that translates *my house is your house*, and it is the equivalent of "make yourself at home." In Portuguese, we say "Fique à vontade," which carries the idea of "make yourself comfortable." These phrases are used to make guests feel welcome and relaxed. However, it does not mean that the guests can do whatever they want. As we know, no matter where we are in the world, all homes have implicit and explicit rules or boundaries either set by society, culture, or the family who lives in the house. As expected, hospitality involves some basic rules or boundaries to protect our guests, ourselves, and our family.

When we invite someone to be a guest in our house, we need to consider a few boundaries and dynamics to minimize conflict and to maximize the experience. Additionally, we need to ensure that we are not engaging in hospitality out of guilt, social pressure, or inability to say "no." Let us look at a few essential considerations.

First, we need to consider that guests may have different rules in their households and may be unable to understand our rules, unless we communicate those to them. Of course, you may not need to share all your household rules if the person will only stay in your house for a few hours or a couple of days. Think of creative ways to communicate some of your basic household rules. We remember having dinner at a home where the homeowners had a framed picture that depicted a list of guest expectations, almost like a procedure manual, posted on a wall of the house. We thought it was funny, but it made it easier for us as guests to conduct ourselves in a way that pleased our host.

Second, we need to understand that our guests can influence us positively and negatively. This is because each guest brings his or her own set of beliefs and behaviors. We remember when we had a guest evangelist leading a revival in our church, and we invited him to stay with us in the parsonage. He was happy to do so, and that allowed us to have meaningful conversations with him. As we ministered and prayed together that week during the revival, God used him to encourage us to take a step of faith, which eventually led us to change our ministry direction. That was a huge step for us. We believe that having that man in our house was a divine appointment in which we became open to receiving a new assignment from God. His presence in our house influenced us positively as a couple.

Third, we need to determine how long the person will stay with us. In American culture, it is entirely acceptable to ask the guest how many hours or days the person is planning to spend with you. This may vary in other cultures. Usually, most guests will give you this information before they come to your house out of respect for your family. However, there are situations in which this might be a little unclear, such as when your guest is escaping a severe storm, tornado, or hurricane. They may need extended stay if their house suffers significant damage. Nevertheless, in emergency situations, you can help your guests think of all housing options they may have and find more permanent housing through government or church programs if needed.

Fourth, we need to make sure we are not enabling people to continue any unhealthy behavioral patterns. This is particularly true when we are hosting guests who are staying with us for longer than a week and who may be struggling with mental illness, addiction, or any relational problems. Perhaps they are staying with you because they are running away from personal responsibilities, avoiding dealing with consequences, or struggling with addictive behaviors. In this case, we need to be wise and partner with God in what He is doing in our guest's life and be cautious about over-involvement with the guest. Furthermore, we need to understand the reason why God wants us to have that particular guest in our house and how our hospitality can empower him or her to grow.

Hospitality and the Couple's Mindset

The way we practice hospitality as a couple may be influenced by our family of origin, culture, and even our country of origin. A survey conducted by the *Expat*

Insider shows that Portugal, Taiwan, and Mexico are ranked as the friendliest countries toward outsiders.[13] It seems that how these countries embrace the idea of hospitality feeds a sense of pride in the nation. However, despite our backgrounds, Christians from all over the globe are called to practice hospitality and go beyond their cultural norms to reach out to others in order to influence the world with the gospel.

So, what is our mindset about hospitality? Is it different from the way our non-Christian neighbors practice hospitality? What type of hospitality do we practice as a couple? Exclusive or inclusive? Do we limit hospitality to only relatives? Do we extend hospitality only to church members and exclude non-believers? Have we missed the opportunity to be hospitable today?

Dustin Willis and Brandon Clements in their book, *The Simplest Way to Change the World: Biblical Hospitality as a Way of Life*, explain that our understanding about hospitality is linked to how we view our home.[14] If we view our home with an individualistic lens, we tend to see it as the place that keeps us away from outsiders; a place only for us. However, if our view is collectivistic or communal, we may be more open and influential to advance the kingdom of God.

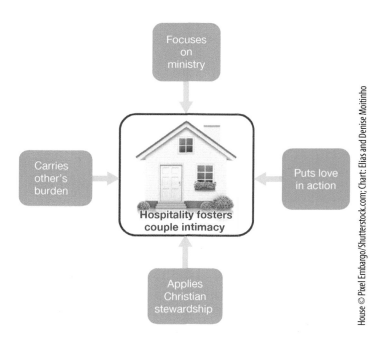

Hospitality as Ministry

When we have the right mindset about hospitality, we are more likely to practice it. If we see hospitality as a ministry, love in action, Christian stewardship, and an opportunity to carry another's burdens, we can find eternal meaning in hospitality. Thus, we can join God in what He is already doing in our guests' lives and, as a couple, become salt and light. We will share some personal examples of hospitality in a variety of circumstances that were indeed ministry opportunities for us.

Hospitality and Friendship

A few years ago, a friend of ours who is a pastor in the Amazon region in Brazil came to speak in a prominent church in Dallas. Our friend and his family were staying at a church member's house in Dallas when he contacted us in Fort Worth. He got excited about spending the night in our home during the week. Our friend and his family were very dear to us in many ways, and, needless to say, we were very excited about receiving them. In fact, he had attended Southwestern Baptist Theological Seminary in Fort Worth, Texas, with us. He was then married and had two children about our children's age. We had so much fun reminiscing about our time in seminary that one night was not enough, and they ended up staying for three wonderful days. We remember that his wife exclaimed joyfully at the table, "I have not seen my husband laughing so hard in a long time." We were glad we were able to encourage and cheer up our friend and think of how God refreshed our souls through that visit.

Hospitality and Homelessness

We believe that something amazing happens when hospitality meets homelessness. Research shows that homelessness comes in many forms: chronic, episodic, transitional, and hidden.[15] Most of us understand that caution and wisdom need to be used when inviting a homeless person who might have a mental disorder or severe addiction into our house. Perhaps it is better to partner with other people or organizations to provide hospitality to the person. We do have a duty to protect our spouse and children as we practice hospitality. However, there is a chance that we might have or will have the opportunity to provide hospitality to someone who might be homeless for one reason or another.

When we were students living on campus at the seminary in Texas, a friend of ours, who was involved in an urban ministry in downtown Fort Worth, called us one day and asked if he could bring someone to our house to bathe. He explained that the man was homeless and hopeless. Our friend indicated that the man was sober, and thus, he felt that he could bring him to our house. He also told us that he felt that we would be willing to extend hospitality to this individual. Our friend shared the gospel with this man and our story of how the Lord opened many miraculous doors for us to study at the seminary. We were not sure if the man was experiencing chronic, episodic, or transitional homelessness, but we were able to share with him God's grace and love for that moment.

Temporary homelessness happens almost every time we hear the word tornado or hurricane. During a hurricane season, we remember receiving a call from a seminary friend who had moved to the coastal area of Texas. His call sounded urgent as he explained that he was evacuating his town and bringing his wife and children and his ill mother with him to the Dallas-Fort Worth area. However, he did not have a place to stay. Understandably, after the aftermath of the terrible Hurricane Katrina, people started paying closer attention to hurricanes and heeding evacuation orders. We had no idea how long our friend and his family would need to stay, but we were committed to helping them. All our bedrooms were upstairs, but since his mother could not walk upstairs, we transformed our family room into her bedroom. As we watched on television the hurricane passing over their city, we praised God that their house was not destroyed.

Hospitality and Graduation

If you live in a college town, you probably have noticed that close to graduation, local hotels, Airbnbs, and bed and breakfasts get booked quickly. This seems to always be the case in Lynchburg, Virginia, where we live. A couple of years ago, a friend called us asking us to help host a family who was coming from Brazil for their son's graduation. Although we recall meeting the young man once at our friend's house, we knew very little about him. Nevertheless, we were glad to receive his family in our house since we had a guest bedroom. The young man and his family came to our house, and we met his parents, younger brother, and girlfriend. We hosted them for a few nights and celebrated with them a special time in their family's life. Months later, we received an invitation to attend his wedding in Brazil. Although we could not attend his wedding, we were glad to know that a friendship was established between that young man and our family.

Hospitality and Tragedy

Several years ago, when we lived and served in a local church in Texas, tragedy hit a family in our church. A young mother from our church had gone for a walk but never returned home. A drunk driver lost control of the car and hit and killed this dear sister. Upon receiving the news, we immediately drove to the family's home to be with them during this tragic moment of loss in their lives. The couple formed a blended family and had many children, including a pre-schooler. We invited the girls to stay with us in the parsonage during the days leading up to the funeral, while Elias spent time ministering to the husband and other adults. During those sorrowful days, we realized that opening our home to the girls who had a broken heart was a way to show God's love for them. It was not a time to try to explain why bad things happen. No, it was a time to "mourn with those who mourn" (Rom 12:15 NIV). As a couple in ministry, we were able to serve others together and use the gifts God gave us to minister to His children. Engaging in hospitality in the midst of tragedy allowed us to work as a team and to be part of a larger group of church members that pulled together to offer support to this sweet family.

Hospitality and the Holidays

A fond memory we have of hospitality is from our first Christmas in the U.S. We arrived in Texas for the fall semester of 1992 and made several friends quickly. One of these friends was from Pensacola, Florida. He gladly invited us to spend Christmas with him and his family. He drove us all the way from the seminary to his house. When we got there, his family had prepared a guest bedroom for us with everything we needed. Every day, they had all the meals prepared for us. They even made us part of their Christmas tradition and had Christmas gifts for us. We spent almost a couple of weeks with them and could experience first-hand Christmas and New Year's celebrations in America. Our seminary friend was such a host that he took us to several of his friends' homes for holiday celebrations. He also took us to his church, touristic spots in Pensacola, and even to the Aquarium of the Americas in New Orleans. This experience exceeded our expectations and allowed us to experience the blessings of hospitality. Receiving hospitality as a young married couple provided us with the assurance that God cared for our needs, as this was our very first Christmas in the U.S. It showed us that Christian hospitality can involve a whole family opening their home and hearts to a couple of strangers.

Benefits of Hospitality

The benefits of hospitality are bidirectional. Both the host and the guest can experience positive outcomes. The Bible clearly states, "it is more blessed to give than to receive" (Acts 20:35 NIV). We already know that hospitality is a blessing to the guests. However, this verse affirms the principle that hospitality has even more benefits to those who practice it. What blessings do hosts and guests receive from hospitality?

The benefits to the recipient of hospitality are numerous and multidimensional. There are times when guests receive material or physical benefits such as food, clothing, or a place to rest and sleep. Other times, they enjoy some psychological benefits, including a sense of belonging, feeling of being cared for, and affirmation as a fellow human being. Guests also receive relational benefits, such as love, care, attention, and make connections with others, potentially, creating new friendships. Finally, they receive spiritual benefits, including experiencing God's grace, love, and provisions through others.

The host experiences spiritual growth and can become less self-centered. As John Piper states,

> we experience the thrill of feeling God's power conquer our fears and our stinginess and all the psychological gravity of our self-centeredness. And there are few joys, if any, greater than the joy of experiencing the liberating power of God's hospitality making us a new and radically different kind of people, who love to reflect the glory of his grace as we extend it to others in all kinds of hospitality.[16]

We also believe that hospitality helps the hosts experience relational growth and cultural enrichment. The Bible teaches us to love our neighbors regardless of their ethnic or cultural backgrounds. Therefore, as we open ourselves up and interact with people who are from diverse backgrounds, we

 When you and your spouse practice hospitality by focusing on it as a ministry, putting love in action, practicing Christian stewardship, and carrying another's burdens, it will foster your spiritual intimacy.

have the opportunity to grow in our relationship skills and knowledge of other cultures. It makes us step out of our comfort zone and learn from other cultures. In addition, we move away from *ethnocentrism*, which is a tendency to see our own culture as normative or superior to other cultures. As a couple, we have opened our home to people from different parts of the world. These encounters and relationships have been enriching to us as a family, as well as the people we allowed into our homes and, most importantly, into our lives.

When you and your spouse practice hospitality by focusing on it as a ministry, putting love in action, practicing Christian stewardship, and carrying another's burdens, it will foster your spiritual intimacy. You will have the privilege of watching your spouse show the love of Christ to others and become a Christian influencer in the community.

Congratulations, you have completed your walkthrough of your dream home! Now, you want to maintain it in a pristine condition, so we encourage you to review the home maintenance checklists in the next chapter.

Endnotes

1. Hannah Martin and Lindsey Mather "Twenty-one Warm and Welcoming Guest Room Ideas," January 10, 2017, accessed September 29, 2019, https://www.architecturaldigest.com/gallery/decorating-ideas-guest-bedroom.

2. Jim Schnorrenberg, *Couples in the Bible: The Good, the Bad, and the Downright Evil* (Bloomington, IN: WestBow Press, 2014).

3. Rosaria C. Butterfield, *The Gospel Comes with a House Key: Practicing Radically Ordinary Hospitality in Our Post-Christian World* (Wheaton, IL: Cross Way Books, 2018).

4. Butterfield, *The Gospel Comes with a House Key*.

5. Butterfield, *The Gospel Comes with a House Key*.

6. Dustin Willis and Brandon Clements, *The Simplest Way to Change the World: Biblical Hospitality as a Way of Life* (Chicago, IL: Moody Publishers, 2017), 12.

7. Jim Ozier and Fiona Haworth, *Clip In: Risking Hospitality in Your Church* (Nashville, TN: Abingdon Press, 2014), 5.

8. Butterfield, *The Gospel Comes with a House Key*.

9. Butterfield, *The Gospel Comes with a House Key*, 216.

10. Butterfield, *The Gospel Comes with a House Key*, 215–216.

11. Butterfield, *The Gospel Comes with a House Key*, 216.

12. Willis and Clements, *The Simplest Way to Change the World*, 19.

13. "Quality of Life–There's a Country for Every Expat," Expat Insider, accessed October 3, 2019, https://www.internations.org/expat-insider/2019/quality-of-life-index-39831.

14. Willis and Clements, *The Simplest Way to Change the World*.

15. Barrett A. Lee, Kimberly A. Tyler, and James D. Wright, "The New Homelessness Revisited," *Annual Review of Sociology* 36 (2010): 501–21; National Health Care

for the Homeless Council, "Are There Different Types of Homelessness?" accessed October 2, 2019, https://nhchc.org/understanding-homelessness/faq/.

16. John Piper, "Strategic Hospitality," August 25, 1985, accessed October 4, 2019, https://www.desiringgod.org/messages/strategic-hospitality.

PART III

THE CLOSING: Putting It All Together

CHAPTER 12

Home Maintenance: Caring for Your Dream Home

"If the Lord doesn't build the house,
the builders are working for nothing."
Psalm 127:1 (ICB)

Homeowners know that taking care of their homes pays off in the long run. For this reason, they check their homes carefully to ensure that the home is in good condition. Multiple home maintenance checklists are available online. Some of them focus on seasonal required maintenance, while others include the essential areas and systems of the house, such as electrical, heating, air, and plumbing.

Moreover, the goal of a maintenance checklist is to ensure that homeowners do not overlook essential areas of the house and keep their homes in great shape for many years.

Similarly, you are putting a lot of effort into creating your dream marriage. You may even have your checklists, and we applaud you for that. To support your effort, we have included checklists covering the various areas of your marriage. You will need to continue to pay attention to these areas regularly to ensure that your dream marriage, or should we say your dream home, is in excellent condition. We realize that sometimes, problems arise, and homeowners need to call experts to do the difficult repairs they cannot do themselves. Therefore, if you find that you have marital problems beyond what you and your spouse can handle, we recommend that you connect with a Christian marriage counselor, a pastoral counselor, or your pastor to help you deal with complex issues.

In this chapter, we review some essential topics that we cover in the book and help you identify some potential red flags or warning signs of marriage trouble. We provide checklists for you to complete individually or as a couple. Although the checklists in this chapter are not statistically validated, they are helpful, practical, and based on the research presented in this book. We believe they can serve as a guide for you to reflect on how you are caring for your dream home.

———— Creating a Shared Vision for Your Marriage ————

We hope that by now, you and your spouse have already developed a shared vision and mission statements for your marriage based on your Christian values. We also hope that you considered the seven essential areas of life, set many SMART goals, and developed a plan with specific action steps you can take to reach your goals. However, we understand that you may still be working on creating a vision and a mission along with SMART goals for your marriage. We encourage you to keep going. Life can be busy, and perhaps you have not had the opportunity to sit down with your spouse to accomplish these essential tasks.

We want to motivate you to share with your spouse what you are reading in this book and start this incredible process of creating a vision for your marriage. We believe the checklist will help you accomplish just that.

 A vision is always *future-oriented*; therefore, it requires reflection and contemplation.

As you have heard, a vision is always *future-oriented*, and it requires reflection and contemplation. You reflect on where you are now and where you want to be, or we should say, where you believe God wants you to be as an individual and as a couple. More specifically, it also requires imagining and contemplating what kind of couple you want to be, or God wants you to be 5, 10, or 20 years from now. While many people make vision boards and try to manifest their desired future, we believe a vision comes from God as we seek His will and purposes for our lives. As you and your spouse get together and envision your amazing dream home, be sure to do what the prophet says, "Write the vision and make it plain" (Hab. 2:2 NKJV).

—— CHECKLIST: OUR HOUSE HUNTING ——

Our Values, Vision, Mission, SMART Goals, and Strategic Plan

For the following items, use the Likert scale below and answer each question.

Definitely Not Too busy, no time!	Probably Not Too much work!	Possibly Considering it!	Definitely Working on it!	Definitely Done!
1	2	3	4	5

1. We have a clear and compelling vision statement _____
2. We have a Christ-centered mission statement _____
3. We have set SMART goals in these seven areas: physical, psychological, relational, financial, professional, recreational, and spiritual _____
4. We have developed a strategic plan to reach our SMART goals _____
5. We evaluate our progress regularly _____

Please rate the extent to which you agree or disagree with the following statements:

Strongly Disagree	Disagree	Undecided	Agree	Strongly Agree
1	2	3	4	5

6. Our vision statement is based on Christian values _____
7. Our vision statement is transformational _____
8. Our vision encompasses seven areas of life _____
9. Our vision is future-oriented and considers the stages of the life cycle _____
10. We believe our vision will lead us out of our comfort zone _____

Total _____

45–50 = Your Dream Home is in great shape!

40–44 = Your Dream Home is in good shape!

35–39 = Identify the areas of your marriage that need improvement.

34 and below = You have several growth areas that need attention. You may need some help.

RED FLAG: If you do not have a long-term vision for your marriage, you may be only living day to day (survival mode). Thus, you may be missing out on a great future together.

Providing Stability

The foundation for marriage that God established in the Garden of Eden remains the same outside the Garden as well. For instance, when some Pharisees asked Jesus about divorce, Jesus provided an answer that took everyone back to God's original design for marriage. He stated, "'Haven't you read,' he replied, 'that at the beginning the Creator made them male and female,' and said, 'For this reason a man will leave his father and mother and be united to his wife, and the two will become one flesh'?" (Matt. 19:4-5 NIV). We continue to encourage you to ensure that your dream home is on a solid biblical foundation.

As we have discussed, homeownership brings social stability to marriage and family. In fact, after reviewing several research studies, the National Association of Realtors concluded that homeownership provides couples and families with a boost of self-esteem and a sense of achieving the "American Dream." It increases responsibility for the home and the neighborhood, enhances children's academic performance, fosters community involvement, improves health care outcomes, lowers crime rates, and reduces welfare dependency.[1] These are indeed great benefits.

Having a dream marriage goes beyond social stability. It provides spiritual stability and, in turn, can improve all other areas of marriage and family life. Thus, we believe that as you and your spouse focus on moving closer to God, the best location for your dream home, you will grow in your marital intimacy, strengthen your marriage, and experience peace of mind.

 The best location for your dream home (dream marriage) is near the heart of God. In this location, you will grow in your intimacy, flourish as a couple, and find shelter from life's fiercest storms.

——— CHECKLIST: OUR LOCATION ———

Building Your Dream Home on a Solid Foundation Creates Stability

Please rate the extent to which you agree or disagree with the following statements:

Strongly Disagree	Disagree	Undecided	Agree	Strongly Agree
1	2	3	4	5

1. Our beliefs on marriage reflect a Christian worldview _____
2. We believe in God's ideal for marriage as established in the Garden _____
3. We believe God's ideal for marriage remains the same outside the Garden _____
4. In terms of location, we are moving toward God together _____
5. We believe that we are experiencing consummate love, including (intimacy, passion, and commitment) in our marriage _____
6. We are experiencing Agape love in our marriage regularly _____
7. We are renewing our minds _____
8. We saturate our minds with the Word of God by reading it and studying it _____
9. We replace false beliefs with biblical truth _____
10. We practice new behaviors based on our renewed mindset _____

Total _____

45–50 = Your Dream Home is in great shape!

40–44 = Your Dream Home is in good shape!

35–39 = Identify the areas of your marriage that need improvement.

34 and below = You have several growth areas that need attention. You may need some help.

RED FLAG: If you or your spouse are not intentionally moving toward God and you are not renewing your minds to align them with a biblical worldview, you may be running the risk of being weak spiritually.

Creating an Influential Marriage

We may look at a house that has a fantastic curb appeal and conclude that the couple inside the house has it all together. Unfortunately, sometimes, this is not the case. According to the American Psychological Association, "about 40 to 50 percent of married couples in the United States divorce [and] the divorce rate for subsequent marriages is even higher."[2] Therefore, a beautiful curb appeal can be an illusion of stability because inside of the apparent dream home, the marriage is chaotic, and a real nightmare.

We emphasize that the curb appeal for our dream marriage is our testimony in the community. People are looking at us and our spouse, and they see something. The question is, what do they see? Hopefully, what they see on the outside

 A Christian influencer is someone used by God to change people's minds and hearts toward Him.

is a true reflection of Christ inside your hearts. We believe that as Christian couples, we need to make a distinctive mark in the community by making a difference in the lives of those around us.

Though not new, the term *influencer* has grown in popularity and use in the last few years. The original meaning of the word *influencer* was used "broadly to refer to someone or something with the power to alter the beliefs of individuals, and as a result, impact the course of events."[3] Our hope is that you and your spouse will become *Christian influencers* in your community by allowing God to use you to change people's minds and hearts toward Him, and influence the course of events in your community in a way that brings glory to God.

CHECKLIST: OUR CURB APPEAL

Our Reputation and Influence in Our Community

Please rate the extent to which you agree or disagree with the following statements:

Strongly Disagree	Disagree	Undecided	Agree	Strongly Agree
1	2	3	4	5

1. We seek to have a godly reputation that reflects a solid Christian character   _____
2. We agree that we are God's representative in our community   _____
3. We have developed a solid Christian identity as a couple   _____
4. We believe that the secular culture in the U.S. tends to be unfriendly and even antagonistic toward the Christian perspective on marriage _____
5. We display the fruit of the Spirit in our daily interactions with each other   _____
6. We seek to practice the following ethical principles: autonomy, nonmaleficence, beneficence, justice, veracity, and fidelity   _____
7. We seek to demonstrate integrity rather than hypocrisy in our marriage   _____
8. We have a good understanding of the socioeconomic (SES) status and challenges of our community   _____
9. We know our neighbors fairly well   _____
10. We engage our neighbors and offer help in times of need   _____

Total _____

45–50 = Your Dream Home is in great shape!

40–44 = Your Dream Home is in good shape!

35–39 = Identify the areas of your marriage that need improvement.

34 and below = You have several growth areas that need attention. You may need some help.

RED FLAG: If you are not displaying the fruit of the Spirit (love, joy, peace, patience, kindness, goodness, faithfulness, gentleness, and self-control) toward your spouse regularly, then there is something essential missing in your marriage.

Communicating Effectively

Clear, effective, and positive communication is the key to having a dream marriage. We hope that you are taking advantage of the *loveseat* in your living room and spending quality time talking and listening to each other. When you implement the communication skills we presented in the book, you are taking the initiative to connect with your spouse at a deeper level. We firmly believe that listening with your heart can help you understand and empathize with your spouse.

Positive communication can encourage and strengthen your spouse. So, being mindful of what you say and ensuring that what comes out of your mouth pleases God first is key to having positive communication with your Do not allow technology gadgets and social media to distract you from your interaction with your spouse. spouse. David says, "May the words of my mouth and the meditation of my heart be pleasing to you, O Lord" (Ps. 19:14 NLT). Thus, make it a habit of using kind words that will lift up your spouse because "Kind words are like honey— sweet to the soul and healthy for the body" (Prov. 16:24 NLT).

Engaging the Do's of positive communication and avoiding the Don'ts we provided in Chapter 4 can certainly help you focus fully on your spouse. We would like to remind you not to allow technology gadgets and social media to distract you from your interaction with your spouse. Besides, being aware of the potential danger of infidelity that is lurking beneath the surface in the various social media platforms is a must. As previously mentioned, Facebook creates a setting that can lead to flirtations, emotional and even physical affairs,[4] and even to the devastation of a dream home.

——————— CHECKLIST: OUR LIVING ROOM ———————

Effective Communication in Marriage

How often do you engage in the following behaviors?

Never	Rarely	Sometimes	Often	Always
1	2	3	4	5

1. We use the idea of the *loveseat* and listen with empathy _____
2. We have positive communication and speak the truth in love _____
3. We use healthy social media boundaries _____
4. We maximize our communication (G.I.F.T.S.) in all five levels: Greeting, Information, Feelings, Thoughts, and Self _____
5. We avoid engaging in these destructive patterns of communication: criticism, defensiveness, contempt, and stonewalling _____
6. We avoid negative behaviors that interfere with communication (Don'ts of communication) _____
7. We implement positive behaviors that improve communication (Do's of communication) _____
8. We use active listening skills regularly in our communication: Paraphrasing, reflecting feelings, reflecting meaning, and summarizing _____
9. We use the Speaker–Listener Technique appropriately _____
10. We engage in open and honest communication _____

Total _____

45–50 = Your Dream Home is in great shape!

40–44 = Your Dream Home is in good shape!

35–39 = Identify the areas of your marriage that need improvement.

34 and below = You have several growth areas that need attention. You may need some help.

RED FLAG: If criticism, contempt, defensiveness, and stonewalling are part of your relationship regularly, these destructive patterns are going to be detrimental to your marriage.

Feeding Body, Mind, Soul, and Relationships

The story of Moses helps us understand our need for self-care. Moses was leading the people of Israel and giving his best from morning to evening. Jethro, his father-in-law, came to visit Moses and observed his hectic schedule and his frenetic activity. Then, Jethro said to Moses, "This is no way to go about it. You'll burn out, and the people right along with you. This is way too much for you—you can't do this alone" (Ex. 18:17 MSG). Even though Moses' motivation and intentions were good, the work and responsibility were too much for him. Thankfully, Moses heard the wise counsel and delegated some of his tasks to other leaders.

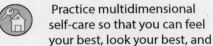

Practice multidimensional self-care so that you can feel your best, look your best, and give your best to your spouse.

Stress is detrimental to our physical, mental, and emotional health. Chronic, ongoing stress can cause many mental health problems, including anxiety and depression, and it can lead to burnout. All these adverse effects of stress are also damaging to relationships. Therefore, we recommend that you develop a multidimensional self-care plan and practice it regularly. Take care of your body, mind, soul, and relationships.

Acknowledging the reality that marriage requires a lot of work and that life is very demanding in various areas is a crucial step to accept help and practice self-care. We encourage you to take the next step and be intentional about taking care of yourself, so that you may feel your best, look your best, and give your best to your spouse.

CHECKLIST: OUR KITCHEN AND DINING ROOM

Caring for Our Bodies, Minds, Souls, and Relationships

How often do you engage in the following behaviors?

Never	Rarely	Sometimes	Often	Always
1	2	3	4	5

1. We avoid living a busy, fast-paced lifestyle because it can be detrimental to our overall health and marriage _____
2. We value multidimensional self-care for our lives and marriage _____
3. We feed our souls through engaging in spiritual activities, including: worship, prayer, and Christian meditation or devotionals _____
4. We feed our bodies by living an active lifestyle _____
5. We feed our bodies by having a healthy diet _____
6. We feed our bodies by having adequate sleep (7–9 hours per day) _____
7. We feed our bodies by resting and relaxing _____
8. We feed our minds by renewing our thinking _____
9. We practice emotion regulation/self-control _____
10. We deal with unmet expectations with grace and wisdom _____

Total _____

45–50 = Your Dream Home is in great shape!

40–44 = Your Dream Home is in good shape!

35–39 = Identify the areas of your marriage that need improvement.

34 and below = You have several growth areas that need attention. You may need some help.

RED FLAG: If you are not taking care of your body (living an active lifestyle, having a healthy diet, adequate sleep, and resting), you will not be able to give your best self to your spouse.

Keeping Finances in Check

The way we manage money is a true reflection of the condition of our hearts. Giving to the Lord's work and helping others is a sign that we have a generous heart. On the other hand, if our primary focus is to accumulate wealth and material possessions without any thought of sharing, then we may be developing a greedy heart. Unfortunately, the health and wealth prosperity gospel in many Christian circles overemphasizes health and wealth above all things. As a result, many Christians erroneously focus on the gifts, rather than on growing a loving relationship with God, the greatest giver (James 1:17). We need to acknowledge that the God who blesses us is more important than the blessings.

Ron Blue notes that everyone, regardless of their backgrounds, asks the same questions, "Will I ever have enough? Will it continue to be enough? Our God who blesses us is more important than the blessings.

How much is enough?"[5] As you and your spouse consider these questions, it is essential to embrace the biblical truths that God is the owner of everything (Ps. 24:1; Ps. 50:10-12; Job 41:11; Hag. 2:8), He is the provider and giver of all blessings (Gen. 2:1-12; 2 Cor. 9:10; Jam. 1:17; Phil. 4:19), and that we are responsible managers (Matt. 25:14-30). Reflecting on the principle of contentment will also be vital in helping you and your spouse overcome the temptation of consumerism and manage money and material possessions wisely.

CHECKLIST: OUR HOME OFFICE

Our Finances in Check

Please rate the extent to which you agree or disagree with the following statements:

Strongly Disagree	Disagree	Undecided	Agree	Strongly Agree
1	2	3	4	5

1. We believe God is the owner of everything   _____
2. God is the provider and giver of all blessings   _____
3. We believe our responsibility is to be managers   _____

For questions 4–10 read the statements and consider the frequency of these actions.

Never	Rarely	Sometimes	Often	Always
1	2	3	4	5

4. We save consistently   _____
5. We spend wisely   _____
6. We avoid debt at all cost   _____
7. We invest prudently   _____
8. We give generously   _____
9. We have a plan to manage our finances   _____
10. We have a budget and live within our means   _____

Total _____

45–50 = Your Dream Home is in great shape!

40–44 = Your Dream Home is in good shape!

35–39 = Identify the areas of your marriage that need improvement.

34 and below = You have several growth areas that need attention. You may need some help.

RED FLAG: If you do not have a budget and you are living above your means, you may be getting deep into debt.

Cleaning Up Our Conflict

Every once in a while, we have to clean up our dirty laundry or conflict. Conflict is always part of relationships, and it does not always need to be negative. In fact, couples can grow through conflict, learn about themselves, and practice repentance, forgiveness, and acceptance. As couples deal with conflict collaboratively and constructively, they can reconnect, restore their relationship, and heal their emotional hurts.

Gary Chapman and Jennifer Thomas developed the *5 Languages of Apology* that help couples deal with conflict and emotional hurt in their relationships.[6] We have found this practical approach helpful for couples. So, we are sharing it here with you:

#1 Expressing Regret: "I am sorry."

- You will need to acknowledge how your behavior hurt your spouse's feelings and show remorse.

#2 Accepting Responsibility: "I was wrong."

- You will need to be specific and take responsibility for your hurtful actions.

#3 Making Restitution: "What can I do to make it right?"

- Do your best to repair the damage caused by your actions and restore the relationship.

#4 Genuinely Repenting: "I'll try not to do that again."

- Express your repentance and desire to change your behavior.

#5 Requesting Forgiveness: "Will you please forgive me?"

- Be patient with your spouse and seek forgiveness and reconciliation.

We believe that this technique can be a great cleaning agent for dealing with your dirty laundry effectively. When couples offer a genuine apology that is followed by true forgiveness, they can experience peace and harmony.

CHECKLIST: OUR LAUNDRY ROOM

Resolving Our Conflicts

How often do you engage in the following behaviors?

Never	Rarely	Sometimes	Often	Always
1	2	3	4	5

1. We are aware of the spiritual dimension of conflict _____
2. We engage in self-examination when handling conflict _____
3. We have a Christ-like attitude during conflict _____
4. We promote grace-filled interactions in our marriage _____
5. We identify the causes of our conflicts without blaming or attacking each other _____
6. We use a collaborative approach to managing our conflicts _____
7. We forgive each other when in conflict _____
8. We practice self-control (emotion regulation) and take Time-Out to protect the marriage _____
9. We make time to communicate and to listen to each other respectfully before engaging in problem-solving _____
10. We implement a collaborative problem-solving approach _____

Total _____

45–50 = Your Dream Home is in great shape!

40–44 = Your Dream Home is in good shape!

35–39 = Identify the areas of your marriage that need improvement.

34 and below = You have several growth areas that need attention. You may need some help.

RED FLAG: If you have unresolved conflict and are feeling resentful toward your spouse, your intimacy is probably suffering.

Keeping Passion and Intimacy Alive

All rooms of your dream home influence your marital intimacy. By this, we mean that all interactions you have with your spouse can potentially bring you closer to each other or can create a distance in your marriage. For instance, you can show genuine love, kindness, and grace toward your spouse, whether you are handling finances, your kids, or even the dirty laundry. In addition, by communicating openly with your spouse, you are creating intellectual, emotional, and spiritual intimacy. Consequently, you set the stage to express your love physically. Peter reminds husbands, "give honor to your wives. Treat your wife with understanding as you live together. She may be weaker than you are, but she is your equal partner in God's gift of new life" (1 Pet. 3:7 NLT).

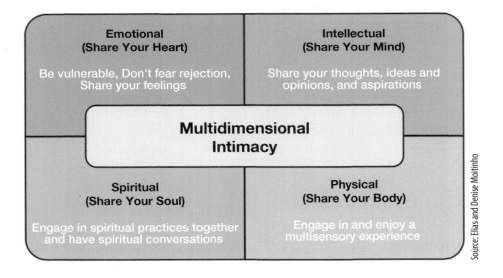

It is your responsibility as a couple to make your home a safe place for your spouse. Real intimacy only happens when a spouse feels loved, secure, and appreciated. The last reminder is to get to know your spouse's needs and seek to meet them to the best of your abilities.

———— CHECKLIST: OUR MASTER BEDROOM ————

Creating Multidimensional Intimacy

Please rate the extent to which you agree or disagree with the following statements:

Strongly Disagree	Disagree	Undecided	Agree	Strongly Agree
1	2	3	4	5

1. We believe that sexuality is part of God's creation _____
2. We believe that God has guidelines and boundaries for the expression of our sexuality _____
3. We believe that intimacy is a multidimensional experience that includes emotional, intellectual, physical, and spiritual areas of our life _____
4. We understand the sexual response model for males and females _____
5. We are aware of multiple factors that influence physical intimacy _____
6. We discuss our preferences regarding sexual behavior in our marriage _____

How often do you engage in the following behaviors?

Never	Rarely	Sometimes	Often	Always
1	2	3	4	5

7. We communicate openly before, during, and after our sexual relationships _____
8. We express Agape love daily _____
9. We catch each other doing good and praise each other _____
10. We maximize a multisensory experience during our sexual intimacy _____

Total _____

45–50 = Your Dream Home is in great shape!

40–44 = Your Dream Home is in good shape!

35–39 = Identify the areas of your marriage that need improvement.

34 and below = You have several growth areas that need attention. You may need some help.

RED FLAG: If your intimacy is lacking in one area (emotional, intellectual, physical, or spiritual), it may create a negative domino effect in your overall intimacy.

Growing Spiritually

Growing spiritually is not an option for Christians. Throughout the New Testament, the message is clear, God wants us to grow in our faith. For example, Peter states, "you must grow in the grace and knowledge of our Lord and Savior Jesus Christ" (2 Pet. 3:18 NLT). God wants us to be mature in the faith and no longer infants easily deceived by false teaching (Eph. 4:12-14). The only way to grow spiritually is to follow the example set by Christ himself and connect with our Heavenly Father daily. We can engage in meaningful worship, prayer, fasting, meditation on Scriptures, and serving people, for example, to pursue godliness (1 Tim. 4:7). The beautiful thing about Christian marriage is that you and your spouse can practice spiritual disciplines together. As a result, these practices lead you to know God more intimately and to live a life that pleases Him through the power of the Holy Spirit.

> When you are *in sync*, pursuing God together, you are going to hear God's will, plan, and purposes for you as a couple.

In Chapter 9, we provided several tips for you to grow spiritually with your spouse. We encourage you to review the tips and talk with each other to decide which one works best for you. Being on the same page is vital. We also recommend that you respect each other's preferences because there is no cookie-cutter approach to growing spiritually.

The key is growing spiritually *together*. When you are in harmony pursuing God together, you are going to hear God's will, plan, and purposes for you as a couple. Then, as you identify the vision and mission God has for you, it will be wonderful for you together to embark on this adventure of creating a dream marriage that honors God and fulfills His purpose for your lives.

CHECKLIST: OUR CLOSET

Our Spiritual Growth Matters

Since in this chapter we emphasized that spiritual growth goes beyond a checklist of behaviors, we do not want to create a checklist to measure your spiritual growth. Rather, we want to encourage you to reflect on your relationship with God within your marriage. So, please complete the statements below.

I believe my spouse and I are growing in our relationship with God *together*

because: _____

_____

_____

The steps my spouse and I are taking to grow spiritually *together* include:

_____

_____

_____

When my spouse and I engage in spiritual conversations, we talk about:

_____

_____

_____

When my spouse and I engage in spiritual practices such as worship, Bible study, or prayer *together,* I feel _____

because _____

_____

_____

RED FLAG: If you find it difficult to answer these questions or if your answers are mostly negative, we encourage you to talk with a pastor or a mature Christian friend.

Parenting with Purpose

Several years ago, we read the book *How to Be a Hero to Your Kids* by Josh McDowell and Dick Day. In the book, they shared several nuggets of wisdom on parenting that we implemented throughout the years when raising our kids. Thoughtfully, they emphasized the importance of acceptance, appreciation, affection, and availability.[7]

Acceptance	Accepting your child will build the child's sense of security and self-worth.
Appreciation	Appreciating your child for the things your child does right will give a sense of significance.
Affection	Engaging in physical contact with your child, including hugs, will make your child thrive.
Availability	Spending time with your child makes your child feel loved.

The parenting years become a time of creating a memorable legacy for your children. It happens one day at a time, one interaction at a time. When you and your spouse agree on being intentional and consistent in your parenting, as previously discussed, you are on track to be successful parents. Above all, we want to remind you of your responsibility to pass your Christian faith and values to your children. Do not delegate or outsource your parenting responsibility to others. By this, we do not mean that you cannot have babysitters, or you should not put your children in a daycare center. Rather, we want to emphasize the importance of spending time with your child and investing in your child's life to the best of your ability. The joys of seeing your children grow and become responsible adults who love God and love people, and contribute positively to society and to God's kingdom outweigh any challenges you may face.

 Do not delegate or outsource your parenting responsibility to others.

CHECKLIST: OUR KIDS' ROOM

Parenting Our Kids with Purpose

Please rate the extent to which you agree or disagree with the following statements:

Strongly Disagree	Disagree	Undecided	Agree	Strongly Agree
1	2	3	4	5

1. We are aware of the U-Shaped curve of marriage happiness and how having a child-centered marriage can be detrimental to marital happiness _____
2. We acknowledge that it is essential to learn about our child's physical, psychological, social, and spiritual development _____
3. One of the primary purposes of parenting is to teach children to love God and to love people _____
4. We are seeking to develop an *Authoritative* parenting style _____
5. We will be on the alert regarding these potential issues: childhood obesity, technology and social media, friendships and peer pressure, and special needs _____
6. We are (we will be) responsible for the spiritual development of our children _____

How often do you engage in the following behaviors?

Never	Rarely	Sometimes	Often	Always
1	2	3	4	5

7. We agree on parenting goals and discipline strategies _____
8. We spend or plan to spend quantity and quality time with our child/children _____
9. We have or plan to have positive and fun activities with our children _____
10. We are (will be) wise regarding our posts on social media about our child _____

Total _____

45–50 = Your Dream Home is in great shape!

40–44 = Your Dream Home is in good shape!

35–39 = Identify the areas of your marriage that need improvement.

34 and below = You have several growth areas that need attention. You may need some help.

RED FLAG: If you find yourself disciplining your child out of anger and frustration, you need to consider the effects it will have on your relationship with your child. If you do not have children yet, we encourage you to reflect on these items.

Practicing Hospitality

Practicing Christian hospitality has the power to contribute to your overall intimacy. Hospitality gives you and your spouse the opportunity to love others, and witness each other's kindness toward family members, friends, and even strangers. Additionally, it gives you a picture of your spouse's commitment to pursue a Christ-like life. Thus, hospitality can be an important tool to build couple intimacy.

You may have been the recipient of the hospitality, or you may have provided the gift of hospitality to many people. Perhaps, they were family members, friends, or even strangers. Since you took the time to host them, they experienced God's love through you.

Hospitality involves intentionality. When you are intentional, all your excuses fall apart. Intentionality fosters creativity and helps you think of ways to engage in hospitality. For instance, perhaps you cannot welcome a person into your home, but you can prepare a meal and take it to someone who is hosting a guest. Intentionality with creativity can empower you and others to practice hospitality.

 Christian hospitality is about loving and serving others with Christ-like compassion and humility.

Christian hospitality is different from the act of purely entertaining guests at home. It is more than merely opening our homes. It is about intentionally opening our hearts and sharing our ordinary lives with others. It is about becoming approachable and opening ourselves up to receive people into our world. Every time you open your home to others, you are reminded that hospitality transcends culture and languages because it is about loving and serving others with Christ-like compassion and humility.

CHECKLIST: OUR GUEST ROOM

Intentionally Engaging in Everyday Hospitality

Please rate the extent to which you agree or disagree with the following statements:

Unimportant	Slightly Important	Moderately Important	Important	Very Important
1	2	3	4	5

1. Opening our house to others _____
2. Hosting relatives or friends for a meal _____
3. Opening our home to church activities such as Bible study group _____
4. Intentionally inviting people of other cultural backgrounds to our home _____
5. Hosting family, friends, and/or church members on Thanksgiving _____
6. Hosting family, friends, and/or church members for Christmas _____
7. Showing hospitality to someone in need of a place to stay _____
8. Hosting people in our house for longer than a day _____
9. Hosting parties or celebrations (i.e., baby shower) in our home _____
10. Partnering with others who are hosting someone in their home _____

Total _____

45–50 = Your Dream Home is in great shape!

40–44 = Your Dream Home is in good shape!

35–39 = Identify the areas of your marriage that need improvement.

34 and below = You have several growth areas that need attention. You may need some help.

RED FLAG: If you cannot remember the last time you had someone over your house, you may be missing the opportunity to practice hospitality as a couple.

Congratulations! You have just completed your dream home maintenance checklists. Now, you have a good idea of the condition of your dream home. We recommend that you work on the growth areas that you have identified, and if you need help from experts, please do not hesitate to contact one. Use these checklists periodically to ensure that you are on the right track and not overlooking any essential area of your marriage.

Endnotes

1. "Social Benefits of Homeownership and Stable Housing National," Association of Realtors, accessed October 2, 2019, https://www.nar.realtor/sites/default/files/migration_ files/social-benefits-of-stable-housing-2012-04.pdf.
2. "Marriage & Divorce," American Psychological Association, 2019, accessed September 27, 2019, https://www.apa.org/topics/divorce/.
3. "The Meteoric Rise of The Word "Influencer,'" accessed October 2, 2019, https://www.dictionary.com/e/influencer/.
4. Irum Saeed Abbasi and Nawal G. Alghamdi, "When Flirting Turns Into Infidelity: The Facebook Dilemma," *The American Journal of Family Therapy* 45, no. 1 (2017): 1–14.
5. Ron Blue and Michael Blue, *Master Your Money: A Step-By-Step Plan For Experiencing Financial Contentment* (Chicago, IL: Moody Publishers, 2016), 17.
6. Gary Chapman and Jennifer Thomas, *The Five Languages of Apology* (Chicago, IL: Northfield Publishing, 2008).
7. Josh McDowell and Dick Day, *How to Be a Hero to Your Kids* (Waco, TX: Word Books Publisher, 1991).

Conclusion

As you complete the walkthrough of your dream home, we hope you will take a moment to reflect on what you have read in this book. We also hope you will continue to put into practice the strategies and skills you have learned to create and maintain your dream home or, should we say, your dream marriage. As you know, creating a dream home or dream marriage is a process that requires intentionality and work on the various areas of marriage. When you and your spouse work together with open hearts and minds to address these areas of your marriage, you empower each other to experience multidimensional intimacy in your Christian marriage.

We hope the metaphors and analogies in this book helped illustrate gracefully some essential topics in marriage life. You may recall that we started our journey with the *house hunting* metaphor to encourage you and your spouse to envision your dream marriage together. We also shared our thoughts with you about foundational biblical principles for Christian marriage. As you have read, creating your dream home on a solid foundation can ensure stability in all areas of your marriage.

The following chart reminds you of the metaphors in the book and some of their benefits. We hope and pray that you will continue to grow as a couple and continue to create an intimate Christian marriage.

Your Dream Home	A Benefit
House Hunting	You have a compelling vision for your future as a couple.
Location	Your marriage is firm on the solid foundation of a biblical worldview.
Curb Appeal	You are Christian influencers in your community.
Living Room	You feel connected through positive communication.
Kitchen & Dining	You are giving your very best to your spouse.
Home Office	You have a strategic plan to manage your finances.
Laundry Room	You clean up your conflicts quickly and effectively.
Master Bedroom	You enjoy multisensory and multidimensional intimacy.
Closet	You are growing closer to God and to each other.
Kids' Room	You are ready to parent with purpose.
Guest Room	You open your heart and your home to others.

Our prayer and desire is that you continue to enjoy your dream home for the years to come.

Drs. Elias and Denise Moitinho

Index

T